"Groundwater, and especially transboundary aquifers, are fundamental sources of freshwater for billions of people worldwide. Yet, little has been written on how international law for these critical resources intersects with the human right to water and sanitation. This timely book masterfully fills this gaping void in the literature with in-depth analyses and explanations that will be welcomed by legal, policy, and science professionals, as well as students, practitioners, and policy makers, working in these fields."

Gabriel Eckstein, *Professor of Law and Director of the Energy, Environmental, and Natural Resource Systems Law Program, Texas A&M University, United States*

"This book represents truly excellent research. It is intellectually ambitious, highly relevant with potential for significant practical impact, and exhaustive in its execution. The author's ambition lies in the fact that he seeks to address a range of important, yet difficult legal issues through the narrow lens of international groundwater resources law. Such issues include the complex interrelationship between the established corpus of international water law and the emerging human rights of access to water and sanitation, an area quite under-explored in academic literature. It also addresses other critical issues, including that of the risk of 'fragmentation' and resulting incoherence in international (water) law. The author very ably tackles further difficult issues, including that of the extra-territorial application of human rights obligations. Above all else, however, this book stands out for the depth and intensity of the author's analysis of the quite particular field of international law relating to transboundary groundwater and aquifers."

Owen McIntyre, *Full Professor at the School of Law, University College Cork, Ireland*

"Groundwater is fundamental for life on earth, it provides more than half of all drinking water worldwide Groundwater plays a fundamental role in achieving the Sustainable Development Goals, beyond the water goal only. It is also critical to realize the human right to water and sanitation. Most of the available groundwater flows under the territory of two or more States, representing an important shared resource. Ibrahim's book represents an important and comprehensive contribution to the existing literature on the international law regarding transboundary aquifers. Ibrahim adds a novel approach by searching not only international water law, but also the human right to water and sanitation. The book presents a scrupulous and detailed research and a critical analysis of the legal frameworks at stake. It is highly recommended for all experts have an interest in improving their understanding of the laws relating to transboundary aquifers."

Raya Marina Stephan, *Water law expert, Consultant/Deputy Editor in Chief Water International, International Water Resources Association*

"The new book addressees a crucial topic for the future of our planet. Focusing on how International Water Law and the Human Rights to Water and Sanitation can be harmonized in the context of transboundary aquifers, this book is a must read for all scholars and practitioners working at the intersection of these two areas of international law. The argument that agreements or arrangements on transboundary aquifers should include provisions on human rights has to be welcomed as an innovative approach that must be considered by States in their negotiations processes."

Mara Tignino, *Reader at the Faculty of Law of the University of Geneva and Lead Legal Specialist of the Platform for International Water Law at the Geneva Water Hub, Geneva, Switzerland*

"The research and conclusions in this book speak to the importance of multilateralism, international law and international cooperation for the sustainable management of our finite land and water resources, as well as of the imperative to put people, and their rights, front and center of any debate or decision. Its voyage through history to explain concepts and agreements, as well as its clear conclusions on the importance of reconciling International Water Law and the Human Right to Water and Sanitation when addressing challenges related to the access to transboundary waters worldwide, are essential contributions to the global conversations on how to truly transition towards a sustainable future for people and planet."

Miriam Medel Garcia, *Former Chief of Global Policy Advocacy and Regional Cooperation, United Nations Convention to Combat Desertification Secretariat*

"This is a terrific book, a must-read for experts in water law and public international law. An enriching and well-structured volume that develops sounds and interdisciplinary research."

Giuseppe Martinico, *Full Professor of Comparative Public law at the Scuola Superiore Sant'Anna, Pisa, Italy*

International Water Law and the Human Right to Water

This book examines the development of international law applicable to Transboundary Aquifers (TBAs) considering the Human Right to Water and Sanitation (HRWS). The purpose is to determine how International Water Law (IWL) and the HRWS can be harmonized in the context of TBAs. This is important given rules and instruments adopted to address this topic are relatively nascent, and the field itself is still in the process of developing regulatory frameworks. Taking the application of the HRWS to shared aquifers as a case study, the work discusses whether IWL and International Human Rights Law complement each other. The response to this question requires an analysis of the development of International Groundwater Law and its challenges, the evolution of the HRWS, the nature of transboundary groundwaters, and the interplay between these two fields. The author argues that IWL agreements should contain a provision related to the HRWS to ensure the protection of this right with a stipulation included in the nonbinding instrument that tackles shared groundwaters: the Draft Articles on the Law of Transboundary Aquifers adopted in 2008 through the United Nations General Assembly Resolution. The book will be of interest to international lawyers, water and human right experts, geologists, and anyone interested in water and human rights issues.

Imad Antoine Ibrahim is an Assistant Professor of Environmental Law and Governance at the Section of Governance and Technology for Sustainability, Faculty of Behavioural, Management and Social Sciences, at the University of Twente, the Netherlands. He is a Senior Research Associate at gLAWcal – Global Law Initiative for Sustainable Development, Essex, United Kingdom, and a Non-Resident Research Fellow at the Center for Innovation in Gas Research and Utilization (CIGRU) and Institute of Water Security and Science (IWSS), West Virginia University, United States. Dr. Ibrahim is an Independent Expert Member of the Intergovernmental Working Group on Drought under the United Nations Convention to Combat Desertification.

Transnational Law and Governance

Series Editor: Paolo Davide Farah, West Virginia University, USA and gLAWcal – Global Law Initiatives for Sustainable Development, UK

In recent years the concepts of "transnational law" and "governance" have been explored by both scholars and practitioners with the terms taking on new meaning and significance, particularly in light of the ongoing economic crisis and a corresponding critical reappraisal of global institutional structures and governance. This multidisciplinary series aims to provide a home for research exploring these issues.

Transnational law covers a broad theoretical definition which includes studies emerging from disciplines such as international law, comparative law, international economic law and administrative law undertaken by legal scholars but also features extensive research undertaken by scholars from other disciplines, including but not limited to, political sciences, international relations, public administration, sociology, history, philosophy, and geography. Governance in particular is now seen as important when we refer to the general stability of the markets, to good faith and other key principles which are fundamental to the notion of a fair market which is responsive to the needs of governments and citizens as well as businesses.

This series features cutting-edge works which critically analyse the relationship between governance, institutions, and law from a variety of disciplinary perspectives.

Available titles in this series include:

The Crisis of Multilateral Legal Order
Causes, Dynamics, and Consequences
Edited by Lukasz Gruszczynski, Marcin J. Menkes, and Veronika Bilkova

Sustainability in Public Procurement, Corporate Law, and Higher Education
Edited by Dr. Lela Mélon

US Trade Policy, China, and World Trade Organization
Nerina Boschiero

Science, Technology, Policy, and International Law
Edited by Justo Corti Varela and Paolo Davide Farah

International Water Law and the Human Right to Water

The Case of Transboundary Aquifers

Imad Antoine Ibrahim

Routledge
Taylor & Francis Group
LONDON AND NEW YORK

First published 2025
by Routledge
4 Park Square, Milton Park, Abingdon, Oxon OX14 4RN

and by Routledge
605 Third Avenue, New York, NY 10158

Routledge is an imprint of the Taylor & Francis Group, an informa business

British Library Cataloguing-in-Publication Data
A catalogue record for this book is available from the British Library

Library of Congress Cataloging-in-Publication Data
Names: Ibrahim, Imad Antoine, author.
Title: International water law and the human right to water: the case of transboundary aquifers / Imad Antoine Ibrahim.
Description: Abingdon, Oxon [UK]; New York, NY: Routledge, 2024. | Series: Transnational law and governance | Includes bibliographical references and index.
Identifiers: LCCN 2024031037 (print) | LCCN 2024031038 (ebook) | ISBN 9781032076447 (hardback) | ISBN 9781032884301 (paperback) | ISBN 9781003537724 (ebook)
Subjects: LCSH: Water rights (International law) | Groundwater–Law and legislation. | Water–Law and legislation. | Water resources development–Law and legislation. | Right to water.
Classification: LCC KZ3686 .I37 2024 (print) | LCC KZ3686 (ebook) | DDC 341.4/2–dc23/eng/20240714
LC record available at https://lccn.loc.gov/2024031037
LC ebook record available at https://lccn.loc.gov/2024031038

ISBN: 978-1-032-07644-7 (hbk)
ISBN: 978-1-032-88430-1 (pbk)
ISBN: 978-1-003-53772-4 (ebk)

DOI: 10.4324/9781003537724

Typeset in Galliard
by Deanta Global Publishing Services, Chennai, India

Contents

Foreword

Dr. Paolo Farah

Natural resources management has been subject to countless articles and studies addressing it from a legal perspective over the previous years and decades.[1] In the transboundary context, the management of natural resources is considered to be extremely complicated given the need for a set of international rules, policies, and institutions that provide guidance for states. In that sense, international law applicable to natural resources has been developed progressively, taking into account various terms and concepts from national sovereignty to allocated resources between countries.[2] Still, natural resources law is not clearly defined or developed in a systemic matter but rather applies general principles and rules of international law contained within binding and non-binding mechanisms. These instruments are established through state practice, international governance frameworks, institutions, etc. Given that natural resources are considered scarce and extremely valuable, various bodies of rules have developed to allocate states rights for exploitation of these natural resources.[3] On that basis, international conventions, customary international law, and general principles of international law, in addition to arbitral and judicial decisions have all played a role in the development of natural resources law at the global level.[4] Over the years, various rules have been adopted providing

1 See for instance, Jérémie Gilbert, Natural Resources and Human Rights: An Appraisal (Oxford University Press 2018); Shawkat Alam, Jahid Hossain Bhuiyan, Jona Razzaque eds., International Natural Resources Law, Investment and Sustainability (Routledge 2017); Elisa Morgera & Kati Kulovesi eds., Research Handbook on International Law and Natural Resources (Edward Elgar Publishing 2016); Francesca Romanin Jacur, Angelica Bonfanti, & Francesco Seatzu, Natural Resources Grabbing: An International Law Perspective (Brill 2016); Daniëlla Dam-de Jong, International Law and Governance of Natural Resources in Conflict and Post-Conflicts Situations (Cambridge University Press 2015).

2 Richard B. Bilder, *International Law and Natural Resources Policies*, 20(3) Natural Resources Journal. 451, 453 (1980).

3 Owen McIntyre, *The making of International Natural Resources Law*, in Research Handbook on the Theory and Practice of International Lawmaking 442, 442 (Catherine Brolmann & Yannick Radi eds., Edward Elgar Publishing 2016).

4 *Id.* at 447-456.

"(1) national control over natural resources; (2) common access to natural resources; (3) joint national control of resources; and (4) international ownership and control of resources."[5] Despite that, international law faced multiple challenges resulting mainly from disagreements among states over the way natural resources must be shared; uncertainty over the existing rules and institutions in the general framework of a division between developed and developing countries.[6] All the challenges led to disputes before international courts over natural resources. Examples include China – Rare Earths and China – Raw Materials disputes adjudicated before the World Trade Organization panel and appellate body. These cases highlight the importance of sound management of transboundary natural resources that are being heavily mismanaged at the global, regional, and transboundary level especially given the interdependence of natural systems. Sound management is needed to ease the tensions that are rising.[7]

In this context, transboundary freshwater resources have been subject to great controversies where various studies and articles have attempted over the years to address the complexities surrounding the governance of shared freshwater resources.[8] This is extremely important given the existence of more than 500 shared water resources globally while this number is constantly increasing. In that sense, the majority of countries share a water basin with other nations. Moreover, various water conflicts have been recorded, especially in the last century while water agreements and river basin organizations are being established to regulate water governance.[9] Such regulations are extremely difficult given the existence of multiple boundaries that must be addressed which are mainly political, social, and jurisdictional in addition to physical, ecological, and biogeochemical. The main issue is that various stakeholders compete to realize their own interests within frameworks established by institutions, regulations, and society in addition to science and technology.[10] In other words, the problem is political by nature as governments, citizens, and companies are all seeking to use the same within

5 Bilder, *supra* note 1, at 453.

6 *Id.* at 465–467.

7 Marie-Claire Cordonier Segger, *Exploring the Role of International Law in Sustainable Natural Resources Management for Development* (Lauterpacht Centre for International Law, Mar. 18, 2021), https://www.lcil.cam.ac.uk/blog/exploring-role-international-law-sustainable-natural-resources-management-development-prof

8 See for instance, Enamul Choudhury & Shafiqul Islam, Complexity of Transboundary Water Conflicts: Enabling Conditions for Negotiating Contingent Resolutions (Anthem Press 2018); Claudia Pahl-Wostl, Water Governance in the Face of Global Change: From Understanding to Transformation (Springer 2015).

9 Gloria Salmoral et al., *Water Diplomacy and Nexus Governance in a Transboundary Context: In the Search for Complementarities*, 690 Science of the Total Environment. 85–96 (2019).

10 Enamul Choudhury & Shafiqul Islam, *Nature of Transboundary Water Conflicts: Issues of Complexity and the Enabling Conditions for Negotiated Cooperation*, 155(1) Journal of Contemporary Water Research & Education. 43, 43–44 (2015).

a given state but also across various nations.[11] This is further worsened due to changes in "population growth, socioeconomic conditions, and ecosystem functions and services",[12] as well as the fragmentation of institutions within at the domestic level.[13] To address these complexities, scholars have attempted to provide solutions such as regulating water resources at the various level be it international, regional, and local while global organizations like the United Nations are seeking to address the challenges.[14] Yet, the task of ensuring sound water management remains very difficult given the need to have social policies and institutional frameworks accepted by society and by the various nations while providing all the necessary support such as financial and technical to ensure the implementation of these policies.[15] Nonetheless, sound water governance is the only strategy that can work in the transboundary context.

Sound water governance is extremely relevant when it comes to shared aquifers as it accounts for 97% of non-frozen freshwater resources globally.[16] This resource is being used for various purposes such as drinking, agriculture, and households requiring its rational and reasonable exploitation,[17] as it also sustains ecosystems.[18] It is the most extracted resource globally and is the safest drinking water source providing water supply to numerous megacities such as Sao Paulo and Bangkok and is used for irrigation systems in places such as Western Asia and Northern Africa.[19] In this regard, there are more shared groundwater bodies when compared with transboundary surface water while the volume of accessible groundwater is much higher than the one of surface water. In this context, numerous countries exploit this resource unilaterally without considering the implications of their activities across the

11 Kurt Mørck Jensen & Rane Baadsgaard Lange, *Transboundary Water Governance in a Shifting Development Context New Development Finance, Development Spaces and Commitment to Cooperation: A Comparative Study of the Mekong and the Zambezi River Basins*, 19 (DIIS Report 2013:20).

12 Choudhury & Islam, *supra* note 10, at 44.

13 Christian Bréthaut & Laura Turley, *Exploring the Politics of Institutional Fragmentation in Transboundary River Basins*, Environmental Science. 1–24 (2020).

14 Michele-Lee Moore, *Perspectives of Complexity in Water Governance: Local Experiences of Global Trends*, 6(3) Water Alternatives. 487–505 (2013).

15 Peter Rogers & Alan W. Hall, *Effective Water Governance*, 16 (Global Water Partnership Technical Committee (TEC), 2003).

16 Christina M. Fraser et al., *A Methodology to Identify Vulnerable Transboundary Aquifer Hotspots for Multi-Scale Groundwater Management*, 45(7/8) Water International. 865, 865 (2020).

17 Ekaterina Golovina, *Environmental Peculiarities of Transboundary Groundwater Management*, 10(2) International Journal of Mechanical Engineering and Technology. 511, 511 (2019).

18 Fraser et al., *supra* note 16, at 865.

19 Alice Aureli & Raya M. Stephan, *Transboundary Aquifers: International Law and Politics?*, 102 Proceedings of the Annual Meeting (American Society of International Law). 356, 356–357 (2008).

borders. This was further worsened with the lack of focus on groundwater resources within international law for a long period given its invisible nature resulting in the existence of very few treaties addressing transboundary aquifers.[20] This is because groundwater was considered a local resource until the Second World War where new technologies emerged allowing the extraction of bigger quantities like the spread of advanced pumps while the need for water resources grew exponentially since then.[21] For all these reasons, groundwater, especially in the transboundary context, is considered as the hidden blue gold,[22] where its management faces great challenges stemming from overconsumption and contamination as well as the inability of the various stakeholders to state their interests clearly and the great difficulties facing cooperation in the transboundary water context.[23] Various factors impacting transboundary groundwater governance are associated with the existence of separate jurisdictions; different cultures and different languages, as well as socio-economic and political settings.[24] This reality is further worsened because of climate change affecting the quantity and quality of the resource,[25] where international organizations like the World Bank are paying a particular attention to this resource.[26]

This book addresses the topic of transboundary aquifers in international law from a new angle which was not examined before. The book highlights the interplay between international water law applicable to shared groundwaters and the Human Right to Water and Sanitation (HRWS). The author, through the analysis, is providing an overview of the development of international groundwater law and the HRWS in parallel. Throughout the book, the author argues for the need to consider the HRWS within the emerging and evolving international groundwater law regime. This is an interesting approach to take given the great value of groundwater as a drinking water source in comparison to surface water. This approach is analyzed in the transboundary groundwater context which adds huge complexities to this topic as various states need to agree on adopting a human right approach to shared aquifers. Nonetheless, this is not evident especially as very few articles in the literature examined this matter while existing international water conventions and instruments did not

20 Gabriel Eckstein, *International Law for Transboundary Aquifers: A Challenge for Our Times*, 115 American Journal of International Law. 201, 202 (2021).

21 Joseph W. Dellapenna, *The Customary Law Applicable to Internationally Shared Groundwater*, 36(5) Water International. 584, 584 (2011).

22 Aureli & Stephan, *supra* note 17, at 359.

23 Jamie Lintona & David B. Brooks, *Governance of Transboundary Aquifers: New Challenges and New Opportunities*, 36(5) Water International. 606-618 (2011).

24 Jac van der Gun, *Transboundary Groundwater Resources: Sustainable Management and Conflict Resolution*, 44(1) Water International. 74–76 (2019).

25 Aureli & Stephan, *supra* note 17, at 359.

26 Salman M.A. Salman, *The World Bank Policy and Practice for Projects Affecting Shared Aquifers*, 36(5) Water International. 595–605 (2011).

discuss this interplay. It is for these reasons that this book has great value in terms of bridging this gap in the literature through a detailed analysis of the interplay between international groundwater law and the HRWS. Such analysis is taking place in the general context of fragmentation of international law which is acknowledged by the author and considered all along the book.

Preface

Water is a scarce and finite resource. It is a resource without an alternative, and on which humanity depends fully, not only for economic and social development, but for its entire survival. However, the resource is facing major challenges, including, *inter alia*, population growth, poor management and protection, climate change and environmental degradation, urbanization and industrialization, and the lack of good faith cooperation to resolve the competing demands between and at all levels. Such levels include individual users, districts, provinces, and particularly nation states; as well as between the different uses within each state itself.

Most of the freshwater resources are located beneath the ground, and as a result, groundwater is faced with the bulk of these challenges. It is a resource that is completely out of sight, and this leaves it out of the immediate minds of planners and policy makers. Detailed and reliable technical information and data are still lacking for many aquifers; and management and protection rules and institutions, where they exist, are inadequate. The unchecked extraction of fossil aquifers, and the unsustainable utilization of the replenishable ones, pose a real danger to the very existence of these aquifers. Consequently, and in the absence of full and genuine cooperative efforts between most of the riparian states, managing and sharing of transboundary aquifers have continued to be a daunting challenge.

The principle of equitable and reasonable utilization has gained acceptance as the cardinal principle of international water law. Yet, because of lack of trust and cooperation between states, difficulties remain in operationalizing the various factors of the principle. Those difficulties have gradually led, in parallel, to the evolution of the concept of water as a vital human need, and to the birth of the human right to water and sanitation, which is now an established principle of international law. However, the implementational challenges to this principle have been staggering. Lack of political commitment in most countries has resulted in the failure to adopt the necessary legislative framework and to establish the appropriate institutions. And where such frameworks and institutions exist, implementation and enforcement remain poor. Under these circumstances, the concept of the extraterritorial application of the obligation of the human right to water, particularly groundwater, has become quite challenging, and indeed, a secondary matter to the national concerns in many states.

Connecting the above two issues of transboundary aquifers and the human right to water is, no doubt, a complex and demanding endeavor. It requires thorough research and full comprehension of the history and context of the two concepts. Moreover, it requires analytical skills and approaches for digging deep in the bottoms of groundwater, as well as in the fragmented international human rights law.

This book addresses these complex and intricate issues in a well-defined and methodical manner. The research is all-encompassing, the analysis is deep and thorough, and the findings are presented in a clear and succinct manner. This makes the book a major addition to the literature on the law of transboundary aquifers and the human right to water law.

Dr. Salman M.A. Salman
Distinguished Honorary Member and Fellow
International Water Resources Association (IWRA)

Acknowledgement

I am deeply grateful to the people who helped me along my PhD journey resulting in this book. I would like to thank first Dr. Paolo Davide Farah, the editor of the series "Transnational Law and Governance" with Routledge, with whom I have been working since 2014. I am also grateful to Dr. Giuseppe Martinico, my former PhD supervisor who provided much needed insights to this work. Finally, I would like to thank international water lawyers who equally contributed with their valuable comments.

Abbreviations and Acronyms

CBD	Convention on Biological Diversity
CESCR	Committee on Economic, Social, and Cultural Rights
UNWC	Convention on the Law of the Non-Navigational Uses of International Watercourses
UNECE Water Convention	Convention on the Protection and Use of Transboundary Watercourses and International Lakes
Draft Articles	Draft Articles on the Law of Transboundary Aquifers
EIA	Environmental Impact Assessment
FAO	Food and Agriculture Organization
GC 15	General Comment 15
HRC	Human Rights Council
HRWS	Human Right to Water and Sanitation
AIDA	International Association for Water Law
ICJ	International Court of Justice
ICCPR	International Covenant on Civil and Political Rights
ICESCR	International Covenant on Economic, Social, and Cultural Rights
IEL	International Environmental Law
IGL	International Groundwater Law
IHRL	International Human Rights Law
IHL	International Humanitarian Law
ILO	International Labour Organization
ILA	International Law Association
ILC	International Law Commission
IWA	International Water Association
IWL	International Water Law
IWRA	International Water Resources Association
MEAs	Multilateral Environmental Agreements

MNCs	Multinational Companies
NGOs	Non-Governmental Organizations
PIL	Public International Law
SADC	Southern African Development Community
SDGs	Sustainable Development Goals
TBAs	Transboundary Aquifers
UDHR	Universal Declaration of Human Rights
UK	United Kingdom
UNECE	United Nations Economic Commission for Europe
UNGA	United Nations General Assembly
US	United States
WFD	Water Framework Directive
WHO	World Health Organization

Introduction

This book aims to examine the development of international law applicable to Transboundary Aquifers (TBAs) and simultaneously considering the Human Right to Water and Sanitation (HRWS) adopted in the last decade. The purpose is to determine how International Water Law (IWL) and the HRWS can be harmonized in the context of TBAs. This is important given that the rules and instruments adopted to address this topic are relatively nascent, and the field itself is still in the process of developing global regulatory frameworks. The book seeks to answer the following question: Taking the application of the HRWS to shared aquifers as a case study, can IWL and International Human Rights Law (IHRL) complement each other? The response to this question requires an analysis of the progressive development of International Groundwater Law (IGL) and its challenges, the evolution of the HRWS, the nature of transboundary groundwaters, and the interplay between these two fields. The author will argue that IWL agreements should contain a provision related to the HRWS to ensure the protection of this right. Particularly, a stipulation must be included in the nonbinding instrument that tackles shared groundwaters: the Draft Articles on the Law of Transboundary Aquifers (hereafter Draft Articles) adopted in 2008 through the United Nations General Assembly (UNGA) Resolution. This introduction will provide a brief overview of the interaction between these different topics.

Generally, most freshwater resources are located underground. As a result, a majority of the world's population rely on such reserves to meet their daily needs.[1] There is no other source being extracted as much as groundwater.

1 Yoram Eckstein & Gabriel E. Eckstein, *Transboundary Aquifers: Conceptual Models for Development of International Law*, 43(5) Ground Water. 679, 679 (2005); Renee Martin-Nagle, *Fossil Aquifers: A Common Heritage of Mankind*, 2(3) Journal of Energy and Environmental Law. 39, 40 (2011); Marguerite de Chaisemartin et al., *Addressing the Groundwater Governance Challenge: A Call from the "Groundwater Governance: A Global Framework for Action" Project*,in Freshwater Governance for the 21st Century 205, 206 (Eiman Karar ed., Springer 2017).

DOI: 10.4324/9781003537724-1

In many places, it is the only reliable freshwater,[2] making it extremely valuable.[3] Rules for its protection vary depending on location.[4] The factors behind this increasing use, however, stem from agricultural and industrial developments occurring due to technological advancements.[5] The fragmentation of institutional mechanisms makes its management at the state-level difficult.[6] Oftentimes, this type of direction does not consider surface water, overconsumption, potential contamination, pollution, or the lack of financial and human resources in the creation of laws and policies.[7] Previous mishandling of regulatory statutes has worsened the above-mentioned challenges.[8] Still, as water scarcity increases, so does the value of groundwater,[9] and the need to protect it.[10]

In this context, the management of TBAs has been considered a very difficult task.[11] Nonetheless, the maintenance of this resource through good governance is a must.[12] International cooperation is vital since nations share aquifers.[13] Efforts are being made for the adoption of rules to preserve and

2 Geert-Jan Nijsten et al., *Transboundary Aquifers of Africa: Review of the Current State of Knowledge and Progress towards Sustainable Development and Management*, 20 Journal of Hydrology: Regional Studies. 21–34 (2018).

3 Water Science School, *Aquifers and Groundwater* (USGS 16 October 2019), available at https://www.usgs.gov/special-topics/water-science-school/science/aquifers-and-groundwater (last accessed 3 August 2022).

4 Marco Doveri, Matia Menichini & Andrea Scozzari, *Protection of Groundwater Resources: Worldwide Regulations and Scientific Approaches*, in Threats to the Quality of Groundwater Resources: Prevention and Control 13, 13–30 (Andrea Scozzari & Elissavet Dotsika eds., Springer 2015).

5 Gabriel Eckstein & Yoram Eckstein, *A Hydrogeological Approach to Transboundary Ground Water Resources and International Law*, 19(2) American University International Law Review. 201, 203 (2003).

6 Pilar Carolina Villar, *Groundwater and the Right to Water in a Context of Crisis,* 19(1) Ambiente & Sociedade. 85, 94 (2016).

7 Kathrin Knüppe & Claudia Pahl-Wostl, *A Framework for the Analysis of Governance Structures Applying to Groundwater Resources and the Requirements for the Sustainable Management of Associated Ecosystem Services*, 25(13) Water Resources Management. 3387, 3390 (2011).

8 Jie Chen et al., *Challenges and Prospects of Sustainable Groundwater Management in an Agricultural Plain along the Silk Road Economic Belt, North-West China*, 34(3) International Journal of Water Resources Development. 354, 354–368 (2018).

9 Henry Vaux, *Groundwater under Stress: The Importance of Management*, 62(1) Environmental Earth Sciences. 19, 19–23 (2011).

10 The Battle Creek Area Clean Water Partnership, *Surface Water vs. Groundwater*, available at https://www.bcwater.org/surface-water-vs-groundwater/ (last accessed 3 August 2022).

11 E I Golovina, *Problems of Groundwater Extraction from Transboundary Aquifers and Complexes,*151(1) IOP Conference Series: Earth and Environmental Science. 1, 1–9 (2018).

12 Andrew Allan, Mara Tignino & Flavia Loures, *The Role and Relevance of the Draft Articles on the Law of Transboundary Aquifers in the European Context*, 8(3) Journal for European Environmental & Planning Law. 231, 232 (2011).

13 Igor S. Zektser, *Investigation of Transboundary Aquifers in Russia: Modern States and Main Tasks*, in Transboundary Aquifers in the Eastern Borders of The European Union:

ensure sustainable use of this resource.[14] Until recently, groundwater was considered a secondary issue. In comparison to surface water, it was not perceived as the main focus by policy-makers and legislators.[15] Nonetheless, the adoption of laws tackling its management challenges requires appropriate legal framework at the national and transboundary water context.[16] These new rules would help preventing its depletion. They might also reduce the negative impacts on human health that result from environmental and natural ecosystems degradation.[17] So far, and by 2021, more than 468 TBAs are recognized worldwide.[18] However, very few agreements currently address matters related to shared aquifers as well as some non-binding arrangements that exist at the local levels.[19] The treaties range from those made in the last century to those as recently adopted in the 2010s,[20] stressing the need for more cooperation given existing complexities.[21]

Regional Cooperation for Effective Management of Water Resources 79, 81 (Tomasz Nałęcz ed., Springer 2012).

14 Justin Carlson, *A Critical Resource or Just a Wishing Well? A Proposal to Codify the Law on Transboundary Aquifers and Establish an Explicit Human Right to Water*,26(5) American University International Law Review. 1409, 1413 (2011).

15 Eckstein & Eckstein, *supra* note 5, at 222–224.

16 Robert G. Varady et al., *Groundwater Governance: A Global Framework for Country Action*, 6 (Thematic Paper No. 5: Groundwater Policy and Governance, April. 2013).

17 Maria Gavouneli, *A Human Right to Groundwater?*, 13(3) International Community Law Review. 305, 312 (2011).

18 International Groundwater Resources Assessment Centre, *Transboundary Aquifers of the World Map*, available at https://www.un-igrac.org/transboundary-aquifers-world-map (last accessed 3 August 2022).

19 Gabriel Eckstein, The International Law of Transboundary Groundwater Resources, 3–6 (Routledge 2017).

20 The agreements are: the 1977 treaty re-negotiated in 2007 on the Genevese Aquifer; three agreements on the Nubian Sandstone Aquifer System, made in 1992 and 2000; the 2010 treaty on the Guarani Aquifer; the 2015 convention on the Al-Sag/Al Disi Aquifer; the 2002 agreement for the "Establishment of a Consultation Mechanism for the Northwestern Sahara Aquifer System"; 2017 Convention de mise à disposition et d'échange de données relatives à la gestion des eaux souterraines des calcaires du carbonifère [Convention for the Provision and Exchange of Data Relating to the Management of Groundwater from Carboniferous Limestone]; the 2014 Memorandum of Understanding for the Establishment of a Consultation Mechanism for the Integrated Management of the Water Resources of the Lullemeden, Taoudeni/Tanezrouft Aquifer System replacing a 2009 Memorandum of Understanding for establishing a trilateral consultative arrangement for the Iullemeden Aquifer System. Imad Antoine Ibrahim, *Factors Affecting the Adoption of Transboundary Groundwater Agreements and Potential Solutions: A Focus on the Nubian Sandstone Aquifer System*, in Cooperating Over Shared Freshwater Resources Using International Law (Gabriel Eckstein et al. ed., World Scientific Publishing, 2023).

21 Raya Marina Stephan et al., *Transboundary Aquifers*, in Groundwater: Making The Invisible Visible 172, 172 (The United Nations World Water Development Report, United Nations Educational, Scientific and Cultural Organization 2022).

There are other international instruments that address TBAs tackling mainly surface water.[22] Nonetheless, shared aquifers have different characteristics requiring special consideration.[23] Any international rule for their governance must take into account the lack of data on groundwater, the potential for contamination, and the perception that water is an *open* resource.[24] The above-mentioned issues exist among a long list of problems affecting water governance that further complicates oversight. These matters include inter alia social, political, and environmental concerns.[25] The difficulties mentioned above should not be viewed from a solely negative perspective as they can also provide incentives to foster international cooperation. Though global regulatory frameworks lack the concrete ability to address the peculiarities of TBAs, efforts have been made in recent decades to establish mechanisms for their governance.[26] In particular, several recent initiatives have attempted to raise awareness of its importance and take concrete action to improve its management.[27] In fact, numerous instruments and conventions already consider surface water and groundwater as an interrelated topic. Furthermore, several joint bodies are addressing TBAs in addition to concerns pertaining to initially shared surface water. Hence, it is important to recognize that these aquifers have gained attention. Nonetheless, a lot of work must be done to reach an appropriate level of cooperation.[28]

Along the developments mentioned above, the international community has taken steps to ensure the establishment of fundamental rights to water and sanitation for citizens worldwide.[29] Existing mechanisms did not expressly include the HRWS in their list of rights. Even though it was stated that the latter is non-exhaustive, implicit rights are still not been considered.[30] To that end, numerous conferences, declarations, statements, and meetings have taken place since the end of the Second World War, leading to the adoption of

22 Eckstein, *supra* note 19, at 3–6.

23 Jamie Linton & David B. Brooks, *Governance of Transboundary Aquifers: New Challenges and New Opportunities*, 36(5) Water International. 606, 606–618 (2011).

24 David B. Brooks & Jamie Linton, *Governance of Transboundary Aquifers: Balancing Efficiency, Equity and Sustainability*,27(3) International Journal of Water Resources Development. 431, 431 (2011).

25 Derek Armitage et al., *Science-Policy Processes for Transboundary Water Governance*, 44 Ambio 353, 353 (2015).

26 Pilar Carolina Villar, *International Cooperation on Transboundary Aquifers in South America and the Guarani Aquifer Case*,59(1) Revista Brasileira de Política Internacional. 1, 1–5 (2016).

27 Sharon B. Megdal, *Invisible Water: The Importance of Good Groundwater Governance and Management*, Npj Clean Water. 1, 1–15 (2018).

28 Raya Marina Stephan, *International Water Law for Transboundary Aquifers – A Global Perspective*, 4(2) Central Asian Journal of Water Research. 48, 56–57 (2018).

29 Amanda Cahill Ripley, The Human Right to Water and Its Application in the Occupied Palestinian Territories, 8–19 (Routledge 2011).

30 Taniya Malik, *Recognition of Human Right to Water Under International Law Regime*, 1(4) International Journal of Applied Research. 169, 169–172 (2015).

the HRWS in 2010.[31] The establishment of this right has fueled a surge in research articles and studies examining all the aspects related to its adoption, implementation, and relevance.[32] That was extremely important as realizing it requires changing the ways decision-makers and experts operate.[33] The recognition of its existence may constitute a very crucial approach to securing water access for communities and individuals lacking it.[34] Despite the progress made in recent decades, regions across the globe still lack basic access to water and sanitation.[35] Nonetheless, the promotion of HRWS is a useful tactic that can be used by those lacking it.[36] In fact, the main question that scholars and researchers have attempted to answer is whether the adoption of the HRWS makes a difference in terms of its fulfilment at the national and local levels.[37] The response has varied, as some have expressed that it provides the necessary legal means for ensuring water access, while others criticized this right for various reasons. For instance, it has been stated that there is a wide range of political and economic avenues that can be used to secure water access to different communities in need.[38]

Discussions concerning the evolution of the HRWS as a concept are also taking place. Academics have begun examining the application of IHRL beyond the borders of states, largely because they have started acting beyond

31 Ben Saul, David Kinley & Jaqueline Mowbray, The International Covenant on Economic, Social and Cultural Rights: Commentary, Cases and Materials, 900–904 (Oxford University Press 2014); Daniel Aguirre, The Human Right to Development in a Globalized World 171–173 (Ashgate 2008).

32 On this point, see for instance, Colin Brown, Priscila Neves-Silva, & Léo Heller, *The Human Right to Water and Sanitation: A New Perspective for Public Policies*, 21(3) Ciencia & Saude Coletiva. 661, 661–670 (2016); Ralph P. Hall, Barbara Van Koppen & Emily Van Houweling, *The Human Right to Water: The Importance of Domestic and Productive Water Rights*,20(4) Science and Engineering Ethics. 849, 849–868 (2014); Takele Soboka Bulto, *The Human Right to Water in the Corpus and Jurisprudence of the African Human Rights System*, 11 African Human Rights Law Journal. 341, 341–367 (2011); Odeh Al Jayyousi, *Water as a Human Right: Towards Civil Society Globalization*, 23(2) International Journal of Water Resources Development. 329, 329–339 (2007).

33 Virginia Roaf, Catarina de Albuquerque, & Leo Heller, *The Human Rights to Water and Sanitation: Challenges and Implications for Future Priorities*, in Equality in Water and Sanitation Services 26, 26–45 (Oliver Cumming & Tom Slaymaker eds., Routledge 2018).

34 Céline Dubreuil, *The Right to Water: From Concept to Implementation*, 3 (World Water Council, 2006).

35 Tiaji Salaam-Blyther, *Global Access to Clean Drinking Water and Sanitation: U.S. and International Programs*, 4-8 (Congressional Research Service, 10 September 2012).

36 Karen Bakker, *Commons Versus Commodities: Debating the Human Right to Water*, in The Right to Water: Politics, Governance and Social Struggles 19, 38 (Farhana Sultana & Alex Loftus eds., Earthscan 2012).

37 John Scanlon, Angela Cassar & Noémi Nemes, *Water as a Human Right?*, 21 (IUCN Environmental Policy and Law Paper No. 51; IUCN – The World Conservation Union, 2004).

38 Jamie Linton, *The Human Right to What? Water, Rights, Humans and the Relation of Things*, *in* The Right to Water: Politics, Governance and Social Struggles 38, 38–47 (Farhana Sultana & Alex Loftus eds., Earthscan 2012).

their national boundaries. This, in turn, impacts the rights of their citizens and the populations of other countries. As a result, the concept of Extraterritorial Application of Human Rights has emerged in the literature.[39] This principle means that a state bears an international legal obligation to respect, comply with, and ensure the realization of IHRL beyond its national territories. This goes against the traditional notion of a government responsibility for human rights violations that usually occurs within a given nation.[40] Stretching the applicability of this framework beyond a country's borders has happened because of globalization and trans-nationalization. States, because of these factors, have begun overtly influencing IHRL. Meanwhile, powerful private actors such as Multinational Companies (MNCs) are also affecting this issue. To this end, there has been a need to address this topic beyond national territories. The debate concerns not only whether states have an obligation to prevent human rights violations, but also whether countries have duties to fulfill these rights in places they are lacking.[41] Nations have been increasingly operating worldwide and transnationally. For these reasons, scholars have argued that a revision of the extraterritoriality principle is necessary to cover these new complex actions. This would ensure that no violations of IHRL can go undetected.[42] Such changes were also suggested to address the global operations of private actors. Few measures have been proposed to hold companies accountable for their performance.[43] Since these actors are constantly asserting their powers abroad, this may affect the rights of individuals located in places where the extraterritorial application of human rights is already a pressing issue.[44] This has been raised before international and national tribunals.[45]

39 See for instance, Joseph Sinchak, *The Extraterritorial Application of Human Rights Treaties: Al Skeini et al. v. United Kingdom (2011)*, 3(12) Pace International Law Review Online Companion. 416, 416–445 (2013); Michał Gondek, The Reach of Human Rights in a Globalising World: Extraterritorial Application of Human Rights Treaties (Intersentia 2009); Galia Rivlin, *Constitutions Beyond Borders: The Overlooked Practical Aspects of the Extraterritorial Question*, 30 Boston University International Law Journal 135, 137 (2012).

40 Ralph Wilde, *The Extraterritorial Application of International Human Rights Law on Civil and Political Rights*, in Routledge Handbook of International Human Rights Law 635, 635–661 (Scott Sheeran & Sir Nigel Rodley eds., Routledge 2013).

41 Ibrahim Kanalan, *Extraterritorial State Obligations beyond the Concept of Jurisdiction*, 19(1) German Law Journal. 43, 43–44 (2018).

42 Abe Chauhan, *A Causal Model for the Extraterritorial Application of Human Rights Treaties*, (VIII) The Oxford University Undergraduate Law Journal. 107, 134–135 (2019).

43 Cantu Rivera Humberto, *Developments in Extraterritoriality and Soft Law: Towards New Measures to Hold Corporations Accountable for their Human Rights Performance?*, 14 Anuario Mexicano de Derecho Internacional. 727, 727–763 (2014).

44 Beth Van Schaack, *The United States Position on the Extraterritorial Application of Human Rights Obligations: Now is the Time for Change*, 90 International Law Studies. 20, 20–21 (2014).

45 Oona A. Hathaway et al, *Human Rights Abroad: When Do Human Rights Treaty Obligations Apply Extraterritorially?*, 43 Arizona State Law Journal. 389, 389–426 (2011).

Among the rights examined in their potential extraterritorial relevance, the HRWS has received considerable attention for its transboundary application. A country can violate this right for citizens residing outside of their borders. State-level actions may for instance reduce the volume of water accessible to the population of another nation. This ultimately spreads pollution from the parent-state to its neighbors downstream.[46] The exterritorial application of human rights occurs every time a state – through its management and use practices – negatively affects the usage of shared water of inhabitants residing in another country.[47] The basis of such a right is found in IHRL.[48] The concept has received criticisms and objections from certain states suggesting they only have an obligation to fulfill it to people within their own borders.[49] In contrast, other actors, including nations and civil society organizations, have been examining this issue to determine its significance and how it can be implemented in the general framework of IHRL.[50] Numerous oppositions to this particular realization were also raised concerning the HRWS.

The extraterritorial application of this right in the context of shared freshwaters is associated with IWL given the existence of such duties within water conventions and instruments.[51] This field has witnessed gradual evolution since World War Two.[52] Nonetheless, the focus has remained on rules that regulate the non-navigational uses of international watercourses. As a result, TBAs have not been granted the same attention as surface waters.[53] The global community has sought to address this by establishing regulations directly tackling TBAs. This resulted in a set of nonbinding rules through an instrument established in 2008.[54] Lawyers and scholars have since been examining the ways through which the various IWL conventions and instruments could be reconciled. Numerous contradictions and overlaps have been noticed between provisions of the various legal mechanisms. Suggestions have been made, both

46 Takele Soboka Bulto, *Towards Rights-Duties Congruence: Extraterritorial Application of the Human Right to Water in the African Human Rights System*, 29(4) NETHERLANDS QUARTERLY OF HUMAN RIGHTS. 491, 500 (2011).

47 Roberta Greco, *The Silala Dispute: Between International Water Law and the Human Right to Water*, 39 QUESTIONS IN INTERNATIONAL LAW. 23, 35 (2017).

48 Colin Brown & Léo Heller, *Development Cooperation in Water and Sanitation: Is it Based on the Human Rights Framework?*,22(7) Ciência & Saúde Coletiva. 2247–2256 (2017).

49 Nora Hansén, *The Human Right to Water and its Status in International Law*, 50 (Thesis in Public International Law, Faculty of Law, Stockholm University, 2018).

50 AMANDA CAHILL-RIPLEY, *Protecting Rights in the Face of Scarcity: The Right to Water*, in UNIVERSAL HUMAN RIGHTS AND EXTRATERRITORIAL OBLIGATIONS 194, 213–214 (Mark Gibney & Sigrun Skogly eds., University of Pennsylvania Press 2010).

51 Greco, *supra* note 47, at 23–37.

52 CHRISTINA LEB, COOPERATION IN THE LAW OF TRANSBOUNDARY WATER RESOURCES, 42–70 (Cambridge University Press 2013).

53 Gabriel E. Eckstein, *Managing Buried Treasure across Frontiers: The International Law of Transboundary Aquifers*, 36(5) WATER INTERNATIONAL. 573, 573–583 (2011).

54 Joseph W. Dellapenna, *The Customary Law Applicable to Internationally Shared Groundwater*, 36(5) WATER INTERNATIONAL. 584, 584–594 (2011).

against and in favor of them.[55] Nonetheless, so far no treaty has been adopted to address TBAs solely. The 2008 instrument requires updating or amending and some call for the formation of a completely new convention.[56]

IWL as a legal field has gone through fragmentation as different water sources require specific regulation that considers their particularities.[57] Therefore, previous discussions addressed the question of harmonization of IWL. The focus remained on tackling this topic, however while the relationship between this field and other legal frameworks remained a secondary matter.[58] This situation occurred as other regimes like IHRL were developing in parallel.[59] Hence, it is important to create synergies between different fields that are connected. Discussions regarding IGL and the HRWS cannot be conducted without also focusing on other problems that affect IWL. Debates over efforts to create connections between these regulatory frameworks require analysis of the fragmentation taking place within IWL.[60]

This book tackles two types of fragmentation simultaneously. Whereas the fragmentation of IWL has been the subject of debate for decades, literature concerning the importance of creating synergies between IWL and the HRWS has only emerged in the last few years.[61] Discussions concerning this issue are extremely relevant since the matters examined concern the need to update water agreements to coincide with scientific, technical, and legal progression. In the decades between the drafting and eventual adoption of the water conventions, many additional subjects have emerged.[62] For instance, the HRWS was adopted in 2010 after the establishment of existing treaties and the 2008 instrument. IWL has created its own version of it referring to it as a vital human need.[63] This discussion holds further importance to TBAs given the

55 Christine Traversi, *The Inadequacies of the 1997 Convention on International Water Courses and 2008 Draft Articles on the Law of Transboundary Aquifers*, 33(2) Houston Journal of International Law. 453, 453–488 (2011).

56 Gabriel Eckstein & Francisco Sindico, *The Law of Transboundary Aquifers: Many Ways of Going Forward, but Only One Way of Standing Still*, 23(1) Review of European, Comparative & International Environmental Law. 32, 32–42 (2014).

57 *Id.*

58 Alistair Rieu-Clarke, Andrew Allan, Sarah Hendry eds., Routledge Handbook of Water Law and Policy (Routledge 2017).

59 On this point see, Jochen Von Bernstorff, *The Changing Fortunes of the Universal Declaration of Human Rights: Genesis and Symbolic Dimensions of the Turn to Rights in International Law*, 19(5) European Journal of International Law. 903, 903–924 (2008).

60 Attila Tanzi, The Consolidation of International Water Law: A Comparative Analysis of the UN and UNECE Water Conventions (Editoriale scientifica 2017).

61 Attila Tanzi, *Reducing the Gap between International Water Law and Human Rights Law: The UNECE Protocol on Water and Health*, 12(3) International Community Law Review. 267, 267–285 (2010).

62 Joyeeta Gupta, *The Watercourses Convention, Hydro-hegemony and Transboundary Water Issues*, 51(3) The International Spectator. 118, 118–131 (2016).

63 See for instance, Claudia Cinelli, *A New Human Rights-Based Approach to the UN Watercourses Convention*, 38(2) Water International. 180, 180–191 (2013).

particularities surrounding aquifers and their relevance for securing drinking water for populations. Moreover, the absence of a binding instrument that exclusively addresses shared aquifers provides an opportunity to examine the ways future provisions can consider the HRWS.[64]

To examine the above issues and their interplay, Chapter 1 addresses the concept of fragmentation giving an overview of it in relation to international law, environmental law, and IHRL. It considers the development of IWL and the existing interactions between the different legal systems. Chapter 2 discusses the historical progress of IGL after World War Two. It tackles all aspects related to its evolution. Chapter 3 analyses the legal dilemmas surrounding the law of TBAs. In particular, it evaluates the 2008 instrument, its scope, substantive norms, and the criticisms against it. Chapter 4 discusses the different sclassification of TBAs (common good, economic good, public good, human right, and quasi commodity) and the implications of each category is assessed. Chapter 5 analyzes the interactions between the HRWS and the law of TBAs considering IWL and the extraterritorial nature of human rights obligations. It draws a conclusion related to the implication of this debate on the 2008 instrument. Chapter 6 discusses the arguments for the inclusion of a human right provision within the Draft Articles. It debates how such a suggestion may fit into the discussion concerning the harmonization of IWL.

64 Chusei Yamada, *Codification of the Law of Transboundary Aquifers (Groundwaters) by the United Nations*, 36(5) Water International. 557, 557–565 (2011).

1 Situating the Debate

This chapter provides a conceptual overview of legal matters related to the discussion on IWL. The objective is to give the readers a general understanding before focusing on the specifics examined in this book. It situates the debate in the framework of fragmentation of international law. This is a concept that has been tackled thoroughly in the literature.[1] It will then focus on the fragmentation of International Environmental Law (IEL). Following this, the author will examine the development of IWL and IHRL, which are the two fields being discussed in this manuscript within the context of TBAs.

On the Phenomenon of Fragmentation of International Law

Fragmentation of the global legal system is not a new phenomenon. Agreements related to issues such as economy, trade, or politics have been adopted mainly since World War II and before that. The difference between this situation and later fragmentation is that the latter highlights a reality where specialized regimes have multiplied. This is pushing scholars to support progression or view it with suspicion.[2] States establish specific universal frameworks when general PIL is viewed as insufficient to address particular issues. Courts created within these regimes push their developments and ensure that legislative needs are met.[3]

1 On the concept of fragmentation of international law, see in general, Philippa Webb, International Judicial Integration and Fragmentation (Oxford University Press 2013); Margaret A. Young (eds.), Regime Interaction in International Law: Facing Fragmentation (Cambridge University Press 2012); Bruno Simma, *Universality of International Law from the Perspective of a Practitioner*, 20(2) European Journal of International Law. 265, 265–297 (2009); Anne van Aaken, *Defragmentation of Public International Law through Interpretation: A Methodological Proposal*, 16(2) Indiana Journal of Global Studies. 483, 483–512 (2009); Martti Koskenniemi & Päivi Leino, *Fragmentation of International Law? Postmodern Anxieties*, 15(3) Leiden Journal of International Law. 553, 553–579 (2002).

2 Tim Stephens, *Multiple International Courts and the 'Fragmentation' of International Environmental Law*, 25 Australian Yearbook of International Law. 227, 228 (2006).

3 *Id.* at 232.

DOI: 10.4324/9781003537724-2

Concerns about fragmentation have surfaced in the post-Cold War era.[4] The collapse of the Soviet Union, the increasing role of new transnational organizations, tribunals, and Non-Governmental Organizations (NGOs) particularly established since the 1990s in addition to MNCs, and acceptance of non-traditional sources of international norms have led to the adoption and ratification of numerous multilateral treaties. This created the fear that such institutions would develop independent interpretations of the system.[5] Fragmentation of international law has sped as universal tribunals have increasingly acted as independent jurisdictions.[6] This reality pushed the International Law Commission (ILC) to tackle this topic in the 2000s, which resulted in the adoption of several reports on the issue.[7] From a functional perspective, fragmentation occurred because of the lack of a centralized global authority with the task of legislating and supervising implementation at the domestic level. This ultimately resulted in the emergence of problems that require specific remedies. From a political perspective, states hold differing ideologies in negotiations that lead to the formation of different regimes.[8]

Specialized cooperation networks are emerging due to globalization. Neither national rules nor international ones are sufficient for regulating them. They also do not have the capacity to tackle the objectives of each network. Therefore, they have created their own laws that may be formal or informal. These are usually developed through cooperative strategies with the help of intergovernmental organizations. The establishment of specific treaties does not take into consideration existing laws globally. This has led to the fragmentation of international law into specialized autonomous subsets that are unconnected.[9] This development occurred due to disregard of existing legislative frameworks and institutional works in different fields. A lack of knowledge on general principles and practices of international law also fueled this phenomenon. The resultant situation has created division within rule-systems and deteriorated the effectiveness of established regulations.[10]

4 Jacob Katz Cogan, *The Idea of Fragmentation,* 105 PROCEEDINGS OF THE ASIL ANNUAL MEETING. 123, 124 (2011).

5 Anne Peters, *"The Refinement of International Law: From Fragmentation to Regime Interaction and Politicization,* 15(3) INTERNATIONAL JOURNAL OF CONSTITUTIONAL LAW. 671, 671–704 (2017).

6 Mario Prost & Paul Kingsley Clark, *Unity, Diversity, and the Fragmentation of International Law: How Much Does the Multiplication of International Organizations Really Matter?*, 5(2) CHINESE JOURNAL OF INTERNATIONAL LAW. 341, 356 (2006).

7 Peters, *supra* note 69, at 671–704.

8 *Id.*

9 Report of the Study Group of the International Law Commission finalized by Martti Koskenniemi, *Fragmentation of International Law: Difficulties Arising from the Diversification and Expansion of International Law* 244–245 (International Law Commission; Fifty-eighth session Geneva, 1 May–9 June and 3 July–11 August 2006).

10 *Id.* at 11.

Despite its negative consequences, fragmentation highlights how transnational legal activity has expanded to cover novel topics and sectors. This is especially true since specific laws are usually developed to respond to a need for regulation of particular concerns.[11] The emergence of these regimes exercising authority through norms, conventions, and institutions does not mean that they are independent of the international legal order. They still must use the existing transnational bodies and rules to fill the gaps within their own systems.[12] One of the many factors that contributed to their appearance was the increase in interstate conflicts that required global solutions through worldwide cooperation.[13] The status of self-contained regimes that have, or are currently emerging, is not the same. For example, international economic law has a well-established base[14] in contrast to international energy law that started evolving mainly in the late 1990s.[15] Fragmentation became further complicated with the increasing reliance on soft law instruments that are not binding. However, they are important in situations where no consensus has been reached on the establishment of compulsory mechanisms.[16]

This phenomenon can have different meanings depending on its interpretation.[17] There are several various forms of fragmentation. For instance, the ILC distinguished three distinct types. The first is associated with diverse understandings of general international law, whereby conflicts may result in diminishing legal security. In this case, it would be unclear how institutions would interpret the rules. Subjects may be discriminated against by the jurisdiction with decision-making powers, depending on the choice.[18] The second is the result of a clash in which an institution deviates from the norm, thus providing a new resolution that would constitute an exception to general rules. The third is related to the confrontation between special laws. This is true where the interpretation plays an important role in deciding which type must apply.[19]

11 *Id.* at 14.
12 Pierre-Marie Dupuy, *A Doctrinal Debate in the Globalization Era: On the "Fragmentation" of International Law*, 1(1) European Journal of Legal Studies. 1–19 (2007).
13 Michele Emily Olivier, *Globalization or Fragmentation of International Law: Challenges for Harmonization*, De Jure. 437, 439 (2008).
14 Ewelina Cala-Wacinkiewicz, *International Law – Between Division (Fragmentation) and Unity (Constitutionalisation). Law of Divisions or Law Beyond Boundaries?*, 12 US-China Law Review. 768, 772 (2015).
15 Alexandra Wawryk, *International Energy Law: An Emerging Academic Discipline*, in Law as Change: Engaging with the Life and Scholarship of Adrian Bradbrook 223, 223–256 (Paul Babie & Paul Leadbeter eds., Cambridge University Press 2014).
16 Pemmaraju Sreenivasa Rao, *Multiple International Judicial Forums: A Reflection of the Growing Strength of International Law or Its Fragmentation?*, 25(4) Michigan Journal of International Law. 929, 931 (2004).
17 Flavia Lattanzi, *Introduction, in* The Diversification and Fragmentation of International Criminal Law 1, 1 (Larissa van den Herik & Carsten Stahn eds., Brill/Nijhoff 2012).
18 Report of the Study Group of the International Law Commission, *supra* note 73, at 31–33.
19 *Id.* at 33–34.

Scholars also have their own understanding of the concept, debating its definition and characteristics.[20]

Pros and Cons of the Concept

Scholars have examined the advantages and disadvantages of fragmentation. Its opponents argue that each new specialized field has its own institutions, communities, academics, negotiators, enforcement mechanisms, and NGOs that make it extremely difficult to create a coherent international system. In the case of conflicts, it is very hard to solve disputes objectively since each specific system has its own provisions. Even when attempts to balance these regimes occur, it is often the values and rules of one field that dominate, while others are viewed as secondary.[21] In fact, the proliferation of tribunals acting in the name of specialized regimes has raised concerns. Given the lack of a centralized structure globally, it is viewed by some as an attempt to further extend the influence of a particular state.[22] Courts addressing these systems disagree over the interpretation and meaning of particular treaties.[23] As a result, a state may be subject to contradictory obligations or decisions issued by different tribunals.[24]

The existence of specialized regimes with their own set of rules may create isolated legal orders. With these systems holding their own understanding of the general principles of PIL, a transformation occurs.[25] The presence of multiple subsets of universal regulations pushes the proponents of each system to provide arguments as to why their rules should apply.[26] The absence of a centralized authority at the global level has led to the adoption of norms that

20 Peters, *supra* note 69, at 672–674; Harlan Grant Cohen, *From Fragmentation to Constitutionalization*, 25(1) Pacific McGeorge Global Business & Development Law Journal. 381, 384–389 (2012); Adrian Nastase & Bogdan Aurescu, *The Strategic Role of International Law in Contemporary International Society*, 1 Romanian Journal of International Law. 15, 19 (2003); Marcelo Dias Varella, *Central Aspects of the Debate on Complexity of International Law*, 27 Emory International Law Review. 1, 20 (2013).

21 Ralf Michaels & Joost Pauwelyn, *Conflict of Norms or Conflict of Laws?: Different Techniques in the Fragmentation of International Law*, 22(3) Duke Journal of Comparative & International Law. 349, 349–376 (2012).

22 Panagiotis Delimatsis, *The Fragmentation of International Trade Law*, 45(1) Journal of World Trade. 87, 87–90 (2011).

23 Harlan Grant Cohen, *Finding International Law, Part II: Our Fragmenting Legal Community*, 44 New York University Journal of International Law and Politics. 1049, 1049–1056 (2012).

24 Salem Hikmat Nasser, *Global Law in Pieces: Fragmentation, Regimes and Pluralism* 13 (São Paulo Law School of Fundação Getulio Vargas – FGV DIREITO SP Research Paper Series – Legal Studies, Paper no. 105, August 2014).

25 N. Jansen Calamita, *Countermeasures and Jurisdiction: Problems of Asymmetry, Fragmentation and Effectiveness*, 42(2) Georgetown Journal of International Law. 233, 237 (2011).

26 Gerhard Hafner, *Pros and Cons Ensuing from Fragmentation of International Law*, 25(4) Michigan Journal of International Law. 849, 856 (2004).

are complex, and thus confuse the applicability of international law within the context of specific conflicts. Each system and interpretation may provide an alternative stance, which further destabilizes situations and presents the opportunity for strife among institutions too.[27] One system may prevent the realization of the objectives outlined by another. Legal certainty may be eroded due to the existence of competing organizations that have overlapping jurisdictions or seek to interpret cases through a different lens. Moreover, there is the possibility of losing the coherence, consistency, and unity of international law.[28] In fact, some do not consider the latter as an actual legal system since the law is unclear. This, therefore, renders it ineffective.[29]

Based on the above analysis, it has been argued that weaker states lose their ability to bargain with stronger ones that possess more resources and are diverse from economic, institutional, and geographic perspectives. This makes reaching a consensus very unlikely given the difference in preferences. Hence, fragmentation through treaty-specific issues provides more advantages to powerful states. Differing institutions allow dominant nations to threaten or favor one institution or specialized legal system over another. This action is often the result of a country pushing its self-interest while small states are further marginalized. A fragmented system is a way to receive the same advantages as before, but in a less visible manner where hierarchies are questioned.[30]

In contrast, proponents argue that having specialized agencies that focus on a particular branch of international law results in the development of a more appropriate regulatory framework. The clash among these organizations provides the necessary incentive for increasing the efficiency of new instruments.[31] The existence of fragmented norms may eventually lead to the development of cohesive sets of ideals as competition may promote the establishment of structuralized systems.[32] These are constantly updated due to healthy rivalry that takes place and is oftentimes beneficial.[33]

Fragmentation highlights the ability of a system to respond to the fast changes in society. This reflects the maturity of international law, where specialized regulations contribute to the provision of necessary rules, despite differences in regimes.[34] As such, the concerns of one system may be more

27 Jack Goldsmith & Daryl Levinson, *Law for States: International Law, Constitutional Law, Public Law*, 122(7) HARVARD LAW REVIEW. 1791, 1803 (2009).

28 Peters, *supra* note 69, at 671–704.

29 Goldsmith & Levinson, *supra* note 91, at 1803.

30 Eyal Benvenisti & George W. Downs, *The Empire's New Clothes: Political Economy and the Fragmentation of International Law*, 60(2) STANFORD LAW REVIEW. 595, 597–598 (2007).

31 Joost Pauwelyn, *Bridging Fragmentation and Unity: International Law as a Universe of Inter-Connected Islands,* 25(4) MICHIGAN JOURNAL OF INTERNATIONAL LAW. 903, 904 (2004).

32 William Thomas Worster, *Competition and Comity in the Fragmentation of International Law*, 34(1) BROOKLYN JOURNAL OF INTERNATIONAL LAW. 119, 146 (2009).

33 *Id.* at 147.

34 Delimatsis, *supra* note 86, at 87–92.

important than those of another. Also, one organization's expertise may be more refined than that of another dealing with the same matter.[35] The existence of various regimes provides flexibility for states that may not be willing to join if given a specific rule set.[36] The increasing complexity of life and modernity requires a more particular approach and the adoption of laws that provide political opportunities for states.[37] These rules and tribunals can better fit the needs of specific situations.[38]

Others point out that, in fact, regulatory coordination among different international agencies has improved.[39] It is in this context that concerns of fragmentation have been downplayed, citing better cooperation between systems and a well-disciplined structure that maintains legal and political stability.[40] Moreover, the threats to legal certainty do not seem dramatically different from those that existed in the past and constitute a healthy part of international law.[41] This phenomenon is a natural one that takes place as a result of gradual evolution. This is why there is no reason to fear it, as the different regimes are interdependent and regulated by the global community.[42] The best argument offered by its supporters is that its alternative is much worse. In that sense, this type of splintering is regarded as a necessary evil.[43] This does not mean that the problems or disadvantages of fragmentation cannot or should not be dealt with.

Fragmentation of IEL

Policies enacted at the state level are unable to tackle global environmental issues,[44] as the growing number of natural resources such as oceans and polar regions, whose degradation impacts the entire globe, is largely considered shared responsibility in today's age.[45] Therefore, there was a need for the establishment of a regulatory framework to tackle transboundary environmental

35 Joel P. Trachtman, *Fragmentation, Coherence and Synergy in International Law*, 2(4) Transnational Legal Theory. 505, 517 (2011).
36 Pauwelyn, *supra* note 95, at 904.
37 Peters, *supra* note 69, at 671–704.
38 Hafner, *supra* note 90, at 859.
39 Benvenisti & Downs, *supra* note 94, at 596.
40 Worster, *supra* note 96, at 146.
41 *Id.* at 146.
42 Davorin Lapas, *Some Remarks on Fragmentation of International Law: Disintegration or Transformation?*, 40(1) The Comparative and International Law Journal of Southern Africa. 1, 28–29 (2007).
43 Anthony J. Colangelo, *A Systems Theory of Fragmentation and Harmonization*, 49 New York University Journal of International Law and Politics. 1, 7 (2016).
44 Theodore Okonkwo, *Adjudicating International Environmental Law Litigation: Recent Development of Case Law*, 8(3) Beijing Law Review. 239, 240 (2017).
45 Albert E. Utton, *International Environmental Law and Consultation Mechanisms*, 12 Columbia Journal of Transnational Law. 56, 60–62 (1973).

matters.[46] This legal foundation evolved in the last six decades to address the relationship between humans and the environment. Originating as a part of PIL to tackle environmental problems, sectoral and regional regimes have been developing since the 1960s to cover different subjects.[47] The Stockholm Declaration of 1972 is defined as the moment at which the emergence of a new discipline was officially recognized.[48] Since then, numerous environmental agreements and soft law instruments have been adopted.[49] The Rio Declaration and Agenda 21 of 1992 constitute another milestone in the creation of this discipline.[50]

IEL possesses a bureaucratic structure with more than a thousand treaties and instruments holding provisions related to ecological protection. The new regimes are characterized by their highly detailed and technical nature, where numerous articles stipulate comprehensive procedures that must be followed. The established institutions are tasked with monitoring and implementing stipulations of their conventions.[51] Environmental problems are very complex and are affected by a wide range of activities. Therefore, decision-makers have the difficult task of taking a holistic approach to solving any issue while simultaneously ensuring an effective solution.[52] The challenges emerging from transboundary harm have led to the proliferation of non-state actors playing a greater role in the environmental sphere. The existing fragmentation and the need for expertise, where different non-state entities have developed, make this especially true. These entities hold either a specific focus or are given a wide range of means to tackle different problems.[53] There are many questions being raised concerning the legitimacy and efficacy of this global regulatory framework.[54] For instance, has this field truly led to protecting the environment, and

46 Alexander Proelss, *International Environmental Law and the Challenge of Climate Change*, 53 German Yearbook of International Law. 65, 65–67 (2010).

47 Stephens, *supra* note 66, at 234–236.

48 United Nations, United Nations Conference on the Human Environment, 5–16 June 1972, Stockholm, available at https://www.un.org/en/conferences/environment/stockholm1972 (last accessed 3 August 2022).

49 Stephens, *supra* note 66, at 234–236.

50 United Nations General Assembly, Report of the United Nations Conference on Environment and Development (Rio de Janeiro, 3–14 June 1992), 12 August 1992, available at https://www.un.org/en/development/desa/population/migration/generalassembly/docs/globalcompact/A_CONF.151_26_Vol.I_Declaration.pdf (last accessed 3 August 2022); Sustainable Development Goals Knowledge Platform, Agenda 21, 1992, available at https://sustainabledevelopment.un.org/outcomedocuments/agenda21 (last accessed 3 August 2022).

51 Stephens, *supra* note 66, at 241.

52 Dave Owen, Mapping, *Modeling, and the Fragmentation of Environmental Law*, 2013 Utah Law Review. 219, 221–222 (2013).

53 Asher Alkoby, *Non-State Actors and the Legitimacy of International Environmental Law*, 3(1) Non-State Actors and International Law. 23, 23–98 (2003).

54 Malgosia Fitzmaurice & Duncan French, *Preliminary Material*, in International Environmental Law and Governance i, i–v (Malgosia Fitzmaurice & Duncan French eds., Brill/Nijhoff 2015).

are developing countries equally participating in the decision-making process and the establishment of Multilateral Environmental Agreements (MEAs)?[55]

IEL developed primarily to respond to ecological crises. It did not have the opportunity to create a comprehensive and holistic approach to the issues. This led to the proliferation of MEAs and the simultaneous fragmentation of the specialized legal system. This complicates the adoption of effective solutions for future generations because it requires the constant establishment of new institutions.[56] The concept of fragmentation became very famous in the environmental field, given the contradiction between MEAs that are sufficiently isolated and those that address environmental issues from a system-level perspective.[57] Examples of specific ones include the 2015 Paris Agreement on Climate Change[58] and the 1992 Convention on Biological Diversity.[59] Division in IEL is the result of systems viewing ecological issues as separate scientific subjects that require the negotiation of specific instruments. This has led to the proliferation of multilateral, regional, and bilateral conventions.[60]

Parties are allowed to negotiate MEAs where they agree on the terms and obligations. Problems arise when states are permitted to continue establishing new agreements even when they overlap, contradict, or have fewer positive results than existing ones. This creates a situation where one party tackles a particular environmental problem without considering consequences.[61] The formation of new MEAs and institutions may result in inconsistencies, overlaps, and contradictions. This eventually affects international relations as these parties are unable to comply with the provisions of agreements. The number of treaties adopted also poses a risk. The potential discrepancies and similarities often lead to having MEAs with soft provisions that do not enjoy enough legal support to be enforced. The creation of numerous conventions allows parties to bypass them without actually being bound by them. In many instances, states try to gain leverage in the negotiation process. This situation negatively impacts those with good intentions who possess a willingness to comply with

55 Steinar Andresen & Ellen Hey, *The Effectiveness and Legitimacy of International Environmental Institutions*, 5 International Environmental Agreements: Politics, Law and Economics. 211, 211–212 (2005).

56 John Carter Morgan III, *Fragmentation of International Environmental Law and the Synergy: A Problem and a 21st Century Model Solution*, 18(1) Vermont Journal of Environmental Law. 134, 138 (2016).

57 Karen N. Scott, *The Dynamic Evolution of International Environmental Law*, 49(4) Victoria University of Wellington Law Review. 607, 621 (2018).

58 United Nations, Paris Agreement, 2015.

59 United Nations, Convention on Biological Diversity, 1992.

60 Harro Van Asselt, *Managing the Fragmentation of International Environmental Law: Forests at the Intersection of the Climate and Biodiversity Regimes*, 44 New York University Journal of International Law. 1205, 1209 (2012).

61 Morgan III, *supra* note 120, at 135–138.

the treaties. This is particularly true when the agreed-upon MEAs do not solve the environmental problem for which they were created.[62]

Numerous articles have been written on the fragmentation of IEL, with the main focus on the proliferation of environmental treaties and institutions.[63] This phenomenon has been criticized by scholars. Weiss, for instance, noted the existence of substantive incompatibilities among the treaties. Furthermore, she noted operational inefficiency among them.[64] Depending on the area of environmental governance and the problem being addressed, the degree of fragmentation differs.[65] Not only is IEL fragmented, but there is division too among specific fields. For example, climate change law has diverged into sector-specific areas.[66] Thus, the debate over the potential establishment of an international court tackling environmental issues has emerged,[67] along with its advantages and disadvantages in comparison with the way courts are handling current claims.[68] The many reasons for the fragmentation of international law also contributed to the split in IEL.[69]

Segmenting not only affects the different treaties and instruments tackling ecological issues, but also the relationship between them and other global fields. This is due to an existing connection within these sectors and between different environmental matters.[70] Indeed, IEL is interlinked with other international bodies of law. The failure to recognize this jeopardizes its effectiveness.[71] For instance, conventions tackling trade or investments may prevent

62 *Id.* at 139–141.

63 Louis J. Kotze, *Fragmentation Revisited in the Context of Global Environmental Law and Governance*, 131(3) South African Law Journal. 548, 549–550 (2014).

64 Asselt, *supra* note 124, at 1209–1210.

65 Fariborz Zelli, *Institutional Fragmentation*, in Encyclopedia of Global Environmental Governance and Politics 469, 470 (Philipp H. Pattberg & Fariborz Zelli eds., Edward Elgar Publishing 2015).

66 William Boyd, *Climate Change, Fragmentation, and the Challenges of Global Environmental Law: Elements of a Post-Copenhagen Assemblage*, 32(2) University of Pennsylvania Journal of International Law, 457, 515 (2010).

67 Lucas Carlos Lima & Mariana Clara DE Andrade, *An International Court for the Environment and its Position Within the Debate on the Fragmentation of International Law*, 67 Rev. Faculdade Direito Universidade Federal Minas Gerais. 373, 373–397 (2015).

68 Christina Voigt, *Introduction – International Courts and the Environment: The Quest for Legitimacy*, in International Judicial Practice on the Environment: Questions of Legitimacy 1, 1–10 (Christina Voigt ed., Cambridge University Press 2019); Susan M. Hinde, *The International Environmental Court: Its Broad Jurisdiction as a Possible Fatal Flaw*, 32 Hofstra Law Review. 727, 727–750 (2003).

69 Gerhard Loibl, *International Environmental Regulations – Is a Comprehensive Body of Law Emerging or is Fragmentation Going to Stay?, in* International Law between Universalism and Fragmentation 783, 783 (Isabelle Buffard et al eds., Brill/Nijhoff 2008).

70 Maryna Medvedieva et al., *Fragmentation and Synergies in International Climate Change Regime*, 48(3/4) Environmental Law and Policy. 160, 160 (2018).

71 David Leary & Balakrishna Pisupati, *Introduction*, in Future of International Environmental Law 1, 8 (David Leary & Balakrishna Pisupati eds., United Nations 2010).

actions that are stipulated within MEAs.[72] IEL faces other challenges such as the need to balance environmental protection with economic growth in developing countries. Here, other concerns, such as lifting people out of poverty, are the main focus of governments.[73] Nonetheless, suggestions are also made to balance both competing objectives through, for example the use of environmental technologies.[74] Fragmentation of this type of law is one of the many reasons why it is often considered ineffective. Despite the increasing focus on this field in the last decades,[75] it has been said that the proliferation of global environmental governance binding and non-binding instruments indicates the complexities involved in regulating it.[76]

Fragmentation of this field has also been viewed in a more positive light under the implication that it fosters innovation that helps enhance environmental governance.[77] Its proponents state that MEAs are necessary and adequate to tackle problems globally. This, they argue, respects cultural differences among states and protects individual sovereignty. The existence of multiple MEAs also increases the efficiency and flexibility of organizations. States have the ability to choose compliance with any agreement they wish. Institutions are also are more efficient, given that they often deal with one particular issue.[78] Expertise in the established institutions, government officials, and general experts focusing on the field is vital to addressing the specific problems tackled by a given convention. Hence, the emergence of specialized regimes that can be interpreted and implemented by environmental experts. These systems interact with other areas of law where environmental issues are considered by institutions like human rights courts and the dispute settlement system of the World Trade Organization.[79] Based on this, various concerns are being considered simultaneously where MEAs defend environmental interests.[80]

72 Harlan Grant Cohen, *Fragmentation* 8 (University of Georgia School of Law Research Paper Series; Paper No. 2015–2022; 27 May 2016).

73 William L. Andreen, *Environmental Law and International Assistance: The Challenge of Strengthening Environmental Law in the Developing World*, 25 Columbia Journal of Environmental Law. 17, 17–23 (2000).

74 Raul R. Cordero, Pedro Roth & Luis Da Silva, *Economic Growth or Environmental Protection? The False Dilemma of the Latin-American Countries,* 8(4) Environmental Science & Policy. 392, 392–394 (2005).

75 Jonathan Verschuuren, *The Role of Sustainable Development and the Associated Principles of Environmental Law and Governance in the Anthropocene*, in Environmental Law and Governance for the Anthropocene 3, 22 (Louis Kotzé ed., Hart Publishing 2017).

76 Harro Van Asselt, The Fragmentation of Global Climate Governance: Consequences and Management of Regime Interactions 5 (Edward Elgar Pub 2014).

77 Frank Biermann et al., *The Fragmentation of Global Governance Architectures: A Framework for Analysis,* 9(4) Global Environmental Politics. 14, 27 (2009).

78 Morgan III, *supra* note 120, at 142–143.

79 Stephens, *supra* note 66, at 241–242.

80 See in general, Joyeeta Gupta, Courtney Vegelin & Nicky Pouw, *Lessons Learned from International Environmental Agreements for the Stockholm + 50 Conference: Celebrating 20 Years of*

Nonetheless, the problem with these conventions is that there are no outlets that allow parties to be forced into compliance with their provisions. Because of this, there are calls for the adoption of innovative approaches that ensure the implementation of obligations bypassing the traditional need of states consent.[81] In fact, numerous suggestions have been made to solve this issue.[82] Moreover, in order to combat the problems emerging from fragmentation, several solutions have been proposed. For instance, formal cooperative arrangements are created to manage existing segments and enhance the efficiency of environmental governance. These solutions represent an attempt to develop mechanisms that manage conflicts and maximize the potential benefits arising from this phenomenon.[83] Despite the recognition of the problems, it is still not clear whether following the proposals will solve the dilemma.[84] Notwithstanding the focus in recent years on reforming this field, not much has been done concerning fragmentation within this type of law.[85]

Relevance of Fragmentation to this Book

Fragmentation of international law and IEL – in this case – affects the regulation of different global issues. Among these, provisions related to water management, including shared ones, are being adopted through various frameworks that address diverse topics.[86] One can mention international climate change law through its various conventions, the United Nations Framework Convention on Climate Change,[87] Kyoto Protocol,[88] and the Paris agreement.[89] All these treaties include provisions that tackle water resources implicitly and explicitly,

INEA, 22 International Environmental Agreements: Politics, Law and Economics. 229, 229–235 (2022).

81 Scott, *supra* note 121, at 607–610.

82 *Id.* at 624–625.

83 Karen Scott, *International Environmental Governance: Managing Fragmentation through Institutional Connection*, 12(1) Melbourne Journal of International Law. 177, 177–216 (2011).

84 Boyd, *supra* note 130, at 516.

85 Asselt, *supra* note 124, at 1210.

86 See, for instance, Erica Lymann, *Rethinking International Environment Linkages: A Functional Cohesion Agenda for Species Conservation in a Time of Climate Change*, 27(1) Fordham Environmental Law Review. 1, 1–56 (2016); Johan G. Lammers, *What is Wrong with International Environmental Law, in* What's Wrong with International Law?: Liber Amicorum A.H.A. Soons 214, 214 (Cedric Ryngaert, Erik J. Molenaar, and Sarah Nouwen eds., Brill / Nijhoff 2015); Marjan Ajevski, *Fragmentation in International Human Rights Law – Beyond Conflict of Laws*, 32(2) Nordic Journal of Human Rights. 87, 87–98 (2014); Saverio Di Benedetto, International Investment Law and the Environment (Edward Elgar Publishing 2013); Turki Althunayan, Dealing with the Fragmented International Legal Environment: WTO, International Tax, and Internal Tax Regulations (Springer 2010).

87 United Nations Framework Convention on Climate Change, 1992.

88 Kyoto Protocol to the United Nations Framework Convention on Climate Change, 1998.

89 Paris agreement, *supra* note 122.

comprising those in the transboundary context.[90] This is despite the fact that this field's main concern is climate change and not water.[91] Another example is the Convention on Biological Diversity (CBD) secretariat, which acknowledged that water plays a crucial part in the protection of biodiversity and the successful implementation of the agreement. It also recognized the existence of synergies and overlaps between the CBD and international water conventions.[92] This highlights the existing interactions between various environmental topics that cannot be seen independently, as the issues addressed within these treaties represent parts of one ecosystem.[93] This remains one of the important challenges to transboundary water management.[94]

Fragmentation also takes place when considering the type of water agreement to be adopted, be it multilateral or bilateral. This can be seen in the context of international watercourses having few treaties or arrangements. The record is better in North America and Europe. Nonetheless, states in many places tend to enter bilateral agreements despite the existence of more than two nations sharing the watercourse.[95] For instance, the Nile river basin, shared between 11 countries, has a huge number of treaties governing it.[96] These lack harmonization and coordination and are signed either bilaterally or among a limited number of states. This results in a situation where some of them are not recognized by all the nations.[97] Examples include the 1959 Agreement between the Republic of Sudan and the United Arab Republic (of Egypt) for the Full utilization of the Nile Waters;[98] the Nile Basin Initiative in

90 Raya Marina Stephan, *Climate Change Considerations Under International Groundwater Law*, 42(6) Water International. 757, 757–772 (2017).

91 Philippe Cullet & Raya Marina Stephan, *Introduction to 'Groundwater and Climate Change: Multi-level Law and Policy Perspectives'*, 42(6) Water International. 641, 641–645 (2017).

92 Owen McIntyre, *The Protection of Freshwater Ecosystems Revisited: Towards a Common Understanding of the 'Ecosystems Approach' to the Protection of Transboundary Water Resources*, 23(1) Review of European Community & International Environmental Law. 88, 89 (2014).

93 Lei Xie & Imad Antoine Ibrahim, *Is the Ecosystem Approach Effective in Transboundary Water Systems: Central Asia as a Case Study?*, 8(5) WIREs Water. 1, 5–9 (2021).

94 Alistair Rieu-Clarke, *From Treaty Practice to the UN Watercourses Convention*, in Research Handbook on International Water Law 11, 13 (Stephen C. McCaffrey, Christina Leb & Riley T.Denoon eds., Edward Elgar Publishing 2019).

95 *Id.* at 13–14.

96 International Waters Governance, *Nile River Basin Initiative*, available at http://www.internationalwatersgovernance.com/nile-river-basin-initiative.html (last accessed 3 August 2022).

97 Salman M.A. Salman, *The Grand Ethiopian Renaissance Dam: The Road to the Declaration of Principles and the Khartoum Document*, 41(4) Water International. 512, 512–527 (2016).

98 United Arab Republic and Sudan Agreement (with annexes) for the full utilization of the Nile Waters. Signed at Cairo, on 8 November 1959. Official text: Arabic. Registered by the United Arab Republic on 7 February 1963, available at https://treaties.un.org/doc/Publication/UNTS/Volume%20453/volume-453-I-6519-English.pdf (last accessed 3 August 2022).

1999[99] and the 2010 Nile Cooperative Framework Agreement.[100] This over-inflation of treaties further complicates the management of the basin even though recent instruments focus on collaboration.

Fragmentation occurs for topics associated with water resources, such as access to it for displaced and stateless people, or simply those residing in war-torn countries such as the Middle East.[101] In this particular case, several frameworks apply to provide a guarantee of basic rights for those facing uncertain legal status within their countries.[102] International Humanitarian Law (IHL), IWL, IHRL, and international criminal law all apply here. Numerous strengths and weaknesses have been noted where this category of people remains vulnerable under international law.[103] In fact, specific instruments have been developed recently to that end, such as the Geneva List of Principles on the Protection of Water Infrastructure. These focus on the protection of infrastructures during armed conflicts.[104] This is despite the fact that IHL has established rules since the 1970s to protect water installations and resources in this context.[105] As such, should this new instrument take precedence over the rest of the frameworks that are equally applicable, considering that the principles are not binding for the time being?

Hence, fragmentation can play a confusing and negative role when it comes to the management of challenges, in this case water resources, since various regimes may apply. This is namely why it has been examined in this book focused on international law applicable to TBAs and the HRWS.

IWL as a Sub-Discipline of IEL

Throughout human civilization, laws have been developed to address the question of water management, given that this resource is a vital element in ensuring the survival of societies. As such, regulations have formed to tackle

99 Nile Basin Initiative, available at https://www.nilebasin.org/index.php/media-center/info-graphics/77-nbi-achievements-1999-2019#:~:text=Since%20it%20was%20established%20in,River%20Nile%20as%20well%20as (last accessed 3 August 2022).

100 Nile Basin Initiative, *Cooperative Framework Agreement*, available at https://www.nilebasin.org/index.php/81-nbi/73-cooperative-framework-agreement (last accessed 3 August 2022).

101 Carly A. Krakow, *The International Law and Politics of Water Access: Experiences of Displacement, Statelessness, and Armed Conflict*, 12(2) WATER. 340, 340 (2020).

102 *Id.*

103 *Id.*

104 Geneva Water Hub, *The Geneva List of Principles on the Protection of Water Infrastructure*, 2019. Available at https://www.genevawaterhub.org/resource/geneva-list-principles-protection-water-infrastructure (last accessed 3 August 2022).

105 MARA TIGNINO, WATER DURING AND AFTER ARMED CONFLICTS: WHAT PROTECTION IN INTERNATIONAL LAW? (Brill 2016).

the questions of water use and allocation.[106] Through a long process that began after World War II, IWL established treaties that were adopted following decades of efforts, non-binding global instruments, and documents.[107] Its role along transboundary water agreements has been analyzed in the literature. Here, scholars have reached various conclusions.[108] The importance of shared water resources led to an explosion of scholarly pieces addressing this topic from a legal perspective. Two institutes paved the way for the adoption of frameworks on shared freshwaters.[109] These are the International Law Association (ILA)[110] and the Institute of International Law (ILI).[111] Other professional membership organizations playing a role in the water field are the International Association for Water Law (AIDA),[112] the International Water Resources Association (IWRA)[113] and the International Water Association (IWA),[114] IWRA and IWA have not been involved in IWL. Meanwhile, AIDA has done so but not in a research capacity. Other relevant entities are the Geneva Water Hub, which is a university research center,[115] and the International Water Law Academy which constitutes a platform for networking and exchanging information.[116]

Initially, laws addressing transboundary freshwaters focused on questions related to boundary demarcation between nations. Domestic legislation regulated other activities such as water use and fishing. In some instances, bilateral agreements were adopted between states. Navigation was the sole issue examined globally because of existing commercial interests. This resulted in the

106 Antoinette Hildering, International Law, Sustainable Development and Water Management 45 (Eburon Publishers 2006).

107 Elisa Aust et al., *Water Resources Law*, in Handbook of Agri-Food Law in China, Germany, European Union: Food Security, Food Safety, Sustainable Use of Resources in Agriculture 347, 350–351 (Ines Härtel ed., Springer 2018).

108 Rafael Emmanuel Macatangay & Alistair Rieu-Clarke, *The Role of Valuation and Bargaining in Optimizing Transboundary Watercourse Treaty Regimes*, 18(3) International Environmental Agreements: Politics, Law and Economics. 409, 409–428 (2018).

109 Dante A. Caponera & Marcella Nanni, Principles of Water Law and Administration: National and International (3rd ed. CRC Press 2019).

110 International Law Association, available at https://www.ila-hq.org/ (last accessed 3 August 2022).

111 Institute of International Law, https://www.idi-iil.org/en/a-propos/ (last accessed 3 August 2022).

112 International Association for Water Law, available at https://www.aida-waterlaw.org/ (last accessed 3 August 2022).

113 International Water Resources Association, available at https://www.iwra.org/ (last accessed 3 August 2022).

114 International Water Association, available at https://iwa-network.org/ (last accessed 3 August 2022).

115 Geneva Water Hub, available at https://www.genevawaterhub.org/ (last accessed 3 August 2022).

116 Wuhan University, International Water Law Academy, available at https://iwla.whu.edu.cn/index.php?id=about (last accessed 3 August 2022).

development of international law explicitly addressing this matter. The 20th century witnessed new forms of water use, such as hydropower. Thus, the protection of water resources became a more significant concern as its usage increased. This led to the adoption of treaties as there was a need to follow the development of nations from economic, technical, and social perspectives.[117] Furthermore, the establishment of water conventions was crucial to water security as it provided the legal systems necessary to protect rights and tackle violations.[118] It also regulates states' behavior when managing and exploiting different shared freshwater bodies.[119]

The rules have taken the form of principles and were stipulated within the provisions of water agreements. They are commonly known as the general principles of IWL. The relationship between them has been discussed in previous decades and will be examined in the following chapters.[120] One must keep in mind that such treaties have led to disputes in many cases. This is especially true since they remain open to interpretation.[121] IWL was perceived from the beginning as controversial.[122] This is why its role along basin water conventions has been evaluated in the literature. Scholars have arrived at various conclusions, however, depending on the analysis conducted.[123] In fact, numerous criticisms have been directed against this field. From this perspective, water laws are seen by many as ineffective and as a baseless fuel for geopolitical claims,[124] since they are conceived as part of power relations.[125]

117 Dante A. Caponera & Marcella Nanni, Principles of Water Law and Administration: National and International 184 (2nd ed. CRC Press 2007).

118 Patricia Wouters & Ruby Moynihan, *Water Security – Legal Frameworks and the UN Watercourses Convention*, inThe UN Watercourses Convention in Force: Strengthening International Law for Transboundary Water Management 336, 343 (Flavia Rocha Loures & Alistair Rieu-Clarke eds., Routledge 2013).

119 Stefano Burchi, *International and Domestic Water Law in Central Asia – Implementing International Law Obligations Regarding Transboundary Waters: The Role of Domestic Water Legislation*, 4(2) Central Asian Journal of Water Research. 59, 59 (2018).

120 See, for instance, Convention on the Law of the Non-navigational Uses of International Watercourses. Adopted by the General Assembly of the United Nations on 21 May 1997. Entered into force on 17 August 2014. In this convention, the different principles are explained in detail.

121 Ruben van Genderen & Jan Rood, *Water Diplomacy: A Niche for the Netherlands?* 8 (Netherlands Institute of International Relations 'Clingendael', December 2011).

122 Jacob D. Petersen-Perlman, Jennifer C. Veilleux, & Aaron T. Wolf, *International Water Conflict and Cooperation: Challenges and Opportunities,* 42(2) Water International. 105, 105–120 (2017).

123 Macatangay & Rieu-Clarke, *supra* note 172, at 409–428.

124 Patricia Wouters, *The Relevance and Role of Water Law in the Sustainable Development of Freshwater: From "Hydrosovereignty" to "Hydrosolidarity"*, 25(2) Water International. 202, 203 (2000).

125 Marwa Daoudy, *Hydro-Hegemony and International Water Law: Laying Claims to Water Rights*, 10 (S2) Water Policy. 89, 89 (2008).

Existing legal frameworks are insufficient when it comes to tackling state control over shared water resources, especially considering their geographic positions, such as being upstream countries.[126] Even recently, criticism regarding the efficiency of IWL has been voiced. Literature indicates that current laws are falling short of their stated goals.[127] It is in this context that calls were made for reimagining this field; in other words, making changes to the regulatory frameworks to address the inability to provide a response to the global water crisis where other aspects, such as economic ones, are considered.[128] In reality, the situation is worse, given the differences in the practices of nations sharing the water resources and due to the diverging political, economic, and religious histories across societies,[129] as well as cultures.[130] In fact, despite the existing rules, water management in the transboundary and national context remains extremely complicated, where numerous water disasters and mismanagement have occurred and are still taking place.[131]

Even though criticism is present, IWL is still the basis for water governance as there is no alternative system.[132] Given that environmental problems have no political boundaries, nations must collaborate to establish structures and frameworks for their management.[133] Shared freshwaters require appropriate systems to ensure cooperation based on specific principles and instruments. In that sense, water laws and regulations create management strategies that facilitate their good governance.[134] Hence, this field should be perceived as an important foundation. The criticism directed against it is justified in some

126 Melvin Woodhouse & Mark Zeitoun, *Hydro-Hegemony and International Water Law: Grappling with the Gaps of Power and Law*, 10 (S2) Water Policy. 103, 103 (2008).

127 Catherine Brölmann, *Sustainable Development Goal 6 as a Game Changer for International Water Law*, 7(5) ESIL Reflections. 1, 1 (2018).

128 Tim Stephens, *Reimagining International Water Law*, 71 Maryland Law Review Endnotes. 20, 21–22 (2012); de Chaisemartin et al., *supra* note 1.

129 Terje Tvedt, Tadesse Kasse Woldetsadik & Owen McIntyre, *"Sovereignty, the Web of Water and the Myth of Westphalia*, in A History of Water 3, 17 (Volume 2: Sovereignty and International Water Law, Terje Tvedt, Tadesse Kasse Woldetsadik & Owen Mcintyre eds., I.B. Tauris, 2015).

130 Lisa Hiwasaki, *'Water for Life'... Water for Whose Life? Water, Cultural Diversity and Sustainable Development in the United Nations*, in Water, Cultural Diversity, and Global Environmental Change: Emerging Trends, Sustainable Futures? 509, 527 (Barbara Rose Johnston et al. eds., Springer 2012).

131 Erfan Goharian & Mohamad Azizipour, *Integrated Water Resources Management in Iran*, in Integrated Water Resource Management: Cases from Africa, Asia, Australia, Latin America and USA 101, 113 (Edson de Oliveira Vieira et al. eds., Springer 2020).

132 Ariel Dinar et al., Bridges Over Water: Understanding Transboundary Water Conflict, Negotiation, and Cooperation 57 (World Scientific Publishing 2013).

133 David J. Lazerwitz, *The Flow of International Water Law: The International Law Commission's Law of the Non-Navigational Uses of International Watercourses*, 1(1) Indiana Journal of Global Studies. 247, 248–249 (1993).

134 Barbara Janusz-Pawletta & Mara Gubaidullina, *Transboundary Water Management in Central Asia: Legal Framework to Strengthen Interstate Cooperation and Increase Regional Security*, 25 Cahiers d'Asie Centrale. 195, 202–210 (2015).

circumstances but does not negate its importance. Indeed, the inefficiency of water agreements is the result of states' approach to this topic. They often focus, for example, on ensuring sovereignty and not on making compromises through negotiation. Another reason for the failure of IWL is the lack of institutional support provided by international donors who are not perceived as neutral actors. These factors, in addition to the ones mentioned previously, result in a negative perception of this sector.[135]

Nonetheless, support for IWL has reached a new milestone in the last decades. In this time, two water conventions (which will be discussed later in the book) have been adopted and ratified. This is why the non-legal water community is contemplating whether it should become accustomed to the debates taking place in this field[136] and become involved in them.[137] In fact, a consensus is emerging over the need to have, for instance, science contributing to water law[138]. This is being increasingly supported by the legal community.[139] The importance of IWL is seen through its current evolution. This has ranged from traditional approaches that tackle the need to regulate different water uses to addressing novel and complex challenges that face this sector. These include matters such as the protection of the environment and economic development. These changes reflect the existence of a sense of urgency given the threats emerging from the freshwater crisis requiring immediate response. This trend faces many uncertainties as this is an ongoing process, and new problems are continually growing. Each issue requires further development of this sector. For instance, there are calls for adapting this field to the realities of climate change,[140] to consider other sectors such as energy and food in the general framework of a water-energy-food nexus,[141] and to tackle the impact of disruptive technologies such as artificial intelligence and big data[142] on water governance. The changes occurring reflect the new values that IWL is attempting to embrace regarding environmental preservation, humanization,

135 Alex Grzybowski, Stephen C. McCaffrey, & Richard K. Paisley, *Beyond International Water Law: Successfully Negotiating Mutual Gains Agreements for International Watercourse*, 22 Pacific McGeorge Global Business & Development Law Journal. 139, 154 (2010).

136 Mark Zeitoun, *The Relevance of International Water Law to Later-Developing Upstream States*, 40(7) Water International. 949, 949 (2015).

137 Tuomas Kuokkanen, *Water Security and International Law*, 20 Potchefstroom Electronic Law Journal. 1, 1 (2017).

138 T.N. Narasimhan, *Water, Law, Science,* 349(1/2) Journal of Hydrology. 125, 125 (2008).

139 See Mara Tignino et al., eds., Legal Perspectives on Bridging Science and Policy (Routledge 2019).

140 Paulo Canelas de Castro, *Trends of Development of International Water Law*, 6 Beijing Law Review. 285, 292–293 (2015).

141 Paolo Davide Farah & Imad Antoine Ibrahim, *Water-Energy-Food Nexus: A Legal Analysis*, in Handbook on the Water-Energy-Food Nexus 381, 381–397 (Floor Brouwer ed., Edward Elgar Publishing, 2022)

142 Christina Leb, Data Innovations for Transboundary Freshwater Resources Management: Are Obligations related to Information Exchange Still Needed? (Brill 2020).

and economization.[143] Such developments did not happen without clashes and disagreements among different stakeholders.[144]

Development of IHRL

Debates over the evolution of IHRL have been ongoing for several decades.[145] This framework was added to the body of international law at a later stage. Initially, global rules in the 17th and 18th centuries only concerned the regulation of relationships among states. Since nations constituted the only subject of international law, the rights of citizens were beyond the scope of these legislations.[146] Exceptions include the rights of diplomats and citizens living abroad, leading in some cases to bilateral agreements based on the principle of reciprocity providing privileges or protection. Global focus on human welfare emerged in the 19th century with the abolishment of slavery and the push towards more protections during armed conflicts, especially for civilians and prisoners. After World War I, the League of Nations established several instruments such as minorities treaties. Meanwhile, an International Labor Organization (ILO) was created, forming conventions and standards related to work and social needs.[147] The development of this field largely took place after World War II.[148] The consequences of the First World War paved the way for its expansion. The Second World War prompted citizens to call for additional contributions to international rights.[149] Its horrors led to a focus on the advancement of this body of law.[150]

The foundational era was the period from 1945 to 1950. The resultant factor was the adoption of many binding documents. For instance, the UN Charter and the Universal Declaration of Human Rights (UDHR) endorsed the universality of these rights.[151] Meanwhile, conditions related to the latter were stipulated within peace treaties.[152] The UDHR is considered the founding

143 Joseph W. Dellapenna & Joyeeta Gupta, *The Evolution of International Water Law*, *in* The Evolution of the Law and Politics of Water 3, 3–19 (Joseph W. Dellapenna &Joyeeta Gupta eds., Springer 2009).

144 Erica J. Thorson, *Sharing Himalayan Glacial Meltwater: The Role of Territorial Sovereignty*, 19 Duke Journal of Comparative & International Law 487, 500 (2009).

145 See, for instance, Philip Alston, *A Third Generation of Solidarity Rights: Progressive Development or Obfuscation of International Human Rights Law?*, 29(3) Netherlands International Law Review. 307, 307–322 (1982).

146 Ilias Bantekas & Lutz Oette, International Human Rights Law and Practice 11–12 (Cambridge University Press 2016).

147 Louis Henkin, *Law and Politics in International Relations: State and Human Values*, 44(1) Journal of International Affairs. 183, 191–192 (1990).

148 Bantekas & Oette, *supra* note 210,at 12.

149 *Id.* at 17.

150 *Id.* at 11 & 18–21.

151 *Id.* at 11 & 18–21.

152 Henkin, *supra* note 211, at 193.

document of IHRL.[153] Following this, the field gradually developed. Huge efforts were made that contributed to the formation of various conventions such as the International Covenant on Economic, Social, and Cultural Rights (ICESCR)[154] and the International Covenant on Civil and Political Rights (ICCPR)[155] in 1966. The international community also formed agreements targeting groups facing discrimination. Examples include the International Convention on the Protection of the Rights of All Migrant Workers and Members of their Families.[156] After 2000, treaties and non-binding instruments addressing the rights of collective groups were established,[157] such as the 2007 UN Declaration on the Rights of Indigenous People.[158]

Literature on the development and evolution of IHRL is huge.[159]This field, despite being part of international law, has a different project and purpose than regulating states relations,[160] as its focus is on a country's actions and their impact on its population. This was only possible due to the state's progressive acceptance of human rights,[161] although such commitment on their

153 Bantekas & Oette, *supra* note 210, at11 & 18–21.

154 United Nations Human Rights Office of the High Commissioner, International Covenant on Economic, Social and Cultural Rights. Adopted 16 December 1966. By General Assembly resolution 2200A (XXI), available at https://www.ohchr.org/en/instruments-mechanisms/instruments/international-covenant-economic-social-and-cultural-rights (last accessed 3 August 2022).

155 United Nations Human Rights Office of the High Commissioner, International Covenant on Civil and Political Rights. Adopted 16 December 1966. By General Assembly resolution 2200A (XXI), available at https://www.ohchr.org/en/instruments-mechanisms/instruments/international-covenant-civil-and-political-rights#:~:text=In%20this%20respect%2C%20the%20law,property%2C%20birth%20or%20other%20status (last accessed 3 August 2022).

156 United Nations Human Rights Office of the High Commissioner, International Convention on the Protection of the Rights of All Migrant Workers and Members of Their Families. Adopted 18 December 1990. By General Assembly resolution 45/158, available at https://www.ohchr.org/en/instruments-mechanisms/instruments/international-convention-protection-rights-all-migrant-workers (last accessed 3 August 2022).

157 Bantekas & Oette, *supra* note 210, at25.

158 UnitedNations General Assembly, 61st Session; Agenda item 68, Resolution adopted by the General Assembly on 13 September 2007. 61/295. United Nations Declaration on the Rights of Indigenous Peoples. 2 October 2007, available at https://documents-dds-ny.un.org/doc/UNDOC/GEN/N06/512/07/PDF/N0651207.pdf?OpenElement (last accessed 3 August 2022).

159 See, for instance, Final Report on the Impact of International Human Rights Law on General International Law; Report of the 73rd Conference of the International Law Association, pp. 663–685, 2008.

160 Frederic Megret, *International Human Rights Law Theory, in* Research Handbook on the Theory and History of International Law 199, 200–214 (Alexander Orakhelashvili ed., Edward Elgar 2011).

161 Rhona K. M. Smith, *Human Rights in International Law, in* Human Rights: Politics and Practice 58, 60 (Michael Goodhart ed., Oxford University Press 2009).

behalf needs to be reflected through domestic enforcement.[162] Among the many reasons for its creation were moral justifications[163] arguing mainly the existence of individual moral rights that are sufficient for the establishment of this field.[164] The relationship between this sector and PIL is complicated since its binding force comes from it. Simultaneously, this framework challenges several of its tenets as it is always attempting to play by its own rules.[165] Nonetheless, it remains a PIL branch given its reliance on its principles and instruments for its further progress.

This field not only holds the objective of protecting citizens from potential human rights violations stemming from other states, but also from nonstate actors, corporations, terrorist organizations, armed groups, and individuals.[166] Meanwhile, the international community, alongside other stakeholders, can protest in case of any violation of these rights.[167] Tribunals play a vital role in enforcing IHRL and in interpreting domestic legislation. They take into account global human rights, including both binding and non-binding mechanisms.[168] Their implementation has proved to be problematic as it does not always occur.[169]

IHRL was, for the most part, considered progressive by the 20th century. The most important development in this framework is the understanding that states and the international community must protect the rights of citizens, including but not limited to political, cultural, and economic rights. This reality makes it difficult for nations that do not want to recognize the existence of such obligations.[170] Countries positions concerning this issue evolved with the gradual advancement of this system. Human rights regimes are currently capable of affecting governmental policy to a degree in numerous countries. Therefore, this field has become subject to increasing criticism because of its growing influence,[171] despite its aims to provide a set of neutral values that

162 Oona A. Hathaway, *Why Do Countries Commit to Human Rights Treaties?*, 51(4) The Journal of Conflict Resolution. 588, 588–590 (2007).
163 Michael J. Perry, *The Morality of Human Rights: A Nonreligious Ground?*, 54(4) Emory Law Journal. 97–150 (2005); Michael J. Perry, *The Morality of Human Rights*, 50 San Diego Law Review. 775 (2013).
164 Andrea Sangiovanni, *Are Moral Rights Necessary for the Justification of International Legal Human Rights?*, 30(4) International Affairs. 471, 471–480 (2016).
165 Megret, *supra* note 224, at 19.
166 David Weissbrodt & Connie de la Vega, International Human Rights Law: An Introduction 234 (University of Pennsylvania Press 2007).
167 Richard Bilder, *An Overview of International Human Rights Law, in* Guide to International Human Rights Practice 3, 3 (4th ed., Hurst Hannum ed., Transnational Publishers, 2004).
168 Weissbrodt & de la Vega, *supra* note 230, at 243.
169 Bilder, *supra* note 231, at 11.
170 Thomas Buergenthal, Dinah Shelton, & David Stewart, International Human Rights in a Nutshell 25–28 (West Academic Publishing 2009).
171 Randall Peerenboom, *Human Rights and Rule of Law: What's the Relationship?*, 36 Georgetown Journal of International Law. 809, 809–898 (2005).

should be embraced and acknowledged by all reasonable people.[172] Indeed, it is extremely relevant to the global constitutional order given the growing need for rules guiding actions of various natures.[173]

This resulted in several interpretations,[174] and attempts to classify IHRL evolution. For instance, it has been stated that the development of human rights has occurred over three generations. The first refers to civil and political rights like those stipulated in the ICCPR. The second mentions economic, social, and cultural ones such as those included within the ICESCR. Finally, the third case of emerging rights encompasses an overarching approach toward human rights that facilitates the common interest of mankind.[175] This idea was criticized as opponents of this theory considered that all different sets of rights represent one generation in the general framework of international law.[176] Moreover, the application of human rights obligations for non-state actors has been, and is still, developing.[177] These include MNCs, armed groups and international organizations which may violate or threaten to affect citizens' rights.[178] IHRL also influences other global frameworks that can be used to regulate the same events. For example, this field along with IHR applies to a state's conduct during an armed conflict or occupation.[179]

There are many questions posed concerning IHRL. For instance, can it be effective? Could it push states to protect their citizens and lead to a behavioral change at the administrative level?[180] This regime only recently began to formulate a consistent theory and still lacks sufficient practical implementation in protecting populations from any violation.[181] It contains numerous rights and

172 Tony Evans, *International Human Rights Law as Power/Knowledge*, 27(3) Human Rights Quarterly. 1046, 1052 (2005).

173 *Id.* at 1062; Stephen Gill, *Globalization, Market Civilization and Disciplinary Neoliberalism*, 24(3) Millennium: Journal of International Studies. 399. 399–423 (1995).

174 Stephen Gardbaum, *Human Rights as International Constitutional Rights*, 19(4) European Journal of International Law. 749, 768 (2008).

175 Patrick Macklem, *Human Rights in International Law: Three Generations or One? Abstract*, 3(1) London Review of International Law. 61–92 (2015).

176 *Id.* at 61–92.

177 Andrew Clapham, *Human Rights Obligations for Non-State Actors: Where are We Now?*, in Doing Peace the Rights Way: Essays in International Law and Relations in Honor of Louise Arbour (Fannie Lafontaine & François Larocque eds., Intersentia 2018).

178 Andrew Clapham, *Human Rights Obligations of Non-State Actors*, Collected Courses of the Academy of European Law (2006; online ed., Oxford Academic, 1 Jan. 2010).

179 John Cerone, *Jurisdiction and Power: The Intersection of Human Rights Law & the Law of Non-International Armed Conflict in an Extraterritorial Context*, 40(2) Israel Law Review. 396, 396–452 (2007); Noam Lubell, *Parallel Application of International Humanitarian Law and International Human Rights Law: An Examination of the Debate*, 40(2) Israel Law Review. 648, 648–660 (2007).

180 Ryan Goodman & Derek Jinks, *How to Influence States: Socialization and International Human Rights Law*, 54(3) Duke Law Journal. 621, 621–703 (2004).

181 Dinah Shelton, Remedies in International Human Rights Law 1 (Oxford University Press 1999).

obligations stipulated in many international instruments. It also encompasses states' reluctance to establish jurisdictions for hearing human rights complaints in the early years. This has begun to change as a number of suggested remedies have developed.[182] Despite its gradual and progressive development, massive human rights violations have occurred in the last decade. All the while, implementation of these guaranteed rights has been very slow.[183]

It is in this context that IHRL has been condemned. Its proponents have had difficulty tackling the criticism since they consider human rights as self-justificatory. Numerous scholars and activists saw such justification as quasi-blasphemous and preferred to focus on the means to implement and enforce this regime.[184] It has been pointed out that the process of adopting it is fundamentally undemocratic and challenges the field's own authority. Such a reality has also led to a disapproval of the claim that IHRL should either be applied directly at the national level or displace and affect domestic human rights law and amend national legislations.[185] Another issue is that it has limits within international law, mainly states' consent, where the application of human rights domestically requires a country's willingness to do so.[186] In fact, it has been stated that its golden era is over. The current period is defined as the post-human rights age because of the challenges facing its implementation; the emergence of more authoritarian states and their increasing influence over the global legal order in addition to the surge in nationalism and populism.[187] Despite all this, this field has managed to provide the necessary support for individuals who have faced or are facing human rights violations. At the same time, it has failed in several instances.[188]

Interplay between IHRL and IEL

Concerns regarding human rights and environmental issues have emerged in the last century. Often, instruments related to both regimes have developed in isolation from each other. Nonetheless, there are numerous links between these topics.[189] For instance, environmental pollution affects the realization

182 *Id.* at 1–2.

183 BILDER, *supra* note 231, at 14.

184 SAMANTHA BESSON, *Justifications*, in INTERNATIONAL HUMAN RIGHTS LAW 22, 35 (Daniel Moeckli et al eds., Oxford University Press 2010).

185 John O. McGinnis & Ilya Somin, *Democracy and International Human Rights Law*, 84(4) NOTRE DAME LAW REVIEW. 1739, 1745–1747 (2009).

186 Margaret E. McGuinness, *Exploring the Limits of International Human Rights Law*, 34(2) GEORGIA JOURNAL OF INTERNATIONAL AND COMPARATIVE LAW JOURNAL, 393, 393–421 (2006).

187 Ingrid Wuerth, *International Law in the Post-Human Rights Era*, 96(2) TEXAS LAW REVIEW. 279, 279 (2017).

188 Dinah L. Shelton, *An Introduction to the History of International Human Rights Law* 28 (GW Law Faculty Publications & Other Works. Paper 1052, 2007)

189 Dinah Shelton, *Human Rights, Health & Environmental Protection: Linkages in Law & Practice* 3 (Health and Human Rights Working Paper Series No 1; A Background Paper for the World Health Organization, 2002).

of a wide range of human rights, including the right to water, food, and health. States have an obligation in the context of IHRL to prevent violations, including those resulting from environmental degradation. Moreover, several human rights instruments include provisions related to ecological matters at various levels.[190]

The importance of creating synergies between these fields is based on the fact that environmental law claims always involve other areas of law, including human rights.[191] IEL interacts with other branches of international law, including IHRL.[192] These regimes have the task of protecting different values through diverse techniques and avenues.[193] The existing interplay between them has pushed lawyers to raise matters related to such connections to human rights tribunals[194] such as the Inter-American Court of Human Rights.[195] However, not everyone is enthusiastic about such interaction. Some academics, for instance, argue that synergies minimize the issues prevalent within each branch of law[196] and diminish the need to provide immediate focus on concerns such as extrajudicial killings and torture.[197]

Acknowledgment of the interconnection between IEL and human rights occurred in the 1970s when the environmental movement realized the

190 Report of the Secretary-General, *Gaps in International Environmental Law and Environment-Related Instruments: Towards a Global Pact for the Environment* 31–32 (Seventy-third session, Agenda item 14, Integrated and coordinated implementation of and follow-up to the outcomes of the major United Nations conferences and summits in the economic, social and related fields, 30 November 2018).

191 Philippe Sands, *Litigating Environmental Disputes: Courts, Tribunals and the Progressive Development of International Environmental Law*, in Law of the Sea, Environmental Law and Settlement of Disputes 313, 313–325 (Tafsir Malick Ndiaye & Rüdiger Wolfrum eds., Brill/Nijhoff 2007).

192 Asselt, *supra* note 124, at 1208.

193 Armelle Gouritin, EU Environmental Law, International Environmental Law, and Human Rights Law: The Case of Environmental Responsibility 11 (Brill/Nijhoff 2016).

194 Tseming Yang, *The Relationship Between Domestic and International Environmental Law* 14 (Santa Clara Univ. Legal Studies Research Paper 21-13, 2013).

195 For instance, the Court in 2020, in the case Indigenous Communities Members of the Lhaka Honhat Association vs. Argentina, decided that Argentina violated the right of the indigenous community to a healthy environment. Corte Interamericana de Derechos Humanos; Caso Comunidades Indígenas Miembros de la Asociación Lhaka Honhat (Nuestra Tierra) Vs. Argentina. Sentencia de 6 De Febrero de 2020. (Fondo, Reparaciones y Costas), available at https://www.corteidh.or.cr/docs/casos/articulos/seriec_400_esp.pdf (last accessed 3 August 2022). See also, Maria Antonia Tigre, *Inter-American Court Recognizes the Right to a Healthy Environment of Indigenous Peoples in First Contentious Case* (IUCN; 4 May 2020), available at https://www.iucn.org/news/world-commission-environmental-law/202005/inter-american-court-recognizes-right-a-healthy-environment-indigenous-peoples-first-contentious-case (last accessed 3 August 2022).

196 Donald K. Anton & Dinah L. Shelton, Environmental Protection and Human Rights 119 (Cambridge University Press 2011).

197 Karin Arts, *Inclusive Sustainable Development: A Human Rights Perspective*, 24 Current Opinion in Environmental Sustainability. 58, 60 (2017).

importance of focusing on it,[198] as both fields have been developing in parallel since World War II.[199] This is why events such as the Stockholm conference of 1972 have gradually recognized this link.[200] For instance, Principle 1 of its Declaration established a direct connection between human rights and the environment, declaring that the state of the environment ultimately impacts the well-being of human settlements and the realization of the most basic rights.[201] Since then, this interplay has been recognized in new instruments, both binding and non-binding, as the UN has progressively tackled this topic.[202]

The 1992 Rio conference also recognized the existing links through Principle 1 of its Declaration, stating that humans represent one of the concerns that must be tackled. This is because citizens have a right to a harmonious existence with nature while undergoing a normal life.[203] Principle 4 mentioned that environmental protection is an important condition for the realization of sustainable development.[204] In fact, throughout the years, different environmental conferences have recognized the link between human rights and the environment.[205] In 2012, an independent expert group created by the Human Rights Council (HRC) confirmed that environmental damage may have already impacted the realization of various human rights, such as the right to life and the right to an adequate standard of living.[206]

According to human rights bodies, states have several obligations to ensure that environmental issues do not infringe on the human rights of individuals.

198 John H. Knox, *Human Rights, Environmental Protection, and the Sustainable Development Goals*, 24(3) Washington International Law Journal. 517, 519 (2015).

199 Alan Boyle & Ben Boer, *Human Rights and the Environment: 13th Informal ASEM Seminar on Human Rights* (Asia-Europe Meeting, Background Paper, 21–23 October 2013); Report of the Special Rapporteur on the Issue of Human Rights Obligations Relating to the Enjoyment of a Safe, Clean, Healthy, and Sustainable Environment 4–9, United Nations Human Rights Council, A/HRC/37/59, January 24, 2018. Human Rights Council, thirty-first session, Agenda item 3, Promotion and protection of all human rights, civil, political, economic, social, and cultural rights, including the right to development, 1 February 2016.

200 Knox, *supra* note 262, at 519.

201 Icelandic Human Rights Center, *Human Rights and the Environment*, available at http://www.humanrights.is/en/human-rights-education-project/human-rights-concepts-ideas-and-fora/human-rights-in-relation-to-other-topics/human-rights-and-the-environment (last accessed 3 August 2022). There are many contexts where the link between human rights and environmental protection is very relevant, such as in the case of extractive industries that may have a great negative environmental impact. See, Sumudu Atapattu, *Extractive Industries and Inequality: Intersections of Environmental Law, Human Rights, and Environmental Justice*, 50 Arizona State Law Journal. 431, 431–454 (2018).

202 International Council on Human Rights Policy, *Beyond Voluntarism: Human Rights and the Developing International Legal Obligations of Companies* 41–43 (International Council on Human Rights Policy, February 2002).

203 Icelandic Human Rights Center, *supra* note 265.

204 *Id.*

205 *Id.*

206 Knox, *supra* note 262, at 520–521.

These include procedural duties such as assessing the environmental impact on human rights and substantive duties related, for instance, to the protection of the freedoms of expression and association. Finally, states have a duty to protect those who are more vulnerable to environmental harm, such as indigenous people.[207] The UN HRC has, in recent years, begun adopting mechanisms that apply human rights standards to environmental matters.[208] In fact, three legal approaches have been provided to environmental human rights, which are mainly 1) reinterpreting them, 2) establishing procedural ones, and 3) adopting a right to the environment.[209] Governments are free to choose the approach that best fits their system.[210]

The justifications for connecting the two fields are many. Environmental influence on rights such as those related to life and health can be tackled explicitly without the need to focus on the state or the environment. Environmental quality standards may increase as nations are obligated to take action to address contamination affecting various rights. The rule of law is further strengthened as countries are held responsible for their inability to implement legislation and protect the environment even when the damage is caused by MNCs. The public benefits greatly as well, since human rights allow their participation in environmental decision-making and ensure their access to information and justice. Finally, this may also lead to the usage of specific aspects of public interest to protect the environment.[211]

The increasing connection between human rights and the environment has led scholars to advocate for a separate right to it,[212] especially in the last decade.[213] A Draft Declaration of Principles on Human Rights and the Environment was prepared on 6 July 1994. However, it was never adopted.[214] The latter failed to generate the necessary support, which prevented

207 *Id.* at 520–524.

208 Marcos A. Orellana, *Typology of Instruments of Public Environmental International Law* 22–23 (Serie Medio Ambiente y Desarrollo No. 158, 2014).

209 Karen Hulme, *International Environmental Law and Human Rights*, in Routledge Handbook of International Human Rights Law 285, 289 (Scott Sheeran & Sir Nigel Rodley eds., Routledge 2016).

210 *Id.*

211 Boer & Boyle, *supra* note 263, at 11; Report of the Special Rapporteur on the Issue of Human Rights Obligations Relating to the Enjoyment of a Safe, Clean, Healthy, and Sustainable Environment, *supra* note 263, at 11.

212 Peter H. Sand, *The Evolution of International Environmental Law*, in The Oxford Handbook of International Environmental Law 15 (Daniel Bodansky, Jutta Brunnée, and Ellen Hey eds., Oxford University Press 2008); see, for instance, Linda Hajjar Leib, Human Rights and the Environment: Philosophical, Theoretical and Legal Perspectives (Martinus Nijhoff Publishers 2011).

213 Boyle & Boer, *supra* note 263; Report of the Special Rapporteur on the Issue of Human Rights Obligations Relating to the Enjoyment of a Safe, Clean, Healthy, and Sustainable Environment, *supra* note 263, at 4–9.

214 *Id.*

the creation of a novel category of rights.[215] Proponents and opponents have made several arguments[216] in addition to attempts to that end. For instance, a French group entitled *Le Club des Juristes* has called for the establishment of a human right to an ecologically sound environment.[217] John Knox, the first Special Rapporteur on human rights and the environment (2012–2018), has been advocating for a Resolution acknowledging that the right to a healthy environment is part of IHRL.[218]

The question of a human right to the environment has prompted scholars to ask whether there is a need for the adoption of such a right,[219] despite the clear relation between environmental degradation and human rights violations.[220] For instance, there have been numerous discussions concerning the synergies between this field and climate change.[221] There have also been debates over the terms that should be used to describe these interconnections.[222] Moreover, one of the challenges is the enforceability of this right.[223] Still, the UNGA officially adopted officially a human right to a clean, healthy, and sustainable environment in July 2022,[224] following a previous HRC Resolution in

215 Cinnamon Piñon Carlarne, *Good Climate Governance: Only a Fragmented System of International Law Away?*, 30(4) Law & Policy. 450, 465 (2008).

216 Abadir Ibrahim, *A Human Rights Approach to Environmental Protection: The Case of Ethiopia*, 1 Contemporary Legal Institutions. 62, 63–65 (2009).

217 Niko Urho et al., *International Environmental Governance: Accomplishments and Way Forward* 79 (Nordic Council of Ministers 2019). The Club represents an independent platform focusing on fostering discussions and proposals from various legal professionals. See, Le Club des Juristes, Le Premier Think Tank Juridique Français, *Qui Sommes-Nous,* available at https://www.leclubdesjuristes.com/qui-sommes-nous/ (last accessed 3 August 2022).

218 International Federation for Human Rights, *Human Rights and Environmental Protection are Interdependent* (Press Release, 05/03/2018), available at https://www.fidh.org/en/issues/globalisation-human-rights/business-and-human-rights/human-rights-and-environmental-protection-are-interdependent (last accessed 3 August 2022).

219 Rebecca Bratspies, *Do We Need a Human Right to a Healthy Environment?*, 13(1) Santa Clara Journal of International Law. 31, 31–69 (2015); see also Dinah L. Shelton, *Problems in Environmental Protection and Human Rights: A Human Right to the Environment* (GW Law Faculty Publications & Other Works.Paper 1048, 2011).

220 Carmen G. Gonzalez, *Environmental Justice and International Environmental Law*, in Routledge Handbook of International Environmental Law 77, 85 (Shawkat Alam & Erika J. Techera eds., Routledge 2013).

221 John H. Knox, *Linking Human Rights and Climate Change at The United Nations*, 33 Harvard Environmental Law Review. 477, 477–498 (2009); John H. Knox, *Human Rights Principles and Climate Change, in* The Oxford Handbook of International Climate Change Law 213, 213–235 (Cinnamon Piñon Carlarne, Kevin R. Gray & Richard Tarasofsky eds., Oxford University Press 2016).

222 Bridget Lewis, *Environmental Rights or a Right to the Environment?Exploring the Nexus between Human Rights and Environmental Protection*, 8(1) Macquarie Journal of International and Comparative Environmental Law. 36, 36–47 (2012).

223 Amedeo Postiglione, *Human Rights and the Environment*, 14(4) The International Journal of Human Rights. 524–541 (2010).

224 United Nations General Assembly, Seventy-sixth session, Agenda item 74 (b) Promotion and protection of human rights: human rights questions, including alternative approaches

2021 recognizing the existence of this right.[225] However, this is not codified within treaties,[226] and remains non-binding upon UN member states.[227] By considering the environment a human right, the international community has answered the question of whether it is an important public good that requires such protection.[228]

Conclusion

The discussion revolving around the synergies between IEL and IHRL is taking place while considering the concept of the extraterritorial application of human rights when violations result from transboundary environmental harm.[229] Different views have emerged considering the existing literature on this notion.[230] Moreover, scholars have begun examining the potential impact of human rights treaties on the environment.[231] Such topics are dealt with at the interstate level via international law.[232] Yet, given that environmental problems such as climate change affect everyone, it seems reasonable that IHRL should apply. IEL has evolved to provide remedies to communities and individuals that have suffered from pollution or the degradation of ecosystems. As such, victims of transboundary environmental problems have rights in international law that can be exercised within the polluting state. It remains unclear whether they can be exercised against the polluting state.[233]

---

for improving the effective enjoyment of human rights and fundamental freedoms: The human right to a clean, healthy, and sustainable environment; 26 July 2022, available at https://digitallibrary.un.org/record/3982508?ln=en (last accessed 3 August 2022).

225 United Nations General Assembly, Human Rights Council; 48th session: 13 September–11 October 2021;

Agenda item 3: Promotion and protection of all human rights, civil, political, economic, social, and cultural rights, including the right to development. Resolution adopted by the Human Rights Council on 8 October 2021, 48/13. The human right to a clean, healthy, and sustainable environment, available at https://documents-dds-ny.un.org/doc/UNDOC/GEN/G21/289/50/PDF/G2128950.pdf?OpenElement (last accessed 3 August 2022).

226 Knox, *supra* note 262, at 519.

227 UN Environment Program, *In Historic Move, UN Declares Healthy Environment a Human Right* (22 July 2022), available at https://www.unep.org/news-and-stories/story/historic-move-un-declares-healthy-environment-human-right#:~:text=In%20historic%20move%2C%20UN%20declares%20healthy%20environment%20a%20human%20right,Photo%20by%20Abigail&text=The%20United%20Nations%20General%20Assembly,decline%20of%20the%20natural%20world (last accessed 3 August 2022).

228 Alan Boyle, *Human Rights and the Environment: Where Next?*, 23(3) European Journal of International Law. 613, 629 (2012).

229 Sumudu Atapattu & Andrea Schapper, Human Rights and the Environment: Key Issues (CRC Press 2019).

230 Boyle, *supra* note 292, at 635–637.

231 *Id.* at 613–642.

232 *Id.* at 633–634.

233 *Id.* at 635.

The main issue that has always been central to the debate is how IHRL can help in the implementation of IEL or affect this field. The question of the potential impact of IEL on the application of human rights law is of equal importance.[234] The increasing interconnection between these fields requires a balancing of the diverging value systems to prevent conflicts.[235] Examining such interdependence in the context of natural resource management is important where commodities such as food and water are being dealt with extensively by these regimes.[236] In fact, the fragmentation of international law or, more precisely, the conflicting sets of laws between two different systems has been witnessed countless times. The clash between IWL and the IHRL is just one example of this reality.[237] This is why the relation between these two fields has been described as complicated.[238]

234 Jorge Vinuales & Stéphanie Chuffart, *From the Other Shore: Economic, Social, and Cultural Rights from an International Environmental Law Perspective, in* Users without a subscription are not able to see the full content. Economic, Social, and Cultural Rights in International Law: Contemporary Issues and Challenges 286, 286 (Eibe Riedel, Gilles Giacca & Christophe Golay eds., Oxford University Press 2014).

235 Dinah Shelton, *Resolving Conflicts Between Human Rights and Environmental Protection, in* Hierarchy in International Law: The Place of Human Rights 206, 235 (Erika De Wet & Jure Vidmar eds., Oxford University Press 2012).

236 Jeremie Gilbert, Natural Resources and Human Rights: An Appraisal 148 (Oxford University Press 2018).

237 Pierre-Marie Dupuy, *Unification Rather than Fragmentation of International Law? The Case of International Investment Law and Human Rights Law, in* Human Rights in International Investment Law and Arbitration 45, 45–62 (Pierre-Marie Dupuy et al eds., Oxford University Press 2009).

238 Douglas Fisher, Legal Reasoning in Environmental Law: A Study of Structure, Form and Language 241 (Edward Elgar 2013).

2 Current State of Customary International Groundwater Law

To understand the interplay between IGL and human rights agreements, it is necessary to examine the historical development of groundwater regulations.[1] An overview of these rules in the global sphere, and within the general framework of IWL will take place before analyzing the legal dilemmas surrounding this field. This will highlight the challenges facing this regime that have emerged in the last decades.[2]

Groundwater Laws in Ancient and Contemporary Civilizations

Several ancient nations elaborated principles to deal with groundwater resources. This is part of a general phenomenon in which past civilizations created sophisticated water management regimes. Examples include the Minoan civilization in Crete; the Incas at Machu Picchu in the Americas; and the Pharaohs in Egypt.[3]

Even though the Chinese legal system was concerned mainly with surface water, the concepts that were established hold much relevance for groundwater. In particular, the principle of equitable distribution of water which appeared for the first time around the year 34 B.C. in the Nan-Yang Commendary. Before that, agreements related to it were carved in stones and put in the fields to prevent conflicts.[4] The Chinese system is considered the

1 On this point, see in general, Thomas C. Cech, Principles of Water Resources: History, Development, Management, and Policy (4d eds. Wiley 2018); Rebecca Nelson & Philippe Quevauviller, *Groundwater Law, in* Integrated Groundwater Management: Concepts, Approaches and Challenges 173, 173–196 (Anthony J Jakeman et al eds., Springer 2016) & Philippe Quevauviller, Okke Batelaan & Randall J. Hunt, *Groundwater Regulation and Integrated Water Planning* at 197, 197–228 of the same book.

2 See for instance, Stefano Burchi & Kerstin Mechlem, *Groundwater in International Law: Compilation of Treaties and Other Legal Instruments* (Food & Agriculture Org, 2005).

3 James Salzman, *Thirst: A Short History of Drinking Water*,17 Yale Journal of Law & the Humanities. 94, 94–100 (2006).

4 Dante A. Caponera & Dominique Alheritiere, *Principles for International Groundwater Law*, 18(3) Natural Resources Journal. 589, 595–596 (1978). The first well was discovered more than 5000 years ago in Zhejiang Province, China. See, Jie Liu & Chunmiao Zheng, *Towards*

DOI: 10.4324/9781003537724-3

earliest one to address the topic of water due to the importance of irrigation to their civilization.[5] Experience and knowledge about its governance were accumulated over the various dynasties resulting in the establishment of institutions for its management in central governments. Indeed, one of the most important missions of Chinese local officials historically was tackling this resource. Formal legislations related to irrigation systems have appeared since the year 111 A.D.[6]

More specific legal norms were established for groundwater resources under Jewish law as the old testament has many references concerning springs and wells. The principal rule is the one of common property since water as a natural resource is given by God and hence belongs to every person. Water emerging from wells was not considered natural as it required labor. Because of that, it was seen as a common property resource but not an open access one. Drinking was given highest priority, then irrigation and grazing. Based on this, those wanting to drink were allowed to regardless of whether they belonged to the community or not,[7] resulting in the recognition of public wells granting travelers a right to use water resources. Moreover, a rule of proximity was applied that allowed the closest irrigator to the well to fill their cistern first. The law would then apply to the rest of the irrigators following the proximity principle.[8] Indeed, parties closer to a water source have priority over those further away according to the Talmud.[9]

Another religious system that established regulations for groundwater resources was Islam. Under Islamic rules, wells were considered public goods and could not be appropriated by an individual. As a general rule, the well belonged to an entire tribe. The only case where a person was allowed to lay claim was when his ancestors dug the well. He would not be granted ownership rights, but rather, exclusive rights to water usage. Muslim water law

---

Integrated Groundwater Management in China, in INTEGRATED GROUNDWATER MANAGEMENT: CONCEPTS, APPROACHES AND CHALLENGES at 455, 461 (Anthony J Jakeman et al eds., Springer 2016). In the context of international water law, the principle of equitable distribution of water means that no states would have leverage over another one given its geographical position and the vagueness of provisions. It also mentions that the institutions that may be established should make sure that such situation does not occur. OLIVIA ODOM GREEN & CHARLES PERRINGS, *Institutionalized Cooperation and Resilience in Transboundary Freshwater Allocation*, in SOCIAL-ECOLOGICAL RESILIENCE AND LAW 176, 181–182 (Ahjond S. Garmestani & Craig R. Allen eds., Columbia University Press 2014).

5 DANTE AUGUSTO CAPONERA, NATIONAL AND INTERNATIONAL WATER LAW AND ADMINISTRATION: SELECTED WRITINGS 403–404 (Kluwer Law International 2003).

6 Shaofeng Jia & Dalong Li, *Evolution of Water Governance in China*, 147(8) JOURNAL OF WATER RESOURCES PLANNING AND MANAGEMENT. 1, 1–2 (2021).

7 Salzman, *supra* note 305, at 99–100.

8 Caponera & Alheritiere, *supra* note 306 at 595–596.

9 RICHARD LASTER, RABBI DAVID ARONOVSKY & DAN LIVNEY, *Water in the Jewish Legal Tradition*, *in*THE EVOLUTION OF THE LAW AND POLITICS OF WATER 53, 53–54 (Joseph W. Dellapenna & Joyeeta Gupta eds., Springer 2009).

adopted the concept of forbidden areas whereby lands that were adjacent to the well would be owned by the same tribe or person utilizing it. This was to prevent the creation of new wells and the depletion of the resource. The principles of Islamic water law are still applicable in some Islamic countries, but the majority of them have adopted rules not directly related to it. They were, instead, inspired by French and British legislations. These laws were also applicable in the Ottoman Empire.[10]

Moreover, Roman law treated groundwater as a resource in which ownership could be claimed merely on the basis of one's capture and possession.[11] A landowner had local control over it,[12] as the owner of the surface land also possessed the water under it,[13] even when potential damage may occur to a third party,[14] unless there is a proof of a willingness to harm the neighbor.[15] This follows the general approach considering that water can be publicly or privately owned[16] as the latter was also privately provided to citizens who can afford this service.[17] On the public side, groundwater was used in the aqueduct system of Rome since most of those were fed by springs.[18] Moreover, water that went from one property to another was seen as belonging to the public.[19] Roman law influenced two main legal systems that impacted the world: the Common Law and Civil Code Systems.[20]

Both regimes originating from Roman law perceived groundwater as part of the land. The owner had the right to exploit this resource which was also considered a commodity that can be owned.[21] English common law developed

10 Caponera & Alheritiere, *supra* note 306, at 596–598. THOMAS NAFF & JOSEPH DELLAPENNA, *Can there be Confluence? A Comparative Consideration of Western and Islamic Fresh Water Law*, in INTERNATIONAL LAW AND ISLAMIC LAW 281, 292–296 (Mashood A. Baderin ed., Routledge 2008); MANUEL SCHIFFLER, THE ECONOMICS OF GROUNDWATER MANAGEMENT IN ARID COUNTRIES: THEORY, INTERNATIONAL EXPERIENCE AND A CASE STUDY OF JORDAN 125–126 (Routledge 1998).

11 ECKSTEIN, *supra* 19, at 51.

12 Cynthia Bannon, *Fresh Water in Roman Law*, 107 THE JOURNAL OF ROMAN STUDIES. 60, 65 (2017).

13 MIGUEL SOLANES, *Institutional and Legal Issues Relevant to the Implementation of Water Markets*,in GROUNDWATER: LEGAL AND POLICY PERSPECTIVES: PROCEEDINGS OF A WORLD BANK SEMINAR 69, 71 (Salman M.A. Salman eds., The World Bank 1999).

14 Dmitry Sivakov et al., *The Fate of Groundwater: A Lawyer's Point of View*, 244 E3S WEB OF CONFERENCES. 1, 9 (2021).

15 MICHAEL C. MEYER, WATER IN THE HISPANIC SOUTHWEST: A SOCIAL AND LEGAL HISTORY, 1550–1850, 178 (The University of Arizona Press 1984).

16 Alberto Quintavalla, *Roman Law and Waters: How Local Hydrography Framed Regulation*, 15(2) WATER ALTERNATIVES. 457, 461 (2022).

17 Salzman, *supra* note 305, at 105–106.

18 David Deming, *The Aqueducts and Water Supply of Ancient Rome*, 58(1) GROUNDWATER. 152, 152 (2020).

19 MEYER, *supra* note 317, at 178.

20 Caponera & Alheritiere, supra note 306 at 598.

21 *Id.* at599–600. On the historical part before the establishment of modern international water law, see CAPONERA, *supra* note 181.

the principle of absolute ownership of groundwater that was then adopted in the United States (US) and Australia.[22] The French Civil Code allowed the landowner to use groundwater on his or her land, as long as such use did not hinder the right of the owners of adjacent properties. Spanish Law followed the reasoning of Roman law. It added that groundwater located under public lands was a public resource.[23] Under both systems, groundwater was rarely regulated in a manner that took into consideration the intrinsic relationship between surface and groundwater. This reality was reflected by the lack of legal schemes that included provisions tackling them simultaneously.[24]

Transboundary Groundwater Norms Before the 1950s

The earliest attempts aiming to ensure a fair distribution of shared groundwaters were recorded in the 18th and 19th centuries. At that time, treaties were established with the objective of securing common access to fountains and wells located at the borders to the nearby population and the livestock. For instance, in 1785, France and Spain conducted negotiations that led to the adoption of the boundary treaty defining the border between Val Carlos and Quinto Real.[25] Likewise, France signed an agreement with the United Kingdom (UK) in 1888, on behalf of Somalia and Djibouti. This pact secured access for both parties to the hadou wells considered as joint property.[26] In all earlier conventions, groundwater was not the main concern, but rather, elements such as surface water.[27] This can be seen when examining the agreements adopted to that end where river basins were the main focus.[28] It is worth mentioning that the Institute of International Law adopted a Resolution on river navigation in 1887;[29] a Declaration on the Use of International Watercourses

22 Nelson & Quevauviller, *supra* note 303, at 176.

23 Eckstein, *supra* 19, at 52.

24 Eckstein & Eckstein, *supra* note 5, at 222–223.

25 Robert E. Hall & James E. Rogers, *Transboundary Groundwater Management: Opportunities under International Law for Groundwater Management in the United States-Mexico Border Region*,21(3) Arizona Journal of International and Comparative Law. 873, 878–879 (2004). See, Peter Sahlins, Boundary: The Making of France and Spain in the Pyrenees 93–102 (University of California Press 1989).

26 *Id.* at 878–879. 3 Sir Edward Hertslet, *The Map of Africa by Treaty* 976–977 (Printed for her Majesty's Stationary Office, by Harrison and Sons, 1896). The wells of hadou are shared between Somalia and Djibouti where France and Britain acted on their behalf.

27 Hall & Rogers, *supra* note 327, at878hadou879. See, Catherine Lu, *Justice and Moral Regeneration: Lessons from the Treaty of Versailles*, 4(3) International Studies Review. 3, 3hadou25 (2002); Council of Foreign Ministers, *Treaty of Peace with Italy* (H.M. Stationery Office, 1948).

28 See for instance, Emmanuel B. Kasimbazi, *The Impact of Colonial Agreements on the Regulation of the Waters of the River Nile*, 35(6) Water International. 718, 720–726 (2010).

29 Institute of International Law, International Regulation on River Navigation; Resolution of Heidelberg, 9 September 1887.

for Purposes other than Navigation in 1911;[30] and a Resolution on regulating the navigation of international rivers in 1934[31] that did not address groundwater resources.

Few agreements were adopted in the early 20th century referring to groundwater. These include the 1925 Treaty on the Ramba Well between Egypt and Italy;[32] the 1927 Convention and Protocol between the Union of Soviet Socialist Republics and Turkey on the use of shared waters;[33] and Minute 242 of the 1944 Treaty between the US and Mexico limiting groundwater pumping within each country's territory.[34] More recently, the world wars constituted an occasion for the inclusion of provisions that dealt with groundwater and springs. Reference to these elements was made in the Versaille Treaty adopted in the aftermath of World War I although it focused more on waterways and territorial waters.[35] The use of springs was also regulated in the 1947 Peace Treaty between the allies and Italy to regulate their use by Italy and Yugoslavia in the Commune of Gorizia.[36] However, the importance of groundwater was acknowledged in the second half of the last century due to growing demand that pushed states to tap into this resource.[37]

Groundwater regulations became increasingly important after the 1950s because of the rising use of submersible pumps and boreholes. Prior to this, its

30 Institute of International Law, International Regulation Regarding the Use of International Watercourses for Purposes Other than Navigation. Declaration of Madrid, 20 April 1911.

31 Institute of International Law, Regulation Governing Navigation on International Rivers; Resolution of Paris, 19 October 1934.

32 Carlos Nagel, *Report on Treaties, Agreements, and Accords Affecting Natural Resource Management at Organ Pipe Cactus National Monument* 718 (University of Arizona/Tuscon; Special Report No. 8, 1988). There are important water agreements adopted back then that have no relevance to groundwater resources. These are: Convention and Statute on the Régime of Navigable Waterways of International Concern; Barcelona, 20 April 1921 and Convention relating to the Development of Hydraulic Power affecting more than one State and Protocol of Signature; Geneva, 9 December 1923.

33 Convention between the Republic of Turkey and the Union of Soviet Socialist Republics Concerning Water Use of Transboundary Waters, signed on 8 January 1927, available at https://unece.org/sites/default/files/2021-11/ECE_ENVWA_32_Bilateral_Multilateral_Agreements_1993.pdf (last accessed 3 August 2022).

34 English Text of Minute 242: International Boundary and Water Commission; United States and Mexico Mexico, D.F. 30 August 1973. Minute No. 242: Permanent and Definitive Solution to the International Problem of the Salinity of the Colorado River, available at https://www.usbr.gov/lc/region/pao/pdfiles/min242.pdf (last accessed 3 August 2022).

35 Hall & Rogers, *supra* note 327, at 878-879. Treaty of Peace with Germany (Treaty of Versailles), signed on 28 June 1919, available at https://www.census.gov/history/pdf/treaty_of_versailles-112018.pdf (last accessed 3 August 2022).

36 *Id.* Treaty of Peace between the Allied and Associated Powers and Italy, Paris, 10 February 1947, available at https://digital-commons.usnwc.edu/cgi/viewcontent.cgi?article=2181&context=ils (last accessed 3 August 2022).

37 M. Dimkic et als., *Groundwater Legislation*, in Groundwater Management in Large River Basins 36, 36–38 (Milan Dimkic, Heinz-Jurgen Brauch & Michael Kavanaugh eds., IWA Publishing 2008).

exploitation was rather limited. Thus, the likelihood of future conflicts among users and the potential for environmental pollution required the adoption of principles to address these matters.[38] IWL focused mainly on developing the legal framework governing transboundary surface waters. The principal reason that such an approach was adopted was the invisible nature of groundwater and the absence of scientific means that enables its complete understanding and mapping.[39] The only occasion in which groundwater was covered was when there was a clear hydrological relationship between this resource and surface water. For instance, when a shared river is connected to groundwater, the relationship was acknowledged. In this case, regulating surface water was the main objective of the treaty.[40] Progressively, the international community acknowledged the shortage of regulations that tackled transboundary groundwaters.[41]

The Development of Customary IGL

Two bodies played the most important role regarding IGL. The ILC[42] and the ILA[43] were responsible for establishing and the further progress of this field. The former was established under the auspices of the UN, while the latter was formed in the 19th century as a result of the efforts of scholarly groups. The ILC is concerned with the progressive codification of international law,[44] while the ILA is focused on its study and clarification. In this case, the global rules affecting transboundary water resources. Since 1947, the ILA has managed

38 Andreas N. Charalambous, Transferable Groundwater Rights: Integrating Hydrogeology, Law and Economics 47–48 (Routledge 2013).

39 Attila Tanzi, *Furthering International Water Law or Making a New Body of Law on Transboundary Aquifers – An Introduction*, 13(3) International Community Law Review. 193, 193–195 (2011). See, Charles A. Job, Groundwater Economics 137–170 (CRC Press 2010).

40 Raya Marina Stephan, *Evolution of International Norms and Values for Transboundary Groundwater Governance*, inGovernance as a Trialogue: Government-Society-Science in Transition 147, 147 (Anthony R. Turton et al eds., Springer 2017); Gabriel E. Eckstein, *Protecting A Hidden Treasure: The UN International Law Commission and the International Law of Transboundary Ground Water Resources*, 5(1) Sustainable Development Law & Policy. 5, 5 (2005).

41 Slavko Bogdanović, International Law of Water Resources: Contribution of the International Law Association (1954–2000) 327–330 (Springer 2001).

42 International Law Commission, available at https://legal.un.org/ilc/ (last accessed 3 August 2022).

43 International Law Association, available at https://www.ila-hq.org/ (last accessed 3 August 2022).

44 Lilian del Castillo-Laborde, *The Law of Transboundary Aquifers and the Berlin Rules on Water Resources (ILA): Interpretive Complementarity*, in Transboundary Aquifers: Challenges and New Directions; Pre-Proceedings of the ISARM 2010 International Conference, Dec. 6–8, 2010, UNESCO, Paris; Carlson, *supra* note 14, at 1413–1415; Guillermo J. Cano, *The Development of the Law of International Water Resources and the Work of the International Law Commission*, 14(4) Water International. 167, 168–170 (1989).

to have a consultative status within the framework of the UN Economic and Social Council. Originally concerned with the adoption of rules that tackle the issue of surface water, both bodies began to include groundwater in the provisions of instruments when there was a clear connection between them.[45] The ILC and ILA gradually acknowledged the importance of groundwater through the adoption of mechanisms specifically targeting it. Despite the great efforts made, none of the decisions or Resolutions that were created were binding upon UN member states.[46] The Convention on the Law of the Non-Navigational Uses of International Watercourses (Watercourses Convention (UNWC)) of 1997[47] became binding. This in addition to the Convention on the Protection and Use of Transboundary Watercourses and International Lakes of 1992 adopted by the United Nations Economic Commission for Europe (UNECE) (UNECE Water Convention).[48]

The Early Days

The interdependence between groundwater and surface water was recognized by the ILA in 1958 in the document connecting international law principles and providing recommendations for the use of shared waters of drainage basins. The document used the terminologies of *water table* and *underground water movements*.[49] The ILA adopted other ones but not all of them tackled this resource.[50] Furthermore, various regional water conventions were established

45 Stephan, *supra* note 342, at 155; Traversi, *supra* note 55, at 462–463; Charles B. Bourne, *The International Law Association's Contribution to International Water Resources Law*, in International Law of Water Resources 3, 3–5 (Slavko Bogdanovic eds., Kluwer Law International 2001).

46 Stephan, *supra* note 342, at 152–164. Salman M.A. Salman, Water Resources and International Law 88–90 (LaMartinus Nijhoff Publishers 2001); Annuka Lipponen & John Chilton, *Development of Cooperation on Managing Transboundary Groundwaters in the Pan-European Region: The Role of International Frameworks and Joint Assessments*, 20 Journal of Hydrology: Regional Studies. 145–157 (2018).

47 Salman M.A. Salman, Notification Concerning Planned Measures on Shared Watercourses: Synergies between the Watercourses Convention and the World Bank Policies and Practice (Brill 2019).

48 Stephan, *supra* note 342, at 152–164; Salman, *supra* note 348, at 88–90; Lipponen & Chilton, *supra* note 348, at 145–157.

49 International Law Association, Resolution on the Use on the Waters of International Rivers, New York, 1958; Eckstein, *supra* 19, at 61.

50 Examples of documents not addressing groundwater in the 1950s and 1960s include International Law Association, Statement of Principles Resolution of Dubrovnik, 1956; International Law Association, Recommendations on the Procedures concerning the Non-Navigational Uses, Hamburg, August 1960; International Law Association, Recommendation on Pollution Control, Hamburg, August 1960. See as well, Ashok Subramanian, Bridget Brown & Aaron Wolf, Reaching Across the Waters: Facing the Risks of Cooperation in International Waters 98 (World Bank Publications 2012). The Institute of International Law also adopted a Resolution on the Use of International Non-Maritime Waters. Resolution of Salzburg, 11 September 1961. The latter also did not address groundwater resources.

where few of them covered groundwater resources but these are beyond the scope of this book.[51] Groundwaters were mentioned for the first time in a non-binding instrument in 1966. At that time, the ILA adopted the Helsinki Rules on the Uses of the Water of International Rivers. This instrument used the terminology of ***underground waters*** where referring to this resource once in Article II.[52] The mechanism itself was not concerned with laying down principles applicable to groundwater. Rather, it considered them to fall under the scope of these rules when they were connected to surface water,[53] in this case a principal river, stream, lake, or different common terminus.[54] Water sources connecting shared surface water and groundwater were seen as an indivisible unit that was named an international drainage basin.[55]

Instead of adopting the concept of riparian states, ILA scholars used the term basin states. The Helsinki Rules were set to cover waters of an international drainage basin. As such, they would apply to basin states, including countries where shared groundwaters exist. This would apply even without a nation being part of the transboundary watercourse but having groundwater connected from a hydrological perspective flowing to another country without reaching the surface. A state that is not part of the drainage basin contributes huge amounts of water resources to the surface flow. This reality forced scholars to use the concept of a drainage basin since a government could interfere with the flow of water. This, in turn, would create conflicts with the countries involved. The adoption of the drainage system allows the sustainable use and protection of the shared resource to the benefit of all countries included in the drainage system. In contrast, the use of the term riparian states would have excluded such groundwaters from being protected.[56] Article 2 of this

51 These treaties include: African Convention on the Conservation of Nature and Natural Resources – Algiers, 15 September 1968; Organization of American States: Draft Convention on the Industrial and Agricultural Use of International Rivers and Lakes – Rio de Janeiro, 1 September 1965; Act of Asunción on the Use of International Rivers – 3 June 1971 and Council of Europe: Draft European Convention for the Protection of International Watercourses against Pollution – Strasbourg, February 1974.

52 Helsinki Rules on the Uses of the Water of International Rivers; adopted by the International Law Association at the 52nd conference, held at Helsinki in August 1966, Article II.

53 *Id.* at Article II; Sarah Mateljan, *Water Wars: Preventing and Resolving Conflicts over Transboundary Groundwater Resources*, 14(2) MURDOCH UNIVERSITY E LAW JOURNAL. 178, 186–188 (2007); David L. Katz & Michael Moore, *Dividing the Waters: An Empirical Analysis of Interstate Compact Allocation of Transboundary Rivers*, 47(6) WATER RESOURCES RESEARCH. 1, 2–3 (2011).

54 The Helsinki Rules on the Uses of the Waters of International Rivers with Comments, London, 1967: Article II, available at https://www.internationalwaterlaw.org/documents/intldocs/ILA/Helsinki_Rules-original_with_comments.pdf (last accessed 3 August 2022).

55 Helsinki Rules, *supra* note 354, at Article II; Mateljan, *supra* note 355, at 186–188; Katz & Michael, *supra* note 355, at 2–3.

56 Helsinki Rules with Comments, *supra* note 356, at Article III; Robert D. Hayton, *The Law of International Aquifers*, 22(1) NATURAL RESOURCES JOURNAL. 71, 73–76 (1982); Eckstein & Eckstein, *supra* note 5, at 228–229. This strategy taken by the ILA prepared the ground

instrument defined international drainage basin as a 'geographical area extending over two or more States determined by the watershed limits of the system of waters, including surface and underground waters, flowing into a common terminus'.[57]

Despite the approach taken by the ILA, scholars did not manage to cover all types of groundwaters within the Helsinki Rules. In particular, it excluded those that are not connected to surface water from its scope. These include reservoirs that were created millions of years ago when the location possessed a different climate such as those found in the deserts. The rules also excluded groundwater that lacks the necessary scientific evidence that would prove its connection with the drainage basin, even when it is a transboundary one.[58] To the credit of the Helsinki Rules, they made clear that the regulations of IWL apply to both surface water and groundwater. Before that, international law had managed to completely avoid this matter. Thus, the instrument asserted the need to regulate groundwater.[59] Indeed, the legal aspects concerning this resource were still ambiguous since the Helsinki Rules were the first to cover it. Even then, none of the provisions dealt with its management. It could be said that these rules provided a model for the potential successive instruments where groundwater could be adequately covered.[60]

The 1970s witnessed the adoption of several non-binding instruments where the majority of them address surface water resources. For instance, the UN approved a Resolution concerning the regulation of international watercourses in 1970 focusing solely on the latter.[61] Meanwhile, the ILA formed instruments on flood control;[62] marine pollution of continental origin[63];

---

for the holistic approach that have been examined in the last decades on the basis of which groundwater and surface water that are connected must be dealt with. Ludwik A. Teclaff, *Evolution of the River Basin Concept in National and International Water Law*, 36(2) Natural Resources Journal. 359, 369 (1996).

57 Helsinki Rules, *supra* note 354, at Article II. Article III of the instrument defined the basin state as one "the territory of which includes a portion of an international drainage basin".

58 Martin-Nagle, *supra* note 1, at 42–43; Hall & Rogers, *supra* note 327, at 879–885. On confined aquifers, see, Eckstein & Eckstein, *supra* note 1, at679, 684–685.

59 Traversi, *supra* note 55, at 462–464. Amy Hardberger, *What Lies Beneath: Determining the Necessity of International Groundwater Policy Along the United States – Mexico Border and a Roadmap to an Agreement (Comment)*, 35 Texas Tech Law Review. 1211, 1227 (2004).

60 Hayton, *supra* note 358, at 75–76; Kerstin Mechlem, *Past, Present and Future of the International Law of Transboundary Aquifers*, 13(3) International Community Law Review. 209, 210–211 (2011).

61 General Assembly Resolution 2669 (XXV) on Progressive Development and Codification of the Rules of International Law relating to International Watercourses. New York, 8 December 1970.

62 Articles on Flood Control, International Law Association, Report of the 55th Conference, New York, 1972.

63 Articles on Marine Pollution of Continental Origin, International Law Association, Report of the 55th Conference, New York, 1972.

protection of water resources; and water installations in times of armed conflict.[64] The only time groundwater was mentioned concerned international water resources administration when defining the scope of territorial competence.[65] The Institute of International Law's Resolution on the pollution of rivers and lakes and international law focused only on these surface waters.[66]

Along the instruments adopted specifically to address transboundary water resources, MEAs, declarations, and conferences that are concerned with preventing environmental damage to other states have also dealt with water issues. For instance, some of the principles of the 1972 Stockholm Declaration address indirectly shared groundwaters. Indeed, principles 21 and 22 expressly request that states prevent transboundary environmental harm resulting from the exploitation of their natural resources, and advocates for cooperation in the establishment of global rules for liability and compensation for potential environmental damages.[67] In fact, environmental concerns played an important role in the development of international law, including the one covering shared freshwaters. However, such a role has been criticized since it is perceived as insufficient.[68] The UN also adopted two Resolutions in 1973[69] and 1979[70] calling for cooperation concerning shared natural resources addressing implicitly groundwater resources.[71]

The first international water conference was held in Mar del Plata, Argentina, in 1977. In this event, norms for water management were suggested through Resolutions, debates, and reports,[72] by the present stakeholders.[73] The confer-

64 Resolution on the Protection of Water Resources and Water Installations in Times of Armed Conflict, International Law Association, Report of the 57th Conference, Madrid, 1976.

65 Resolution on International Water Resources Administration, International Law Association, Report of the 57th Conference, Madrid, 1976.

66 Institute of International Law, Resolution on the Pollution of Rivers and Lakes and International Law. Athens, 12 September 1979.

67 Declaration of the United Nations Conference on the Human Environment, 5–16 June, 1972, Principles 21 & 22. Hayton, *supra* note 358, at 85–90. See, Mark Giordano et al, *A Review of the Evolution and State of Transboundary Freshwater Treaties*, 14(3) International Environmental Agreements: Politics, Law and Economics. 245, 245–264 (2013).

68 Ludwik A. Teclaff, *The Impact of Environmental Concern on the Development of International Law*, 13(2) Natural Resources Journal. 357, 357–390 (1973); Alezah Trigueros, *The Human Right to Water: Will its Fulfillment Contribute to Environmental Degradation?*, 19(2) Indiana Journal of Global Legal Studies. 599, 603 (2012).

69 Resolution 3129 (XXVIII) on Cooperation in the Field of the Environment Concerning Natural Resources Shared by Two of More States. New York, 13 December 1973.

70 Resolution 34/186 on Co-operation in the field of the Environment concerning Natural Resources Shared by Two or More States New York, 18 December 1979.

71 The UN also adopted the Convention on Wetlands of International Importance especially as Waterfowl Habitat in 1971 which holds great importance as wetlands are regulators of water regimes including the ones in the transboundary context.

72 Report of the United Nations Water Conference, Mar del Plata, 14–25 March 1977, available at https://digitallibrary.un.org/record/724642?ln=en (last accessed 3 August 2022).

73 United Nations, UN Photos, available at https://dam.media.un.org/asset-management/2AM9LOF84X28 (last accessed 3 August 2022).

ence also addressed the question of groundwater management through several recommendations that examined issues ranging from their exploitation and knowledge to the relationship with water supply and usage for agricultural and domestic purposes.[74] The final report mentioned the notion of aquifer several times using the terminology of *groundwater aquifers*.[75]

Throughout the 1980s, the UNECE adopted several non-binding documents dealing with the issue of transboundary water resources.[76] These include the 1980 Declaration of Policy on Prevention and Control of Water Pollution, Including Transboundary Pollution[77] and the 1982 Decision on International Cooperation on Shared Water Resources, where the issue of groundwater connected to surface water was covered.[78] The UNECE gradually adopted the 1984 Declaration of Policy on the Rational Use of Water;[79] the 1986 Decision on Cooperation in the Field of Transboundary Waters; the 1989 Charter on Groundwater management;[80] and the 1990 Code of Conduct on Accidental Pollution of Transboundary Waters.[81] Some of these instruments address directly and indirectly groundwater resources or simply do not cover it within their scope. The ILA adopted several similar mechanisms in the same decade where some of them address groundwater in the general context of transboundary water resources. These are the rules on water pollution in an international drainage basin which covers groundwaters connected to surface water[82] and the Articles on the relationship between water, other natural

74 Report of the United Nations Water Conference, *supra* note 374; Malin Falkenmark, *UN Water Conference: Agreement on Goals and Action Plan*, 6(4) AMBIO. 222, 222–227 (1977); Mechlem, *supra* note 362, at 211; Kirstin I. Conti & Joyeeta Gupta, *Global Governance Principles for the Sustainable Development of Groundwater Resources*, 16(6) INTERNATIONAL ENVIRONMENTAL AGREEMENTS: POLITICS, LAW AND ECONOMICS. 849, 852 (2016).

75 *Id.*

76 United Nations Environment Programme, *Hydropolitical Vulnerability and Resilience Along International Waters: Europe* 34 (United Nations Environment Programme 2009).

77 ECE Declaration of Policy on Prevention and Control of Water Pollution, including Transboundary Pollution, November 1980, available at https://unece.org/environment-policy/publications/ece-declaration-policy-prevention-and-control-water-pollution (last accessed 3 August 2022); JOHAN G. LAMMERS, POLLUTION OF INTERNATIONAL WATERCOURSES: A SEARCH FOR SUBSTANTIVE RULES AND PRINCIPLES OF LAW 257 (Martinus Nijhoff Publishers 1984).

78 FADIA DAIBES-MURAD, A NEW LEGAL FRAMEWORK FOR MANAGING THE WORLD'S SHARED GROUNDWATERS: A CASE-STUDY FROM THE MIDDLE EAST 142–143 (IWA Publishing 2005).

79 Draft ECE Declaration of Policy on the Rational Use of Water/prepared by Government rapporteurs, available at https://digitallibrary.un.org/record/99070?ln=en (last accessed 3 August 2022).

80 United Nations Economic Commission for Europe, Charter on Ground-Water Management. Adopted at the 10th meeting, 21 April 1989. Available at https://digitallibrary.un.org/record/73142 (last accessed 3 August 2022).

81 United Nations Environment Programme, *supra* note 377, at 34. See in general, Wiek Schrage, Keith Bull & Albena Karadjova, *Environmental Legal Instruments in the UNECE Region*, 18(1) YEARBOOK OF INTERNATIONAL ENVIRONMENTAL LAW. 3, 3–31 (2007).

82 Rules on the Water Pollution in an International Drainage Basin, International Law Association, Report of the 60th Conference, Montreal, 1982.

resources and the environment where an actual distinction between surface water and groundwater is not made.[83] The ILA also tackled the flow of water of international watercourses which excluded groundwater from its scope.[84]

Unilateral initiatives outside the UN increased in the 1980s. For example, experts from different fields collaborated and drafted the Ixtapa Draft Agreement in 1981. It was ratified after meetings in the cities of Ixtapa and Puerto Vallarta, Mexico. The group made several suggestions to governments addressing the US-Mexican groundwater problems. Experts were seeking to adopt a draft that would be relevant for dealing with groundwater matters globally,[85] considering this resource a shared one.[86] The Draft Agreement defined shared groundwaters as water located within an aquifer crossing political borders. An aquifer was defined as a geological formation that contains water. The objective was to include all types of groundwater resources within its scope.[87]Experts discussed concepts such as conjunctive management of surface water and groundwater; legal rights considering hydrological realities; wells spacing etc.[88] However, since US-Mexican groundwater problems were taken as a case study,[89] a new draft was adopted in 1989 and was named the Bellagio Draft Treaty, or the Draft Agreement Concerning the Use of Transboundary Groundwaters.[90]

At the time, the provisions of the treaty were considered innovative since they aimed at creating a framework for the management of groundwater resources. For instance, the provisions suggested the establishment of a commission that would manage and protect shared water resources.[91] Indeed,

83 Articles on the Relationship between Water, Other Natural Resources and the Environment, International Law Association, Report of the 59th Conference, Belgrade, 1980.

84 Regulation of the Flow of Water of International Watercourses, International Law Association, Report of the 59th Conference, Belgrade, 1980.

85 Ann Berkley Rodgers & Albert E. Utton, *The Ixtapa Draft Agreement Relating to the Use of Transboundary Groundwaters*, 25(3) Natural Resources Journal. 713, 721 (1985); See, Ann Berkley Rodgers, The Ixtapa Draft Agreement Relating to the Use of Transboundary Groundwaters (University of New Mexico. School of Law, 1985); Douglas M. Johnston, Theory and History of Ocean Boundary-Making 318 (McGill-Queen's University Press 1988).

86 Julio A. Barberis, International Groundwater Resources Law 34 (Food and Agriculture Organization 1986).

87 Bogdanović, *supra* note 343, at 337.

88 Albert Utton, Transboundary Resources Law (Routledge 1987).

89 Kyoko Matsumoto, *Transboundary Groundwater and International Law: Past Practices and Current Implications* 9 (A Research Paper Submitted to the Department of Geosciences Oregon State University in partial fulfillment of the Requirements for the degree of Master of Science Geography Program, Dec. 2002); Marilyn C. O'Leary, *The Bellagio Draft Treaty as a Tool for Solving Border Groundwater Issues*,11(11) United States-Mexico Law Journal. 57, 57–60 (2003).

90 *Transboundary Groundwaters: The Bellagio Draft Treaty*, 29 Natural Resources Journal. 676 (1989).

91 *Id.* at Article III and other many other provisions; Tanzi, *supra* note 341, at 197.

detailed stipulations relevant to its function and competences were included.[92] The treaty adopted similar definitions to groundwater and aquifers as the Ixtapa Draft Agreement adding that an aquifer is a formation from which water can be extracted.[93] It also acknowledged that the parties have common interests and responsibility to secure the proper management of shared groundwaters.[94] Each party is considered responsible for taking water quantity and quality measures within its territory[95] while the Commission is tasked with the creation and maintenance of a database containing all relevant information.[96] The parties are also expected to protect water quality and improve it in the transboundary context.[97] Other provisions related for instance to public health emergencies[98]; planned depletion[99]; transboundary transfers[100] and planning for drought[101] were included.

Going back to the work of the ILA and the gaps that emerged due to the adoption of the Helsinki Rules in 1966, scholars at the association decided to resolve existing legal dilemmas. For this reason, the ILA adopted the Seoul Rules in 1986. These mainly addressed transboundary groundwater while also linking its provisions to the Helsinki instrument.[102] It expanded the scope of the latter making them applicable to all types of groundwaters,[103] considering this resource as constituting an international drainage basin or part of it irrespective of whether it is connected to surface water flowing into a common terminus.[104] The Seoul Rules addressed the concept of hydraulic interdependence[105]; groundwater pollution; data exchange[106]; cooperation and management of surface water and groundwater.[107]

With the adoption of the Seoul Rules, the ILA signaled that transboundary groundwater resources were subject to water rules adopted through the Helsinki instrument. In addition, the global frameworks applicable to shared freshwaters were starting to adopt mechanims that were specifically tailored to

92 *Id.* at 197; Kerstin Mechlem, *International Groundwater Law: Towards Closing the Gaps?*, 14(1) Yearbook of International Environmental Law 47, 67 (2003); Hall & Rogers, *supra* note 326, at 890–892.
93 Bellagio Draft Treaty, *supra* note 392, at Article I.
94 *Id.* at Article II.
95 *Id.* at Article IV.
96 *Id.* at Article V.
97 *Id.* at Article VI.
98 *Id.* at Article IX.
99 *Id.* at Article X.
100 *Id.* at Article XI.
101 *Id.* at Article XII.
102 The Seoul Rules on International Groundwaters; adopted by the International Law Association at the 62nd Conference held at Seoul in 1986. Martin-Nagle, *supra* note 1, at 43.
103 Mechlem, *supra* note 394, at 66–67; Eckstein & Eckstein, *supra* note 5, at 228–229.
104 Seoul Rules, *supra* note 404, at Article 1.
105 *Id.* at Article 2.
106 *Id.* at Article 3.
107 *Id.* at Article 4.

the specifics of groundwaters. For this reason, one cannot but acknowledge the vital role the ILA has played in the development of IWL in the last 70 years. This is important, given the significant obstacles that were encountered in the process of doing so. All these efforts culminated in rapid developments on the international scene in the 1990s that resulted in the adoption of the very first conventions addressing transboundary freshwater resources.[108]

Important Developments in 1992

The UN Conference on Environment and Development, held in Rio in 1992, paid great attention to water issues. This is due to new and increasing problems that had emerged since the Stockholm Declaration. Indeed, environmental governance principles adopted through the Rio Declaration and the non-binding action plan Agenda 21 provided much-needed guidance.[109] Despite the fact that the Rio Declaration did not mention water once, several of its principles apply implicitly to it. These include those related to ensuring that environmental damage does not harm other nations;[110] to cooperate with the aim of safeguarding the Earth's ecosystem[111] and to notify other nations of any emergency that may create damage to their environment.[112]

Agenda 21 adopted Chapter 18, entitled, *Protection of the Quality and Supply of Fresh Water Resources: Application of Integrated Approaches to the Development, Management and Use of Water Resources.* This was created to address water problems.[113] It considered groundwater as having the same status as surface water. Chapter 18 expressly stated that successful water resource management required the protection of groundwaters. However, its provisions did not cover the issue of this resource's management, except in a few instances.[114] It called for considering groundwater in the context of integrated water resources planning and management,[115] highlighting the relevance of its

108 Traversi, *supra* note 55, at 464; Mechlem, *supra* note 362, at 212–213; Hall & Rogers, *supra* note 327, at 885–886. See in general, Eyal Benvenisti, *Collective Action in the Utilization of Shared Freshwater: The Challenges of International Water Resources Law*, 90(3) American Journal of International Law. 384, 384–415 (1996).

109 United Nations Conference on Environment & Development Rio de Janerio, *supra* note 114, at Agenda 21, Chapter 18. Mechlem, *supra* note 394, at 62–65; Owen McIntyre, *International Water Resources Law and the International Law Commission Draft Articles on Transboundary Aquifers: A Missed Opportunity for Cross- Fertilisation?*,13(3) International Community Law Review. 237, 240–241 (2011); Mateljan, *supra* note 355, at 194–196.

110 *Id.* at Annex I: Rio Declaration on Environment and Development, 12 August 1992. Principle 2.

111 *Id.* at Principle 7.

112 *Id.* at Principle 18.

113 *Id.* at Agenda 21: Chapter 18. It included seven programme areas for freshwater.

114 Matsumoto, *supra* note 391, at 10–12.

115 United Nations Conference on Environment & Development, *supra* note 114, at Chapter 18: 18.3.

recharge;[116]the need for reliable information[117] especially through institutional arrangements;[118] its protection[119] through various measures;[120] and encouraging its conjunctive management.[121] Groundwater was mentioned in Chapter 13 related to the management of fragile ecosystems when it comes to knowledge dissemination to local people with regards to groundwater recharge[122] and Chapter 14 on the promotion of sustainable agriculture and rural development concerning its protection from chemical pollution.[123]

That same year the International Conference on Water and the Environment was held in Dublin, Ireland. The conference was an attempt to examine emerging water issues. The focus was on sustainable management, use and the protection of freshwater resources and ecosystems.[124] Four principles emerged as a result of the adopted non-binding statement on water and sustainable development. It acknowledged that freshwater was a non-renewable and vulnerable source and that ensuring the participation of the important actors (users, planners, and policy-makers at all levels) was vital for water development and management. The principles recognized the important role women play in the protection and governance of freshwater and the economic value of water considering it an economic good.[125] This resource was mentioned in Principle 1 tackling effective management linking land and water uses.[126] The Action Agenda issued considered the river basin as including surface water and groundwater when it comes to planning and management.[127] It created a framework in which surface water and groundwater constituted the main elements.[128]

1992 witnessed the adoption of the regional UNECE Water Convention.[129] Parties that are members of the treaty committed to protecting shared waters by preventing any transboundary pollution and controlling/reducing pollution in the case of its accidental occurrence. They have an obligation to take

116 *Id.* at Chapter 18: 18.12 (j).
117 *Id.* at Chapter 18: 18.23.
118 *Id.* at Chapter 18: 18.25 (d).
119 *Id.* at Chapter 18: 18.35/18:37.
120 *Id.* at Chapter 18: 18.40 (d) ii and iii.
121 *Id.* at Chapter 18: 18.76 (c).
122 Id. at Chapter 13: 13.22 (a).
123 *Id.* at Chapter 14: 14.40 (c).
124 The Dublin Statement on Water and Sustainable Development, adopted on 31 January 1992 in Dublin Ireland at the International Conference on Water and the Environment. Mechlem, *supra* note 394, at 65.
125 *Id.* at Principles 1 to 4.
126 *Id.* at Principle 1.
127 *Id.* at Action Agenda.
128 Conti & Gupta, *supra* note 376, at 852; Martin-Nagle, *supra* note 1, 44–45.
129 Convention on the Protection and Use of Transboundary Watercourses and International Lakes, done at Helsinki, on 17 March 1992.

all the necessary measures for achieving stated objectives.[130] Shared waters are defined in the agreement as those that mark or cross geographic boundaries of two or more states.[131] The convention emphasized the need to adopt specific measures in addition to those related to prevention, control, and reduction to prevent groundwater pollution.[132] It was adopted as states were seeking to establish an instrument that would provide clear rules on the utilization of international watercourses.[133] It established an institutional framework through which groundwater standards could be enforced.[134] A protocol to the convention was established in 1999 to ensure the proper management of water to protect health including domestic groundwater. Among its many objectives, it sought to guarantee the existence of safe drinking water and sanitation measures. Other follow-ups and amendments to the convention were made afterwards.[135]

The ILA in the 1990s established several instruments applicable to shared groundwater without, however, mentioning the term once. These are those related to cross-media pollution;[136] the one resulting from the use of the waters of an international drainage basin[137] and Articles on private law remedies for transboundary damage in international watercourses.[138] Groundwater is covered within the scope of these instruments since they tackle pollution and remedies for environmental damages within a drainage basin. According to the Helsinki and the Seoul Rules, all types of groundwaters are covered within

130 Philippe Sands et al, Principles of International Environmental Law 363 (4d ed. Cambridge University Press 2018); Philippe Sands, Principles of International Environmental Law 482 (2d ed. Cambridge University Press 2003).

131 UNECE Water Convention, *supra* note 431, at Article 1.

132 *Id.* at Article 3 (k).

133 Malebo Matlala, *Geo-Hydrology of Transboundary Confined Aquifers and International Water Law* 4 (University of South Africa, 2017).

134 Jona Razzaque, Environmental Governance in Europe and Asia: A Comparative Study of Institutional and Legislative Frameworks 132 (Routledge 2013).

135 Conti & Gupta, *supra* note 376, at 852–853; Mechlem, *supra* note 362, at 215. The importance of this convention globally was acknowledged after an amendment that took place in 2003. This allowed states worldwide to become members to the treaty that entered into force after receiving the necessary number of ratifications making it binding internationally. See for instance, Edith Hodl, *Legislative Framework for River Ecosystem Management on International and European Level*, in Riverine Ecosystem Management: Science for Governing Towards a Sustainable Future 325, 328 (Stefan Schmutz & Jan Sendzimir eds., Springer 2018).

136 Rules on Cross-Media Pollution, International Law Association, Committee on International Water Resources, Buenos Aires Conference Report, 1994.

137 Articles on Private Law Remedies for Transboundary Damage in International Watercourses, International Law Association, Committee on International Water Resources, Helsinki Conference (1996).

138 Articles on Cross-Media Pollution Resulting from the Use of the Waters of an International Drainage Basin, International Law Association, Committee on International Water Resources, Helsinki Conference, 1996.

the scope of the instruments considering them as part of the drainage basin.[139] It is worth mentioning that 1994 witnessed the adoption of *the Convention to Combat Desertification in Those Countries Experiencing Series Drought and/or Desertification, Particularly in Africa*. In this treaty, water be it surface or groundwater is considered an important element in fighting desertification requiring effective management and protection.[140]

A First Milestone Reached in 1997

It was mentioned previously that both the ILA and the ILC played an essential role in the development of IWL as it relates to groundwater. While the ILA played an instrumental role in the establishment of non-binding instruments, it was the ILC that managed to create a binding mechanism in the early days. This success only occurred after decades of negotiations and studies.[141] The ILC began studying the topic of the non-navigational uses of international watercourses in the 1970s following a Resolution that recommended such analysis. Before this, the UN operated within the constraints of a 1959 Resolution questioning whether international rivers should be regulated[142] which led to the drafting of the report addressing the legal dilemmas facing the use of international rivers presented to UNGA in 1963.[143]

The ILC was tasked with studying the law of non-navigational usage of international watercourses through Resolution 2669 of 1970.[144] The long-term objective was the codification of this law. It began seriously examining this topic in 1974, and the first report on this matter was submitted in 1976.[145] Many disagreements took place among the members of the Commission

139 Helsinki Rules, *supra* note 354; Seoul Rules, *supra* note 404.

140 1994 United Nations Convention to Combat Desertification in Those Countries Experiencing Series Drought and/or Desertification, Particularly in Africa.

141 Stephan, *supra* note 342, at 152–164; Traversi, *supra* note 55, at 462–464; Bourne, *supra* note 347, at 3–5.

142 Preliminary Studies on the Legal Problems relating to the Utilization and Use of International Rivers with a view of Determining Whether the Subject was Appropriate for Codification.

143 Document:- A/CN.4/274: Legal problems relating to the non-navigational uses of international watercourses. Supplementary report submitted by the Secretary-General pursuant to General Assembly Resolution 2669 (XXV). (Vol.I and II). Topic: Law of the non-navigational uses of international watercourses. Extract from the Yearbook of the International Law Commission:- Document:- vol. I(2). See, Salman M.A. Salman, *The Future of International Water Law: Regional Approaches to Shared Watercourses?*, in Looking to the Future: Essays on International Law in Honor of W. Michael Reisman 907, 908–911 (Mahnoush H. Arsanjani et al eds., Martinus Nijhoff Publishers 2011).

144 General Assembly Resolution 2669, *supra* note 363. There are plenty of other developments that took place since then until the adoption of the UNWC in 1997. See, Salman, *supra* note 445, at 908–911.

145 Document:- A/CN.4/295. First report on the law of the non-navigational uses of international watercourses by Mr. Richard D. Kearney, Special Rapporteur, Topic: Law of the non-

concerning several concepts and important aspects. In particular, disagreements emerged when attempting to determine the scope of any future convention. Additionally, there were no guarantees that groundwater would be included in any new instrument. Yet, the reports of the Special Rapporteur showed that the Commission emphasized its importance. These cited that the majority of freshwater resources were groundwater. The ILC acknowledged the contribution of groundwater to the constant flow of surface water. For this reason, the Special Rapporteur demanded that groundwater contribution to watercourses be considered when establishing principles for their regulation.[146] The position of the ILC faced severe criticism from member states. Still, the Special Rapporteur continued to emphasize the importance of groundwater to a drainage basin and argued that UNGA had made a grave mistake by not considering such hydrological reality. Negotiations continued to adopt the correct terminologies and agree on the scope of the future instrument.[147]

It took the Commission several years, five consecutive Special Rapporteurs, and various reports before successfully submitting a first draft of the future instrument applicable to international watercourses.[148] This was coined as the Draft Articles on the Non-Navigational use of International Watercourses in 1991. The Commission then proposed a final draft in 1994.[149] This one included groundwater in the definition of the watercourse when it is connected to surface water constituting a unitary whole as well as flowing into a common terminus.[150] This final draft resulted from many objections by states and commentators to the initial articles. The 1994 draft was used for the

navigational uses of international watercourses, extract from the Yearbook of International Law Commission:- 1976, vol.II(1).

146 Hayton, *supra* note 358, at 80–85. See for instance, Document:- A/CN.4/462 and Corr.1, second report on the law of the non-navigational uses of international watercourses, by Mr. Robert Rosenstock, Special Rapporteur, Topic: Law of the non-navigational uses of international watercourses. Extract from the Yearbook of the International Law Commission:- 1994, vol. II(1).

147 Joseph W. Dellapenna, *The Customary International Law of Transboundary Fresh Waters*, 1(3/4) International Journal of Global Environmental Issues. 264, 277–278 (2001); Patricia Wouters, *The Legal Response to International Water Conflicts: The UN Watercourses Convention and Beyond*, 42 German Yearbook of International Law. 293, 304–305 (1999); Joseph W. Dellapenna, *The Evolving International Law of Transnational Aquifers*, in Management of Shared Groundwater Resources: The Israeli-Palestinian Case with an International Perspective 209, 236–237 (Eran Feitelson & Marwan Haddad eds., Springer 2001); Nahid Islam, The Law of Non-Navigational Uses of International Watercourses: Options for Regional Regime-Building in Asia 147–149 (Kluwer Law International 2010).

148 *Id.*

149 Draft articles on the law of the non-navigational uses of international watercourses and commentaries thereto. Text adopted by the International Law Commission at its 46th session, in 1994.

150 *Id.* at Article 2..

preparation of a draft convention that was approved by UNGA in 1997.[151] As such, the UNWC was adopted in 1997.[152]

The convention namely aimed to establish rules for the regulation of international watercourses. Its scope covered groundwater when it is connected to surface water where both sources are considered a unitary whole and flowing towards a common terminus.[153] This followed the same scope established within the 1994 Draft. In fact, it was the ILC's decision that was adopted after lengthy negotiations and examination of the possibility of including groundwaters in the codification process. The basis of this decision was the importance of groundwater, as the Commission recognized that it required a separate study on this matter.[154] In 1994, in order to fill the vacuum left as a result of the ILC's decision to not cover all types of shared groundwaters, the Commission adopted a Resolution on confined transboundary groundwater.[155] A confined aquifer is not permeable to surface water resources unlike an unconfined aquifer.[156] The definition used for confined transboundary groundwater is not the same one as adopted by hydrogeologists. In the resolution's preamble, it refered to confined groundwater as one not connected to an international watercourse.[157] Yet, a hydrogeologic definition of confined groundwater refers to groundwater contained between two confining layers (above and below). These definitions are not synonymous nor compatible.[158] The definition adopted by the ILC is the one used in the book in the following

151 Dellapenna, *supra* note 449, at 277–278; Wouters, *supra* note 449, at304–305; ISLAM, *supra* note 449, at 147–149.

152 International Water Law Project, United Nations General Assembly Press Release GA/9248, available at https://www.internationalwaterlaw.org/documents/intldocs/convention_press.html (last accessed 3 August 2022).

153 UNWC, *supra* note 184, at Article 2 Paragraph (a).

154 CHUSEI YAMADA, *Codification of International Law for Transboundary Aquifers by the United Nations*, in THE DILEMMA OF BOUNDARIES: TOWARD A NEW CONCEPT OF CATCHMENT, GLOBAL ENVIRONMENTAL STUDIES 9, 10–11 (Makoto Taniguchi & Takayuki Shiraiwa eds., Springer 2012); UNWC, *supra* note 184, at Article 2, Paragraph a. RAYA MARIA STEPHAN, *Transboundary Aquifers in International Law: Towards an Evolution*, in OVEREXPLOITATION AND CONTAMINATION OF SHARED GROUNDWATER RESOURCES: MANAGEMENT, (BIO)TECHNOLOGICAL, AND POLITICAL APPROACHES TO AVOID CONFLICTS 33, 34–35 (Christophe J. G. Darnault eds., Springer 2008).

155 Resolution on Confined Aquifers. Adopted by the Commission at its 46th session, in 1994, and submitted to the General Assembly as a part of the Commission's report covering the work of that session on the topic *Law of the Non-Navigational Uses of International Watercourses.*

156 JAMES R. MIHELCIC ET AL, *Water: Quantity and Quality*, in ENVIRONMENTAL ENGINEERING: FUNDAMENTALS, SUSTAINABILITY, DESIGN 296, 300–301 (2d ed., James R. Mihelcic & Julie B. Zimmerman eds., Wiley 1992).

157 Resolution on Confined Aquifers, *supra* note 457.

158 Gabriel Eckstein, *A Hydrogeological Perspective of the Status of Ground Water Resources Under the UN Watercourse Convention*, 30(3) COLUMBIA JOURNAL OF ENVIRONMENTAL LAW. 525, 547–558 (2005).

sections unless stated otherwise. Worth mentioning the existence of other definitions and classifications for this resource.[159]

The Resolution refers to the 1994 draft articles on the law of the non-navigational uses of international watercourses in its recommendations since it was adopted the same year.[160] Through it, the ILC recommended that states use initially the provisions of the 1994 Draft Articles and then later on those of the UNWC as guidance for the regulation of shared confined aquifers.[161] The ILC recognized the importance of this resource in the maintenance of ecosystems and healthy lifestyles for citizens.[162] The Resolution acknowledged the need to establish regulations applicable to transboundary confined aquifers. This was especially true since the principles of the convention could be inappropriate for the purpose mentioned above.[163] The adoption of the Resolution was the result of the approach taken by the ILC. In the opinion of the majority of the Commission's members, confined aquifers must be further studied. For this reason, it could not be covered by the UNWC.[164] One must acknowledge the role states have played in this context.[165]

It is obvious that the UNWC suffers from many limitations as it only applies to specific types of groundwater and does not address regulatory problems that are particular to it.[166] Yet, it is still considered a milestone in international law as it made significant advances in recognizing its relationship to the management of groundwater resources. Mainly, it provided the basis for countries sharing TBAs connected to surface water to adopt multilateral and bilateral agreements.[167] Indeed, several IWL principles, such as the principle of equitable and reasonable utilization and the no harm rule, apply to the types of groundwaters covered by the UNWC.[168]

159 Michael Arthur and Demian Saffer, *The Pennsylvania State University*, available at https://www.e-education.psu.edu/earth111/node/911 (last accessed 3 August 2022).

160 Resolution on Confined Aquifers, *supra* note 457.

161 *Id.*; Stephen C. McCaffrey, *The International Law Commission Adopts Draft Articles on Transboundary Aquifers*, 103(2) American Journal of International Law. 272, 274 (2009).

162 *Id.*

163 Resolution on Confined Aquifers, *supra* note 457; Stephen C. McCaffrey, *International Water Cooperation in the 21st Century: Recent Developments in the Law of International Watercourses*, 23(1) Review of European Community & International Environmental Law. 4, 10–11 (2014); Tanzi, *supra* note 340, at 199–200; Stephan, *supra* note 456, at 34–35.

164 Kerstin Mechlem, *Shared Resources: Transboundary Groundwaters – Reports of the Special Rapporteur*, 34(4/5) Environmental Policy and Law. 162, 162 (2004).

165 Daibes-Murad, *supra* note 380, at 126; Pierre-Marie Dupuy & Jorge E. Viñuales, International Environmental Law 135 (2d ed. Cambridge University Press 2018).

166 Kerstin Mechlem, *Moving Ahead in Protecting Freshwater Resources: The International Law Commission's Draft Articles on Transboundary Aquifers*, 22(4) Leiden Journal of International Law. 801, 804–806 (2009).

167 Eckstein & Eckstein, *supra* note 5, at 229–231; Traversi, *supra* note 55, at 464–466.

168 Stephan, *supra* note 456, at 34–35.

A Gradual Development of IGL

The ILC benefited from the momentum created by the UN in 2000 considering 2003 as the international year of freshwater and calling for increasing awareness of its importance at various levels.[169] It also profited from the adoption of General Comment 15 (GC 15) on the right to water[170] and the Declaration of International Decade for Action, "Water for Life", 2005–2015 in 2003 with the goal of further addressing water related issues and implementing existing plans.[171] All these instruments addressed implicitly groundwater resources.

The importance of the ILC's role concerning the codification of international law was acknowledged by UNGA in 2001, which asked the Commission to further develop this field.[172] The ILC chose to work on shared natural resources in 2002. Among the many subjects, the Special Rapporteur decided to study the topic of confined TBAs alongside oil and natural gas, and other matters.[173] He commented on the ILC's description of "confined" and recognized the existence of two definitions: one of the Commission and the other is the scientific meaning. Moreover, when he separated the study of "confined" aquifers from that of oil and natural gas, he specifically noted that he referred to non-recharging aquifers.[174] 2002 also witnessed the adoption of Resolution VIII that directly dealt with groundwater by the Parties to the Convention on Wetlands of International Importance Especially as Waterfowl Habitat. This occurred at the Eighth Meeting of the Conference of the Contracting Parties in November 2002. Through the Resolution, specific guidelines were laid out for ensuring the compatibility of groundwater use with the conservation of wetlands.[175]

169 International Year of Freshwater General Assembly Resolution A/RES/55/196 (December 2000).

170 General Comment No. 15 (2002), The Right to Water, Substantive Issues Arising in the Implementation of the International Covenant on Economic, Social and Cultural Rights, U.N. Economic and Social Council, E/C.12/2002/11 (26 November 2002).

171 International Decade for Action, "Water for Life", 2005–2015, General Assembly Resolution A/RES/58/217 (December 2003).

172 United Nations General Assembly, 55th session; Agenda item 159. Resolution adopted by the General Assembly [on the report of the Sixth Committee (A/55/609)] 55/152. Report of the International Law Commission on the work of its 52nd session. 19 January 2001.

173 Stephan, *supra* note 456, at 34–35; Stephan, *supra* note 342, at 157; Alice Aureli, *UNESCO Inventory of Transboundary Aquifers: Managing Shared Groundwater Resources Wisely*, in Groundwater Management Practices 367, 379 (Angelos N. Findikakis & Kuniaki Sato, CRC Press 2011); Yamada, *supra* note 64, at 557–565.

174 Chusei Yamada, Shared Natural Resources; [Agenda item 9]. Document A/CN.4/533 and Add.1: First Report on Shared Natural Resources: Outlines, p. 125. 30 April and 30 June 2003.

175 "Wetlands: Water, Life and Culture"; 8th Meeting of the Conference of the Contracting Parties to the Convention on Wetlands (Ramsar, Iran, 1971), Valencia, Spain, 18–26 November 2002. Resolution VIII. 40: Guidelines for Rendering the Use of Groundwater

While the ILC was examining the abovementioned issue, the ILA once again stepped in and adopted a new comprehensive non-binding instrument where regulations tackling groundwater were expressly included. The association saw the need to update IWL as a result of the developments that took place since the adoption of the Helsinki Rules in 1966.[176] For this reason, the Berlin Rules on Water Resources were adopted in 2004[177] and were considered controversial since the ILA suggested their application to shared and national freshwaters.[178] The rules were heavily criticized. Others praised them claiming it represented a great summary of international water regulations[179] and the most comprehensive and holistic instrument addressing water governance as its scope and content was much broader than the existing mechanisms and conventions.[180]

The ILA dedicated an entire chapter to groundwater, solely focusing on its inclusion in the instrument.[181] It included seven provisions.[182] Within the rules, the association provided definitions for the terms aquifer and groundwater.[183] More importantly, the rules stated in Article 36 that the principles used for the regulation of surface watercourses would apply to all types of shared aquifers.[184] The provisions tackled conjunctive management; the use of a precautionary approach; the obligation to have the needed information for various purposes; the application of sustainability considering natural and artificial recharge and the adoption of measures to prevent, eliminate, decrease, and

---

Compatible with the Conservation of Wetlands. See in general, Clare Shine & Cyrille de Klemm, *Wetlands, Water, and the Law: Using Law to Advance Wetland Conservation and Wide Use* (IUCN Environmental Policy and Law Paper No. 38, IUCN Environmental Law Centre, 1999).

176 Ved P. Nanda & George Pring, International Environmental Law and Policy for the 21st Century 304–306 (2d ed. Martinus Nijhoff Publishers 2013); Onita Das, *Environmental Protection in Armed Conflict: Filling the Gaps with Sustainable Development*, in War and the Environment: New Approaches to Protecting the Environment in Relation to Armed Conflict 129, 151–152 (Rosemay Rayfuse ed., Brill Nijhoff 2014).

177 International Law Association, Water Resources Law: The Berlin Rules on Water Resources; Berlin Conference (2004).

178 Conti & Gupta, *supra* note 376, at 853; Tanzi, *supra* note 341, at 196. See in general, Salman M. A. Salman, *The Helsinki Rules, the UN Watercourses Convention and the Berlin Rules: Perspectives on International Water Law*, 23(4) International Journal of Water Resources Development. 625, 635–638 (2007).

179 Martin-Nagle, *supra* note 1, at 42–44. See, Joseph Dellapenna, *The Berlin Rules on Water Resources: The New Paradigm for International Water Law* (Conference: World Environment and Water Resources Congress, May. 2006).

180 Irina Zodrow, *International Aspects of Water Law Reforms*, in Water Law for the Twenty-First Century: National and International Aspects of Water Law Reform in India 36, 42 (Philippe Cullet et al eds., Routledge 2010); Hildering, *supra* note 170, at 47.

181 Martin-Nagle, *supra* note 1, at 42–44; Joseph Dellapenna, *Sources of the Berlin Rules on Water Resources* 1–189 (Technical Report, Mar. 2004).

182 Berlin Rules, *supra* note 479, at Chapter VIII.

183 *Id.* at Article 3.

184 *Id.* at Article 36.

control potential pollution.[185] Article 42 expressly focused on TBAs considering that the Berlin Rules apply whether or not connected to a shared surface water as long as it is shared between two or more nations. It also emphasized that TBAs management shall be conducted considering the equitable and reasonable utilization, the obligation not to cause significant harm; cooperation, and exchange of data and information.[186] Throughout the articles that were tackling groundwaters, the essential principles of IWL at the time were used.[187]

In 2006, the Alicante Declaration, emphasizing the relevance of groundwater globally and calling for its responsible use and management through various recommendations, was adopted.[188] Proposals included having comprehensive strategies for its governance considering land use and energy; understanding holistically the rules, rights, and policies pertaining to groundwater, and enhancing the technological and scientific expertise in developing countries.[189]

A Milestone Reached in 2008

Going back to the work conducted by the ILC on TBAs, the decision of the Commission to include this resource in its work program was based on a couple of matters. First, non-recharging aquifers were not regulated in a proper manner. Secondly, groundwaters were increasingly used and exploited. Such a rise has created new problems as heavy reliance is expected to lead to its depletion, if no proper management rules are established. Considering this, the ILC was ordered in 2001 to proceed in accordance with the work program.[190] Shared natural resources were included as a topic in the program in 2002 with the Commission appointing Mr. Chusei Yamada as Special Rapporteur.[191] The UNGA took note of this the same year calling the nations to provide their

185 *Id.* at Articles 37, 38, 39, 40, and 41.

186 *Id.* at Article 42.

187 Tanzi, *supra* note 341, at 197.

188 Alicante Declaration an action agenda that emerged from the International Symposium on Groundwater Sustainability (ISGWAS) held in Alicante, Spain, on 23–27 January 2006, available at https://aguas.igme.es/igme/isgwas/ing/The%20Alicante%20Declaration%20-%20Final%20Document.pdf (last accessed 3 August 2022).

189 *Id.*

190 Stephan, *supra* note 342, at 157; Aureli, *supra* note 475, at 379; Yamada, *supra* note 456, at 10–11. On the increase in groundwater use, see for instance, Fernando López-Vera, *Groundwater: The Invisible Resource*, 28(1) International Journal of Water Resources Development. 141, 141–150 (2012); Xiaosi Su et al, *Responses of Groundwater Vulnerability to Groundwater Extraction Reduction in the Hun River Basin, Northeastern China*, 23(5) Human and Ecological Risk Assessment: An International Journal. 1121, 1121–1139 (2017); Muhammad Arif Watto & Amin William Mugera, *Groundwater Depletion in the Indus Plains of Pakistan: Imperatives, Repercussions and Management Issues*, 14(4) International Journal of River Basin Management. 447, 447–458 (2016).

191 United Nations, Report of the International Law Commission; 54th session (29 April–7 June and 22 July–16 August 2002. General Assembly Official Records; 57th session; Supplement No. 10 (A/57/10) (United Nations, New York, 2002).

views on the topic to the Commission.[192] Yamada proposed in 2003 to address confined transboundary groundwaters (considering both meanings to the term at that stage) as well as oil and gas and other matters. He also suggested to focus first on the former.[193] In fact, given that the Commission already dealt with freshwaters through the UNWC, its Special Rapporteur decided that it is better to address non-recharging transboundary groundwaters.[194] Several suggestions have been made that require further analysis. In this context, states were invited to provide information concerning their domestic laws, existing agreements and arrangements concerning this resource. Particular emphasis was put on the rules tackling quantity and quality.[195]

Although the main reason this topic was included in the work program was that confined aquifers were not covered through the UNWC, the scope of the study was widened as a result of the decision of the Special Rapporteur.[196] The latter emphasized in his reports the vulnerability of all TBAs; the need for specific plans for fossil aquifers; the importance of periodical assessment and monitoring; the importance of conjunctive management and development of laws addressing pollution and potential aquifer depletion.[197] Yamada used the Nubian Sandstone Aquifer System divided between Chad, Egypt, Libya, and Sudan as an example. He highlighted that although it is interrelated to surface water which implies the application of the UNWC, this connection is actually negligible especially as no recharge is occurring. He pointed to a similar case study: the Guarani aquifer shared between Argentina, Brazil, Paraguay, and Uruguay. Based on this and to ensure that these types of aquifers are regulated, he called for covering all types of TBAs within future convention and not only those detached from surface waters.[198] One could notice a shift in the scope of the study that was focusing on adopting rules for regulating transboundary water bodies not covered by Article 2(a) of the UNWC to covering all types of

192 United Nations General Assembly, 57th session; Agenda item 156. Resolution adopted by the General Assembly [on the report of the Sixth Committee (A/57/563)]. 57/21. Report of the International Law Commission on the work of its 54th session. 21 January 2003.

193 United Nations, Report of the International Law Commission; 55th session (5 May–6 June and 7 July–8 August 2003). General Assembly. Official Records: 58th session. Supplement No. 10 (A/58/10). Chapter IX.

194 McCaffrey, *supra* note 463, at 273–274. Arnold Pronto & Michael Wood, The International Law Commission 1999–2009, Volume IV: Treaties, Final Draft Articles, and Other Materials 566 (Oxford University Press 2010).

195 United Nations General Assembly, Fifty-eighth session, Agenda item 152, Resolution adopted by the General Assembly on 9 December 2003 [on the report of the Sixth Committee (A/58/514)]. 58/77. Report of the International Law Commission on the work of its 55th session. 8 January 2004.

196 Mechlem, *supra* note 466, at 162; See, M. Bonell, *Forward, in* Hydrology and Water Law – Bridging the Gap vii, viii (J. Wallace & Patricia Wouters eds., IWA Publishing 2006).

197 Yamada, *supra* note 476, at 132.

198 United Nations, Report of the International Law Commission; Fifty-sixth session (3 May–4 June and 5 July–6 August 2004). General Assembly; Official Records; 59th session; Supplement No. 10 (A/59/10), p. 126–127).

TBAs. In fact, the Special Rapporteur decided not to use the word confined, or words that have a similar meaning. In this, he recognized that the ILC and the hydrogeologists referred to these concepts with different meanings.[199]

In order to acknowledge the concerns of the hydrogeological community, the Special Rapporteur adopted the concept of aquifer. This followed the definition of hydrogeologists who give the same importance to the geological formations as to the water within.[200] Yamada justified his approach of focusing on aquifers instead of groundwater by stating that the use of the term aquifer has more technical and legal precision in contrast to groundwater. This strategy confirms the Special Rapporteur's aim of reconciling the legal provisions with hydrological realities. An advisory group composed of international lawyers and hydrologists was established upon his demand for discussing and studying these issues.[201] The UNGA asked states again to provide their views on various aspects related to this topic especially concerning fossil TBAs[202] and asked them to provide information on this subject.[203] Yamada presented the first Draft Articles in 2004, which were later amended. A new version was presented in 2005. States made several comments and criticisms to which the Special Rapporteur responded.[204] To revise these articles, a working group was established by the Commission. After making the necessary revisions, they were adopted by the Plenary of the ILC in 2006.[205] 19 Draft Articles were approved with commentaries where references to oil and gas were included.[206] The UNGA congratulated the Commission[207] and invited

199 Mechlem, *supra* note 466, at 162; BONELL, *supra* note 498, at vii.

200 *Id.*

201 Eckstein & Eckstein, *supra* note 5, at 201–210; MICHAEL PRICE, INTRODUCING GROUNDWATER 13–19 (2d ed. Taylor & Francis 1996).

202 United Nations General Assembly, 59th session; Agenda item 144; Resolution adopted by the General Assembly on 2 December 2004 [on the report of the Sixth Committee (A/59/510)]. 59/41. Report of the International Law Commission on the work of its 56th session. 16 December 2004.

203 United Nations General Assembly, Sixtieth session; Agenda item 80, Resolution adopted by the General Assembly on 23 November 2005 [on the report of the Sixth Committee (A/60/516)]. 60/22. Report of the International Law Commission on the work of its 57th session. 6 January 2006.

204 United Nations, Report of the International Law Commission; 57th session (2 May–3 June and 11 July–5 August 2005). General Assembly; Official Records; 60th session ; Supplement No. 10 (A/60/10).

205 Nora R. Pincus, *Groundwater and International Law: The Need for Specific Regulation*, 11 UNIVERSITY OF DENVER WATER LAW REVIEW. 313, 320 (2008).

206 United Nations, Report of the International Law Commission; 58th session (1 May–9 June and 3 July–11 August 2006). General Assembly; Official Records; 61st session; Supplement No. 10 (A/61/10).

207 United Nations General Assembly, 61st session, Agenda item 78, Resolution adopted by the General Assembly on 4 December 2006 [on the report of the Sixth Committee (A/61/454)]. 61/34. Report of the International Law Commission on the work of its 58th session. 18 December 2006.

governments to provide information, comments, and observations on the Draft Articles and commentaries.[208] In 2008, a preamble and 19 draft articles on the law of transboundary aquifers were adopted by the ILC on second reading. The Commission incorporated commentaries and references to oil and gas.[209] UNGA again congratulated the Commission on the new version[210] and asked governments to provide their views.[211]

The majority of the states supported the approach adopted by the Commission. Nations had a hard time reaching a consensus over the form that the Draft Articles should take. Primarily, they disagreed whether it should be adopted as a binding or non-binding instrument. The ILC recommended UNGA to take note of these Articles in a Resolution where they would be annexed. It called states to consider its principles when taking necessary legal measures for the management of bilateral or multilateral TBAs. Furthermore, the ILC recommended that the UNGA prepare a convention in the future where the provision of the Draft Articles would constitute its basis. Indeed, the assembly followed the recommendations of the ILC.[212] In 2008 at their 63rd session, the Resolution 63/124 was adopted. The UNGA took note of the Draft Articles and where these provisions were annexed to the document.[213]

208 United Nations General Assembly, 62nd session, Agenda item 82, Resolution adopted by the General Assembly on 6 December 2007 [on the report of the Sixth Committee (A/62/450)]. 62/66. Report of the International Law Commission on the work of its 59th session. 8 January 2008.

209 United Nations, Report of the International Law Commission; 60th session (5 May–6 June and 7 July–8 August 2008). General Assembly; Official Records; 63rd session; Supplement No. 10 (A/63/10).

210 United Nations General Assembly, 63rd session, Agenda item 75, Resolution adopted by the General Assembly on 11 December 2008 [on the report of the Sixth Committee (A/63/439)]. 63/123. Report of the International Law Commission on the work of its 60th session. 15 January 2009.

211 United Nations General Assembly, 64th session, Agenda item 81, Resolution adopted by the General Assembly on 16 December 2009 [on the report of the Sixth Committee (A/64/449)]. 64/114. Report of the International Law Commission on the work of its 61st session. 15 January 2010.

212 Mechlem, *supra* note 468, at 806–807. See for instance, United Nations, Report of the International Law Commission 59th session (7 May–5 June and 9 July–10 August 2007). General Assembly Official Records; 62nd session; Supplement No. 10 (A/62/10). The fact that it is still hard to reach a consensus over the fate of the Draft Articles reinforced the conviction of many scholars concerning the relevance of the ILC. According to this, the latter is either considered an outdated institution with nothing to offer, or as an institution having a less relevant role than in the past. See, Christian Tomuschat, *The International Law Commission – An outdated Institution?*, 49German Yearbook of International Law 78 (2006); Michael Wood, *The General Assembly and the International Law Commission: What Happens to the Commission's Work and Why?, in* International Law Between Universalism and Fragmentation: Festschrift in Honour of Gerhard Hafner 373, 386–387 (Isabelle Buffard et al eds., Martinus Nijhoff Publishers 2008).

213 United Nations General Assembly, Resolution adopted by the General Assembly on 11 December 2008 [on the report of the Sixth Committee (A/63/439)] 63/124. The law of

The provisions of the instrument reflect the intention of the Commission to ensure proper regulation of TBAs through the principles of IWL. These include equitable and reasonable utilization and the obligation to not cause significant harm. They were expressly stated and defined in the Draft Articles.[214] Yet, several articles were criticized by scholars who noticed inconsistencies and overlaps with other mechanisms.[215] Concerning the Resolution, states were encouraged to make all the necessary arrangements for ensuring the proper management of TBAs while making sure that scientific and technical assistance is provided to them by UN agencies.[216] In fact, nations showed a very strong interest in the work of the ILC given that the majority of them have shared aquifers. The position of or relation between the Draft Articles and other IWL instruments was left undecided. This approach was adopted because the instrument had to be first agreed upon through future negotiations. In contrast to the UNWC that was realized in 24 years, the ILC completed the entirety of their work in six years. This reflected the Commission's awareness of the urgency and relevance of this matter.[217]

The discussion revolving around the final form of the Draft Articles began in 2011 and 2013. The parties had to choose among many options such as adopting it as a binding treaty, a Resolution, a declaration, etc. Due to the complexity of this issue, the discussion was postponed and it was agreed that the parties should examine the topic again in 2016. Despite this, a Resolution was adopted in 2013 considering the Draft Articles as guidance and asking governments to use it when attempting to establish bilateral or regional agreements for the management of TBAs.[218] This stands in contrast to the period before when states were requested to only take the Draft Articles into

transboundary aquifers. 15 January 2009; McCaffrey, *supra* note 465, at 11–12; Martin-Nagle, *supra* note 1, at 46–48; Tanzi, *supra* note 341, at 200; Elena Quadri, *The Law of Transboundary Aquifers in the Draft Articles of the International Law Commission and in the UN Convention on the Law of the Non-Navigational Uses of International Watercourses* 1–12 (presented at the XV World Water Congress, 25–29, May. 2015, Edinburgh, Scotland; International Water Resources Association, 2015).

214 *Id.* at Articles 4 & 5; Castillo-Laborde, *supra* note 346. Ryan B. Stoa, *Climate Change Mitigation and Adaptation: The Role of International Ocean and Freshwater Agreements*, in Sustainability of Integrated Water Resources Management: Water Governance, Climate and Ecohydrology 445, 450 (Shimelis Gebriye Setegn & Maria Concepcion Donoso eds., Springer 2015).

215 McCaffrey, *supra* note 465, at 11–12; Martin-Nagle, *supra* note 1, at 46–48; Yamada, *supra* note 456, at 11–12.

216 United Nations General Assembly, 66th session, Agenda item 85, Resolution adopted by the General Assembly on 9 December 2011 [on the report of the Sixth Committee (A/66/477)]. 66/104. The law of transboundary aquifers. 13 January 2012.

217 Yamada, *supra* note 456, at 9–15.

218 United Nations General Assembly, 68th Session, Sixth Committee, Agenda Item 87, The Law of Transboundary Aquifers, Draft Resolution, The Law of Transboundary Aquifers, A/C.6/68/L.25, Distr.: Limited, 11 November 2013.

account.[219] Another Resolution was issued in 2016, which has urged nations to consider the provisions of the 2008 instrument as guidance when drafting their transboundary groundwater agreements.[220] Similar wordings were again reiterated in 2019 via a new Resolution.[221]

The mere fact that the ILC prepared the Draft Articles which were adopted then by a UN Resolution in 2008 is a recognition of the importance of groundwater resources and the need to protect them. The Commission benefited from the already established principles of IWL that were applicable to transboundary surface waters. These principles were used in the regulation of shared aquifers. Other provisions added new concepts and elements that took into consideration the particularities of this resource.[222] Furthermore, in preparing the instrument, the ILC made the wise choice of adopting provisions that would provide states with the necessary practical guidance for the elaboration of treaties. Likewise, the Commission ensured that the instrument granted states much-needed flexibility.[223] One must keep in mind that new legal dilemmas emerged. These issues largely relate to the UNWC and the scope of application of each instrument. In fact, several provisions and principles adopted in the Draft Articles were considered progressive when compared to the provisions of the UNWC. Other articles were perceived as regressive and were considered a setback to the achievements that were accomplished in 1997.[224]

219 Eckstein & Sindico, *supra* note 56, at 33–35; Tanzi, *supra* note 341, at 200.

220 United Nations General Assembly, 71st Session, Agenda Item 86, Resolution adopted by the General Assembly on 13 December 2016 [on the report of the Sixth Committee (A/71/517)]. 71/150. The Law of Transboundary Aquifers, A/RES/71/150, Distr.: General, 20 December 2016. See in general, ECKSTEIN, *supra* note 19, at 1–186.

221 United Nations General Assembly, 74th session, Agenda item 85. The law of transboundary aquifers Resolution adopted by the General Assembly on 18 December 2019 [on the report of the Sixth Committee (A/74/431)]74/193. The Law of Transboundary Aquifers. 30 December 2019.

222 Mechlem, *supra* note 362, at 218–222.

223 NELE MATZ-LÜCK, *The Benefits of Positivism: The ILC's Contribution to the Peaceful Sharing of Transboundary Groundwater*, in PEACE THROUGH INTERNATIONAL LAW 125, 141–142 (Georg Nolte eds., Springer 2009). See in general, Raya Marina Stephan, *The Draft Articles on the Law of Transboundary Aquifers: The Process at the UN ILC*,13(3) INTERNATIONAL COMMUNITY LAW REVIEW. 223, 223–235 (2011). On the agreements established between states for the management of transboundary aquifers, see for instance Laura Movilla Pateiro, *Ad Hoc Legal Mechanisms Governing Transboundary Aquifers: Current Status and Future Prospects*, 41(6) WATER INTERNATIONAL. 851, 851–865 (2016); Eran Feitelson, *When and How Would Shared Aquifers be Managed?* 28(2) WATER INTERNATIONAL. 145, 145–153 (2003).

224 McIntyre, *supra* note 411, at 237–240.

Other Developments in the Last Decade

In 2010, a HRWS was adopted by UNGA[225] as well as by the UNHRC.[226] This occurred after years of efforts made by the international community and different stakeholders to that end. This topic will be examined in great detail later on in the book.

A new milestone was reached in 2014. Seventeen years after of the adoption of the UNWC, and after plenty of scholarly articles, the latter entered into force. This occurred as Vietnam became the 35th country to ratify the convention.[227] In fact, since 2010, one could notice a shift, as during this time, 17 states had ratified the UNWC or prepared the ground for doing so.[228] Still, one has to keep in mind that this process was extremely long and impacted the efficiency and importance of this treaty.[229] By 2014, many of the provisions required revisions due to the technological and legal developments that have occurred since 1997.[230] This led scholars to suggest the adoption of a follow-up to the convention, or the amendment of the UNWC to reflect the nature of the changes.[231] Despite the ratification of the agreement, it still lacks the larger support of states since only a handful of them have done so.[232] This result is expected given the sensitivity of the issue at stake, which is the management of transboundary freshwaters. Though, there is a need to ensure cooperation among the different nations sharing this resource.[233]

225 U.N. General Assembly Resolution on the Human Right to Water and Sanitation, A/64/L.63/Rev.1 (26 July 2010).

226 U.N. Human Rights Council Resolution on Human Rights and Access to Safe Drinking Water and Sanitation, A/HRC/15/L.1 (24 September 2010).

227 On this point see, Salman M.A. Salman, *Entry into Force of the UN Watercourses Convention: Why Should it Matter?*, 31(1) International Journal of Water Resources Development. 4, 4–16 (2015); Ryan B. Stoa, *The United Nations Watercourses Convention on the Dawn of Entry into Force*, 47(5) Vanderbilt Journal of Transnational Law. 1321, 1321–366 (2014).

228 Stoa, *supra* note 227, at 1367; Bennett L. Bearden, Following the Proper Channels: Tributaries in the Mekong Legal Regime 96-97 (Brill / Nijhoff 2018).

229 Joseph W. Dellapenna & Joyeeta Gupta, *Toward Global Law on Water*, 14(4) Global Governance. 437, 437–50 (2008); Salman M.A. Salman, *The United Nations Watercourses Convention Ten Years Later: Why Has its Entry into Force Proven Difficult?*, 32(1) Water International. 1, 1–15 (2007).

230 For instance, the increasing use of artificial intelligence and big data in the water sector is expected to impact the governance of this field. Meanwhile technologies such as blockchain and the metaverse have similar potential.

231 Gupta, *supra* note 62, at 118–131.

232 Ashok Swain, *Running Dry: Water, Development and Conflict*, in The Palgrave Handbook of International Development 749, 757–758 (Jean Grugel & Daniel Hammett eds., Palgrave 2016).

233 See for instance in this regard, Jonathan Chenoweth, *International River Basin Management: Data and Information Exchange under International Law and the Case of the Mekong River Basin*, 18(2) Journal of Energy & Natural Resources Law. 142, 142–158(2000);Patricia Wouters & Huiping Chen, *China's 'Soft-Path' to Transboundary Water Cooperation Exam-*

The UNWC is seen as favoring certain countries interests over others. For instance, in the case of shared river basins, the convention is perceived by upstream states as favoring downstream states, which would discourage upstream nations from signing or ratifying it.[234] Despite these limitations, the recent enforceability of the convention represents an important step for IWL and groundwater resources, in particular. In that sense, the international community is slowly moving towards the progressive codification of water regulations through global frameworks.[235] The ratification sent a clear message to those doubting that efforts are being made for the governance of shared groundwater resources. In this regard, it became apparent that despite the long and tiresome process needed for the ratification of the Draft Articles, the international community will at some point manage to achieve the stated objective.[236]

The final event discussed in this section is related to the 1992 UNECE Water Convention. This regional treaty became enforceable in 1996.[237] It had the objective of fostering and strengthening cooperation among nations in Europe concerning transboundary surface and groundwater resources.[238] The treaty initially played a vital role at the regional level and provided a push for the adoption of the European Union Water Framework Directive (WFD). The experience and knowledge acquired as a result of the implementation of the UNECE Water Convention was used in the drafting process of the directive.[239] The treaty became global in 2012 after receiving the necessary

---

ined in the Light of two UN Global Water Conventions – Exploring the 'Chinese Way', 22(6) Water Law. 229, 229–247 (2013).

234 Green & Perrings, *supra* note 306, at 178–179.

235 Bjørn-Oliver Magsig, International Water Law and the Quest for Common Security 142–143 (Routledge 2015); Patricia Wouters, Sergei Vinogradov & Bjorn-Oliver Magsig, *Water Security, Hydrosolidarity, and International Law: A River Runs Through It*,19(1) Yearbook Of International Environmental 97, 97–108 (2008).

236 Joseph W. Dellapenna, *The Law of Transboundary Groundwater*, in The Earth Charter, Ecological Integrity and Social Movements 77, 77–89 (Laura Westra & Mirian Vilela eds., Routledge 2014); de Chaisemartin et al, *supra* note 1, at 205-225.

237 Owen McIntyre, *Water*, in Research Handbook on International Law and Natural Resources 305, 305–307 (Elisa Morgera & Kati Kulovesi eds., Edward Elgar Publishing 2016).

238 Patricia Wouters & Sergei Vinogradov, *Analysing the ECE Water Convention: What Lessons for the Regional Management of Transboundary Water Ressources*, in Yearbook of International Cooperation on Environment and Development 55, 56 (Patricia Wouterset al eds., Earthscan 2003).

239 Alistair Rieu-Clarke & Flavia Rocha Loures, *Still not in Force: Should States Support the 1997 UN Watercourses Convention?*, 18(2) Review of European Community & International Environmental Law. 185, 196 (2009). The EU Water Framework Directive 2000/60/EC (WFD) is considered the most important European legislation that addresses water resources in Europe. This directive has also been criticized because of problems that have occurred at the implementation stage. Nikolaos Voulvoulis, Karm Dominic Arpon & Theodoros Giakoumis, *The EU Water Framework Directive: From Great Expectations to Problems with Implementation*, 575 Science of the Total Environment. 358, 358–60 (2017).

ratifications.[240] The 2003 amendment introduced and opened the door to non-UNECE countries to become parties to it. This ultimately resulted in a change regarding the scope of the agreement that initially focused on regional matters.[241] The amendment itself became enforceable in 2013, allowing all UN Member States the possibility of accession.[242] New states who have signed and ratified the treaty include Chad, Ghana, Senegal, Azerbaijan, Guinea Bissau, and Togo.[243] Its ratification and transformation meant that the UNWC is no longer the only global convention that deals with transboundary water resources.[244]

Scholars have already expressed that potential synergies can be found between the UNWC and the UNECE Water Convention, allowing both instruments to exist,[245] especially as both treaties are compatible under IWL.[246] Still, one cannot deny that there are some differences. The provisions of both treaties vary in terms of scope, rules, and procedures.[247] The UNWC contains general rules while the UNECE Water Convention has more detailed and

240 Iulia Trombitcaia & Sonja Koeppel, *From a Regional Towards a Global Instrument – The 2003 Amendment to the UNECE Water Convention*, inThe UNECE Convention on the Protection and Use of Transboundary Watercourses and International Lakes: Its Contribution to International Water Cooperation 15, 15–31 (Attila Tanzi et al eds., Brill-Nijhoff 2015).

241 Fitzgerald Temmerman, Trade in Water Under International Law: Bulk Fresh Water, Irrigation Subsidies and Virtual Water 28–35 (Edward Elgar Publishing 2017).

242 Trombitcaia & Koeppel, *supra* note 542, at 15–31; Eckstein & Sindico, *supra* note 56, at 32–42.

243 United Nations Treaty Collection, 5. b Amendments to Articles 25 and 26 of the Convention on the Protection and Use of Transboundary Watercourses and International Lakes; Madrid, 28 November 2003. Available at https://treaties.un.org/Pages/ViewDetails.aspx?src=TREATY&mtdsg_no=XXVII-5-b&chapter=27&clang=_en (last accessed 3 August 2022).

244 Ariel Litke & Alistair Rieu-Clarke, *The UN Watercourses Convention and its Complementary User's Guide: Indispensable Ingredients for Global Water Cooperation, in* Global Water: Issues and Insights 215–216 (R. Quentin Grafton et al eds., ANU Press 2014).

245 Alistair Rieu-Clarke, *A Cure or a Curse? Entry into Force of the UN Watercourses Convention and the Global Opening of the UNECE Water Convention*, 8 Questions of International Law. 3, 3–17 (2014); Alistair Rieu-Clarke & Remi Kinna, *Can Two Global UN Water Conventions Effectively Co-Exist? Making the Case for a 'Package Approach' to Support Institutional Coordination*, 23(1) Review of European, Comparative & International Environmental Law. 15, 15–31 (2014).

246 Remi Kinna & Alistair Rieu-Clarke, The Governance Regime of the Mekong River Basin: Can the Global Water Conventions Strengthen the 1995 Mekong agreement? 1–84 (Leiden: Brill Academic Pub 2017). For instance, both conventions contribute to the development of an ecosystem approach in international water law. The UNECE offers a more detailed framework in this regard. Ruby Moynihan, *Inland Water Biodiversity: International Law on Protection of Transboundary Freshwater Ecosystems and Biodiversity*, in Biodiversity and Nature Protection Law 189, 199 (Elisa Morgera & Jona Razzaque eds., Edward Elgar Publishing 2017).

247 Hodl, *supra* note 437, at 328.

stringent ones.[248] In the grand scheme of things, however, the main provisions of both treaties allow their coexistence simultaneously.[249]

Compared with the UNECE Water Convention, the UNWC has yet to find its place at the international level. The former has proper funding and institutional support as the Secretariat is located in Geneva. Furthermore, it has already influenced the adoption of several bilateral and multilateral agreements to manage shared water basins.[250] When it comes to transboundary groundwater governance, the UNECE Water Convention adopted a different approach covering all types of shared groundwater resources.[251]

In fact, Model Provisions on Transboundary Groundwaters were adopted in 2012 as non-binding instruments providing guidance for states that are members of the UNECE Water Convention. These will help improve transboundary groundwater cooperation and the application of the principles of the convention to this resource.[252] The importance of the UNECE Water Convention and its role in IWL will be discussed later. The UNWC and the Draft Articles will also be analyzed due to the increasing importance of the UNECE Water Convention.[253]

Final Remarks

Throughout this chapter, it has been noted that the evolution of IGL faced several obstacles and challenges. Until recently, the international community has given primacy to surface water over groundwater. The primary outcome

248 *Id.*

249 *Id.* at 328. Attila Tanzi, *UN Economic Commission for Europe Water Convention*, in The UN Watercourses Convention in Force: Strengthening International Law for Transboundary Water Management 231, 240–242 (Flavia Rocha Loures & Alistair Rieu-Clarke eds., Routledge 2013).

250 Hodl, *supra* note 437, at328; Economic Commission for Europe, Convention on the Protection and Use of Transboundary Watercourses and International Lakes, *Guidance on Water and Adaptation to Climate Change* 27 (United Nations 2009).

251 UNECE Water Convention, *supra* note 431, at Article 1 (1).

252 United Nations Economic Commission for Europe, *Model Provisions on Transboundary Groundwater* (United Nations, New York, and Geneva, 2014). Attila Tanzi & Alexandros Kolliopoulos, *The International Water Law Process and Transboundary Groundwater: Supplementing the Water Convention with the 2012 UNECE Model Provisions*, in The UNECE Convention on the Protection and Use of Transboundary Watercourses and International Lakes: Its Contribution to International Water Cooperation 408, 408–420 (Attila Tanzi et al eds., Brill Nijhoff 2015); Dellapenna, *supra* note 538, at 88–89.

253 Ruby Moynihan & Bjorn-Oliver Magsig, *The Rising Role of Regional Approaches in International Water Law: Lessons from the UNECE Water Regime and Himalayan Asia for Strengthening Transboundary Water Cooperation*, 23(1) Review of European Community & International Environmental Law. 43, 43–58 (2014). For instance, the UNECE is conducting climate change adaptation projects in transboundary basins, see, Sonja Koeppel, *Jointly Adapting to Climate Change in Transboundary Basins: The Programme of Pilot projects under the UNECE Water Convention*, in Transboundary Water Management in a Changing Climate 95, 95–96 (Benjamin Dewals & Maïté Fournier eds., CRC Press 2013).

was the emergence of several legal dilemmas that must be resolved to speed up the codification process of IGL. Moreover, this reality became further complicated because of the change of status of the UNECE Water Convention. The enforceability of this treaty and the UNWC has also played a role. Hence, international groundwater rules in the two different global water conventions are currently legally binding. The Draft Articles adopted in 2008 to fill the gaps in the UNWC did not take into account the change in status of the UNECE Water Convention.[254] As such, there is a need to reconcile all of these instruments that have dealt with transboundary water resources while also determining the best approach to regulate shared groundwaters. For these reasons, the following chapter will examine the legal issues that have been discussed by various IWL scholars and experts over the years while highlighting disagreement over ways that such matters could be resolved.

254 Matlala, *supra* note 435, at 7.

3 Dissecting the Main Legal Dilemmas

This chapter will build on the historical overview provided previously. The aim is to examine the principal legal challenges that were raised as a result of the adoption of the Draft Articles.[1] This instrument was created considering the UNWC provisions. The latter were used as a model in the drafting process. Several ones were also added which were not mentioned in the UNWC, but are related to the specific characteristics of groundwater resources.[2] These include tackling hydrological matters, for instance addressing abstraction impacts, pollution vulnerability and persistence, natural quality, resource evaluation, and drought propensity. All of these elements differ when addressing groundwater in comparison to surface water.[3]

Since the 1950s, international lawyers have excluded shared aquifers from discussions. The revival of such debates revolved around the adoption of a new convention. In that sense, the Draft Articles contributed to the further understanding of concepts such as aquifers and hydrology. These terms were included in its provisions. This development proved to be very important considering the lack of understanding of these matters. Various states and government officials did not possess the necessary scientific and legal expertise. Thus, it was crucial to assist nations sharing groundwater resources in drafting future

1 Carlson, *supra* note 14, at 1421–1423.

2 McCaffrey, *supra* note 463, at 281–282. On the characteristics of groundwater resources, see, Olumuyiwa I. Ojo, Fred A.O. Otieno & George M. Ochieng, *Groundwater: Characteristics, Qualities, Pollutions and Treatments: An Overview*,4(6) International Journal of Water Resources and Environmental Engineering. 162, 162–169 (2012).

3 Albert Tuinhof et al., *Groundwater Resource Management: An Introduction to its Scope and Practice* 1–2 (GW.MATE Briefing Note Series, World Bank, 2003).

DOI: 10.4324/9781003537724-4

agreements.[4] Indeed, this instrument could ensure closer cooperation among the countries.[5]

After its adoption, the international community made several attempts to move forward with the codification process.[6] Nonetheless, numerous legal problems emerged that further increased fragmentation of IWL. This is due to the massive technicalities required to deal with TBAs; the previous failure of lawyers and policymakers to address them;[7] and insufficient understanding of the relationship between surface and groundwater,[8] that are connected through the hydrologic cycle affecting the ecology and ecosystem of water basins.[9] This fragmentation resulted in the emergence of many legal dilemmas that will be addressed in this chapter. The focus is solely on the challenges that appeared as a result of the scope and substantive provisions excluding the procedural ones. The objective is to highlight clearly how either overlapping and contradictory provisions were adopted. One has to keep in mind that this reality has been witnessed concerning the procedural rules.

4 McCaffrey, *supra* note 463, at 282–283. Alfonso Rivera, *Transboundary Aquifers Along the CanadaUSA Border: Science, Policy and Social Issues*, 4(Part B) Journal of Hydrology: Regional Studies. 623, 624 (2015); Shaminder Puri & Karen G. Villholth, *Governance and Management of Transboundary Aquifers*, in Advances in Groundwater Governance 367, 370–380 (Karen G. Villholth et al eds., CRC Press 2018); Joseph W. Dellapenna, *Treaties as Instruments for Managing Internationally-Shared Water Resources: Restricted Sovereignty vs. Community of Property*, 26(1) Case Western Reserve Journal of International Law. 27, 29–30 (1994).

5 Tomasz Nalecz & Shaminder Puri, *Implementation of Legal Mechanisms to Strengthen the Process of Transboundary Aquifer Resources Management*, in Transboundary Aquifers in the Eastern Borders of the European Union: Regional Cooperation for Effective Management of Water Resources 1, 5–6 (Tomasz Nalecz ed., Springer 2010).

6 Alistair Rieu-Clarke, *The Treaty Architecture for the Governance of Transboundary Aquifers, Lakes and Rivers*, inRoutledge Handbook of Water Law and Policy 193, 196 (Alistair Rieu-Clarke, Andrew Allan & Sarah Hendry eds., Routledge 2017); United Nations, United Nations Juridical Yearbook 2008, 185 (United Nations Publications 2010); Stefano Burchi, *International Rivers and Lakes/Groundwater*, 1(1) Yearbook of International Environmental law. 211, 211–12 (2011).

7 Margaret J. Vick, *International Water Law and Sovereignty: A Discussion of the ILC Draft Articles on the Law of Transboundary Aquifers*,21(2) Global Business & Development Law Journal. 191, 201–203 (2008); Gabriel Eckstein, *Application of International Water Law to Transboundary Groundwater Resources, and the Slovak-Hungarian Dispute Over Gabcikovo-Nagymaros*, 19 Suffolk Law Review. 67, 70–71 (1995).

8 R. I. Acworth, *Surface Water and Groundwater: Understanding the Importance of their Connections*, 56(1) Australian Journal of Earth Sciences. 1, 1–3 (2009).

9 Sida Jia et al., *Quantitative Evaluation of Groundwater and Surface Water Interaction Characteristics During a Dry Season*, 35(4) Water and Environment Journal. 1348, 1348–1350 (2021).

Problems Arising Due to the Scope of the Draft Articles

A Focus on the Term "Aquifer" Instead of "Groundwater"

The fact that groundwater was neglected for so long by the international community has led to the drafting of agreements where it is not appropriately addressed.[10] In fact, the latter is being solely tackled in very few treaties. In addition to the legal mechanims, surveying, managerial, and planning matters such as the Environmental Impact Assessment (EIA), and economic tools such as groundwater pricing have emerged in previous decades.[11] A new global perspective to transboundary groundwater resources has appeared,[12] based on various developments taking place when it comes to the aspects of this resource. These include the quantification of its stress; simulation and monitoring; recharge zone; sampling etc.[13] All of these approaches are needed to assess the current and future state of the resource to ensure its sustainable use and non-depletion[14] and affect the adoption of groundwater legislations.

In the legal sphere, the concepts used to define this resource contradicted hydrological realities. The UNWC did not offer a universal definition of groundwater. Instead, it mentioned the term once to include it in the scope of a watercourse when connected to surface water and flowing into a common terminus.[15] Such an approach did not provide much guidance on how groundwater should be protected and managed,[16] as the term was only mentioned once in the convention.[17] This is true when considering that the majority of

10 Traversi, *supra* note 55, at 468–472.

11 DE CHAISEMARTIN et al, *supra* note 1, at 209; on the technical understanding of groundwater see, Thomas C. Winter, *Recent Advances in Understanding the Interaction of Groundwater and Surface Water*, 33(S2) REVIEW OF GEOPHYSICS. 985, 985–994 (1995).

12 Robert G. Varady, Christopher A. Scott & Sharon B. Megdal, *Transboundary Aquifer Institutions, Policies and Governance: A Preliminary Inquiry* (International Conference "Transboundary Aquifers: Challenges and New Directions" (ISARM, 2010).

13 Zahra Kayhomayoon et al., *A New Approach for Regional Groundwater Level Simulation: Clustering, Simulation, and Optimization*, 30 NATURAL RESOURCES RESEARCH. 4165, 4165–4170 (2021); MehriTabarmayeh, Mehdi Zarei & Okke Batelaan, *A New Approach to Quantification of Groundwater Resource Stress,* 42 JOURNAL OF HYDROLOGY: REGIONAL STUDIES. 101161 (2022); N. C. Mondal & V. S. Singh, *A New Approach to Delineate the Groundwater Recharge Zone in Hard Rock Terrain,* 87(5) CURRENT SCIENCE. 658, 658–660 (2004); Kristy Case, *A New Approach to Groundwater Sampling: Using Plants and Insects to Monitor Environmental Toxins* (Apr. 1, 2022), available at https://gradschool.wayne.edu/news/a-new-approach-to-groundwater-sampling-using-plants-and-insects-to-monitor-environmental-toxins-47652 (last accessed 3 August 2022); NL Netherlands, *"Approaching Groundwater Problems from an Integrated Approach is Essential"* (June. 30, 2022), available at https://www.dutchwatersector.com/news/approaching-groundwater-problems-from-an-integrated-approach-is-essential (last accessed 3 August 2022).

14 James J. Butler Jr et al., *A New Approach for Assessing the Future of Aquifers Supporting Irrigated Agriculture,* 43(5) GEOPHYSICAL RESEARCH LETTERS. 2004, 2004–2010 (2016).

15 UNWC, *supra* note 184, at Article 2(a).

16 Traversi, *supra* note 55, at 468–472.

17 UNWC, *supra* note 184.

freshwater resources are groundwater.[18] This approach by the ILC reflects a compromise that had to be made to accommodate different states' interests. Still, the very fact that the convention covered groundwater connected to surface water constituted a reason, for instance for Pakistan and Rwanda, to abstain from voting.[19] This is because of the limited scientific understanding of groundwater in the previous decades due to the lack of technical and technological means.[20] The UNECE Water Convention also did not define the term groundwater which was included within the definition of transboundary waters along surface waters.[21] Both agreements did not mention the term aquifer.[22]

The same problem is noticed when it comes to the Draft Articles. This instrument did not define groundwater which was mentioned four times, but rather, used the concept of aquifer. This term reflected the hydrological realities that took place.[23] According to the ILC, the term bounds the field to science and minimizes the risk of creating legal loopholes.[24] This approach created significant confusion as a result of the definition given to the term aquifer, described as an underground layer where water is collected as a result of an impermeable layer beneath it.[25] This explanation highlights that the focus is on geologic formation rather than the water it contains.[26] The instrument comprises definitions of an aquifer system, TBA, aquifer state, utilization of TBAs

18 Stoa, *supra* note 529, at 1335.

19 RAJ KRISHNA & SALMAN M.A. SALMAN, *International Groundwater Law and the World Bank Policy for Projects on Transbounday Groundwater*, in GROUNDWATER: LEGAL AND POLICY PERSPECTIVES: PROCEEDINGS OF A WORLD BANK SEMINAR 163, 175 (Salman M.A. Salman eds., World Bank Technical Paper No. 456, 1999); STEPHEN MCCAFFREY, *The UN Convention on the Law of the Non-Navigational Uses of International Watercourses: Prospects and Pitfalls*, in INTERNATIONAL WATERCOURSES – ENHANCING COOPERATION AND MANAGING CONFLICT 17, 18 (Salman M.A. Salman & Laurence Boisson de Chazournes eds., World Bank Technical Paper No. 414, 1998). It is was impossible to take into consideration the interests of all the states even though the final version of the UNWC reflects a compromise that had to be made. Gabriel Eckstein, *Specially Invited Opinions and Research Report of the International Water Law Project: Global Perspectives on the Entry into Force of the UN Watercourses Convention 2014: Part Two*, 17(1) WATER POLICY. 162, 168–171 (2015).

20 CENTRE FOR STUDIES AND RESEARCH IN INTERNATIONAL LAW AND INTERNATIONAL RELATIONS OF THE HAGUE ACADEMY OF INTERNATIONAL LAW, WATER RESOURCES, AND INTERNATIONAL LAW 88 (Martinus Nijhoff Publishers 2001).

21 UNECE, *supra* note 431, at Article 1(1).

22 UNWC, *supra* note 184 & UNECE Water convention, *supra* note 431.

23 Draft Articles, *supra* note 515, at Preamble & Article 2 (g) and Traversi, *supra* note 55, at 468–472.

24 Report of the International Law Commission, 58th session, p. 196 (1 May–9 June and 3 July–11 August 2006). General Assembly, Official records, 61st Session, Supplement No. 10 (A/61/10).

25 Draft Articles, *supra* note 515, at Article 2 (a).

26 Stephen C. McCaffrey, *Comments on the International Law Commission's Draft Articles on The Law of Transboundary Aquifers* 4 (2006) (Mar. 30, 2008).

or aquifer systems, recharging aquifer, recharge zone, and discharge zone.[27] The rights and obligations of aquifer states constituted its main focus.[28] This led to confusion concerning the subject of regulation. Namely, this concerned whether water itself or the geographic formations that hold them were subject to rules.[29] States that are not aquifer countries and do not have any relationship with the aquifer have specific rights and obligations.[30] For instance, aquifer states must take all measures to prevent causing significant harm to nations having a discharge zone as well as actions to eliminate and mitigate any occurring damage.[31] At the same time, nonaquifer states having a recharge or discharge zone within their territories must cooperate with aquifer nations to protect the aquifer(s) and ecosystems.[32]

The emphasis on geologic formations, instead of water, implied that the Draft Articles moved the focus from freshwater resources. This reasoning is further justified by the fact that groundwater was considered a natural resource and was equated to other vital ones like oil and gas. This classification was made when the ILC studied this topic the first time in 2002. The Commission considered that such topics should be dealt with independently of the work conducted on oil or gas.[33] This is why, for instance, the Special Rapporteur advocated for a particular legal regime applicable to fossil aquifers in 2002–2003 as these can be depleted.[34] The definition provided in this instrument failed to conceive all relevant aspects. It shows that groundwater is seen a secondary issue while its mobility in the aquifer is not considered at all.[35] There were many consequences in opting for aquifer instead of groundwater. Among these was the fact that the ILC adopted the term *Transboundary* in lieu of *International*. This concept was used in reference to the aquifers covered under this instrument. There were several objections over the utilization of the term *International*. There were fears that it would somehow be interpreted

27 Draft Articles, *supra* note 515, at Article 2: (b), (c), (d), (e), (f), (g), (h).
28 *Id.* at 2(b) & (d); Joseph W. Dellapenna, *International Groundwater Law*, in Human Health and Ecological Integrity: Ethics, Law and Human Rights 213, 220–221 (Laura Westra, Colin L. Soskone & Donald W. Spady eds., Routledge 2012).
29 McCaffrey, *supra* note 582, at 4.
30 Dellapenna, *supra* note 538, at 77–89; Joseph W. Dellapenna & Flavia Rocha Loures, *Filling Gaps: A Protocol to Govern Groundwater Resources of Relevance to International Law*, in The UN Watercourses Convention in Force: Strengthening International Law for Transboundary Water Management 270, 276 (Flavia Rocha Loures & Alistair Rieu-Clarke eds., Routledge 2013).
31 Draft Articles, *supra* note 515, at Article 6(1), (2), (3).
32 *Id.* at Article 11(2).
33 Vick, *supra* note 563, at 203–205; Pronto & Wood, *supra* note 496, at 566.
34 United Nations General Assembly, International Law Commission, 55th Session, Geneva, 5 May–6 June and 7 July–8 August 2003, Shared Natural Resources: First Report on Outlines by Mr. Chusei Yamada, Special Rapporteur, p.7, Paragraph 3, A/CN.4/533/Add.1, Distr.: General, 30 June 2003.
35 Traversi, *supra* note 55, at 468–472.

as *Internationalization of Aquifers*. This approach was heavily criticized and represented a step backward in water regulations when compared with the UNWC.[36]

The rationale behind the ILC's decision to focus on aquifers instead of groundwater was that both must be governed and monitored jointly. This is why, the aquifer was chosen to be the basic management unit. This logic, however, is flawed.[37] Indeed, the question of whether groundwater or the aquifer should be selected as the governance unit has been the subject of debate where different factors of political, social, economic, and cultural nature play a role. Based on this, it seems that one cannot ignore groundwater and simply focus on aquifers especially in the transboundary context.[38] In fact, management plans are impacted based on whether the focus is on groundwater or the aquifer.[39] The ILC could have chosen to adopt two definitions for the terms aquifer and groundwater, respectively. An approach like this would have led to the establishment of a parallel system where provisions related to sovereign rights and control of aquifers could have been established for this explicit purpose. Other provisions related to the utilization and management of groundwaters would have also been adopted.[40]

In fact, several problems have been noticed due to the approach adopted by the ILC. First, it is not easy to determine the outer limits of an aquifer. Despite the existence of several methods for estimating the parameters, the limits could only be established with technical methods such as drilling. In several cases, it is not clear whether the aquifer is a transboundary or domestic one. This situation, although not common, requires further examination.[41]

36 2 Alistair Rieu-Clarke, *Determining Sovereign Rights and Duties Over International Watercourses: The Contribution of the International Law Commission and the UN General Assembly*, in A History of Water: Sovereignty and International Water Law 149, 160–165 (Terje Tvedt et al eds., I.B. Tauris 2015). It is important to mention that the terms used by the UNWC for defining the scope were equally criticized. For instance, it was argued that the term "international drainage basin" should have been used instead of "international watercourse". 3 Patricia Wouters, *The International Law of Watercourses: New Dimensions*, in Collected Courses of the Xiamen Academy of International Law 347, 391–393 (The Xiamen Academy of International law eds., Brill 2010). The focus on transboundary would avoid the discussion over whether shared aquifers are a common heritage of mankind requiring international regulations that would go beyond the control of the states sharing groundwaters.

37 Mechlem, *supra* note 362, at 219.

38 Alfonso Rivera, *What Should We Manage: Aquifers or Groundwater?*, 59(5) Groundwater. 624, 624–625 (2021).

39 E. K. White et al., *Can We Manage Groundwater? A Method to Determine the Quantitative Testability of Groundwater Management Plans*, 52(6) Water Resources Research. 4863, 4863–4868 (2016).

40 McIntyre, *supra* note 411, at 248.

41 Mechlem, *supra* note 468, at 809; Kanak Moharir, Chaitanya Pande & Sanjay Patil, *Inverse Modelling of Aquifer Parameters in Basaltic Rock with the Help of Pumping Test Method Using MODFLOW Software*, 8(6) Geoscience Frontiers. 1385, 1385–1395 (2017).

This information is essential since the Draft Articles do not cover domestic aquifers.[42] They do not include domestic ones connected to transboundary surface water. Hence, it holds a much narrower scope[43] than other IWL instruments such as the Berlin Rules[44] and MEAs, like the Carpathian Framework Convention and the African Convention on the Conservation of Nature and Natural Resources.[45]

Moreover, the failure to distinguish groundwater from geological structures has complicated the implementation of the substantive principles of the Draft Articles. In particular, the application of the concept of territorial sovereignty and the one of equitable and reasonable use. They became problematic since national sovereignty claims could be applied to the water resource that is not static. This stands in contrast to the geological formation that is located in an area under the sovereignty of a given state.[46] Indeed, water flows in the transboundary context within a geological formation,[47] and as such a legal regime such as the one related to oil and gas is not adequate. This approach could lead to problems since the focus on geologic formations would affect the management of groundwater resources. This specific issue, however, cannot easily be resolved by focusing on these formations.[48] For instance, groundwater pollution may flow across the borders requiring an urgent need to tackle the contamination.[49] In this case, groundwater governance is more adequate than aquifer regulation. Finally, focus on the term *Aquifer* instead of *Groundwater* led to the exclusion of several potentially problematic situations from the scope of the Draft Articles.[50] For example, domestic aquifers connected to TBAs were all omitted.[51]

Given all of the above, scholars are calling for reshaping this debate since policymakers and hydrogeologists need to be able to properly communicate.

42 Report of the International Law Commission, 58th Session (1 May–9 June and 3 July–11 August 2006), p. 196. General Assembly, Official Records, 61st session, Supplement No. 10 (A/61/10).

43 Mechlem, *supra* note 468, at 809; Jens Newig & Edward Challies, *Water, Rivers and Wetlands*, in ROUTLEDGE HANDBOOK OF GLOBAL ENVIRONMENTAL POLITICS 439, 446 (Paul G. Harris eds., Routledge 2014).

44 Conti & Gupta, supra note 376, at 853; Tanzi, *supra* note 341, at 196.

45 African Convention, *supra* note 353.

46 Russel Frink, *Preserving Trans-Boundary Aquifers: A Precious Resource for our Future Generations*, 26(2) GLOBAL BUSINESS & DEVELOPMENT LAW JOURNAL. 503, 519 (2013).

47 Mechlem, *supra* note 362, at 219.

48 DELLAPENNA & LOURES, *supra* note 586, at 276–277.

49 Ekaterina Golovina et al., *Sustainable Management of Transboundary Groundwater Resources: Past and Future*, 13 SUSTAINABILITY. 1, 1–10 (2021).

50 ADRIEN BODART, *Transboundary Groundwater Management: Comparison Between International Law Codification and EU Water Policy*, in WATER AND LAW: TOWARDS SUSTAINABILITY 108, 110 (Michael Kidd et al eds., Edward Elgar Publishing 2014).

51 JOSEPH W. DELLAPENNA & FLAVIA ROCHA LOURES, *Transboundary Aquifers: Towards Substantive and Process Reform in Treaty-Making*, in ENVIRONMENTAL LAW AND SUSTAINABILITY AFTER RIO 217, 225–226 (Jamie Benidickson et al. eds., Edward Elgar Publishing 2011).

In that sense, hydrogeology professionals cannot expect policymakers to understand all the scientific information. At the same time, the latter must gain a certain understanding of water science to ensure the adoption of effective policies.[52] This is especially the case, as regardless of the focus on TBAs, good groundwater governance remain essential.[53]

Confined Aquifers Covered Under the Draft Articles and the UNWC Simultaneously

Scholars argued that the Draft Articles were not needed since the ILC adopted a Resolution on Confined Transboundary Aquifers in 1994. The latter sought recognition of the fact that the Commission's 1991 and 1994 versions of the Draft Articles on international watercourses did not cover these resources.[54] The ILC managed to cover unconfined through the UNWC, and confined aquifers through the Resolution.[55] The latter stated that the convention's principles could apply and encouraged states to use international surface water rules as guidance. These are meant as a suggestion for action taken in the absence of those applicable to this source. Despite the adoption of the Resolution, there was an explicit acknowledgment of the need to establish comprehensive rules applicable to non-rechargeable groundwaters. The ILC followed this approach as mentioned previously in its 2002 program of work focusing initially on transboundary fossil aquifers, then on all types of groundwater resources resulting in the adoption of the Draft Articles in 2008.[56]

At that time, several arguments were made supporting the inclusion of shared confined aquifers within the scope of the UNWC.[57] A lack of scientific understanding of the nature of this resource, a wish to limit the scope of the 1997 convention, and a decision to deal with this topic through a separate

52 Shammy Puri & Karen G. Villholth, *I Say 'Aquifer' and She Says 'Groundwater' … Let's Call the Whole Thing Off … (With Apologies to Ella Fitzgerald & Satchmo)*, (Water Alternatives Forum, 15 May 2021), available at https://www.water-alternatives.org/index.php/blog/aquifer (last accessed 3 August 2022).

53 Megdal, *supra* note 27, at 1–5.

54 Resolution on Confined Transboundary Groundwater, *supra* note 457; Stephen C. McCaffrey, *The 1997 U.N. Watercourses Convention: Retrospect and Prospect*, 21(2) Pacific McGeorge Global Business and Development Law Journal. 165, 166–171 (2008).

55 Megdal, *supra* note 27, at 2–3; Markus Aufleger & Michael Mett, Handshake across the Jordan: Water and Understanding 78 (Innsbruck University Press 2011).

56 Stephan, *supra* note 342, at 162; Stephen C. McCaffrey, *The Codification of Universal Norms: A Means to Promote Cooperation and Equity?*, in International Law and Freshwater: The Multiple Challenges 125, 132 (Laurence Boisson de Chazournes, Christina Leb & Mara Tignino eds., Edward Elgar Publishing 2013); Michelle R. Sergent, *Comparison of the Helsinki Rules to the 1994 U.N. Draft Articles: Will the Progression of International Watercourse Law Be Dammed*, 8(2) Villanova Environmental Law Journal. 435, 455 (1997); Dupuy & Viñuales, *supra* note 467, at 135; Eckstein, *supra* note 575, at169.

57 Mechlem, *supra* note 394, at 54–55.

instrument have all played a role in the final outcome.[58] The insufficient scientific understanding was evident since the definition provided by the ILC for shared confined aquifer differs.[59] Another matter that created problems is related to the geologic formation of an unconfined aquifer. In this sense, the formation housing an aquifer might change due to factors such as drought. This would impact the amount of existing water in it and reflects the vast complexities revolving around its regulation.[60] Again, one could see how the lack of understanding of hydrological realities has complicated the ILC's tasks.

In fact, the Commission created strict criteria to determine which shared aquifer was covered within the UNWC. In that sense, only those that have some type of relationship with surface water could be considered. This approach has been criticized as the ILC should have focused instead on whether the aquifer plays an important role in the hydrological cycle and its potential transboundary impact.[61] There is a lack of clarity in the UNWC and subsequent commentaries on whether the transboundary element should be found only in a river, or in an aquifer. In that sense, a shared river connected to a domestic aquifer falls under the UNWC. However, the convention did not clarify whether a TBA connected to a domestic river falls under the convention. Unfortunately, the ILC and the Special Rapporteurs did not clarify this matter. Scholars stated that this exclusion is indefensible. There were criticisms directed toward the convention in relation to the inclusion of the term *common terminus*. It is argued that this could not have been applied to many types of aquifers that were connected to surface water. Such terminology within the scope of the convention led to many debates.[62] Surface water, in general, flows to a common terminus, which is usually the sea. Aquifers, on the other hand, could have multiple termini. Hence, the requirements of the UNWC in which groundwater and surface water must flow to a common terminus, creates some instances of aquifers beyond the scope of the convention. Moreover, surface water and groundwater do not necessarily constitute a whole unit despite the statement made in the UNWC declaring otherwise. This may be

58 See, Maurizio Arcari, *The Draft Articles on the Law of International Watercourses Adopted by the International Law Commission: An Overview and Some Remarks on Selected Issues*, 21(3) Natural resources Forum. 169, 172 (1997); Stephen C. McCaffrey, *An Assessment of the Work of the International Law Commission*, 36(2) Natural Resources Journal. 297, 318 (1996).

59 Stephan, *supra* note 342, at 154.

60 Eckstein, *supra* note 460, at 548–550.

61 *Id.* at 552.

62 UNWC, *supra* note 184, at Art. 2 (a); Vick, *supra* note 563, at 196; Lilian del Castillo, *The La Plata Basin System Against the Background of Other Basin Organizations*, in Managing Transboundary Waters of Latin America 89, 92 (Asit K. Biswas eds., Routledge 2013). The term "Common Terminus" was included in previous international water law Instruments within the provisions defining their scope such as Article 2 of the Helsinki Rules on the Uses of the Waters of International Rivers of 1966.

inaccurate. Accordingly, two rivers that are hydrologically connected through a TBA could not be covered under the convention.[63]

Additionally, even though Article 2 of the UNWC expressly mentioned that this convention is applicable to specific types of transboundary groundwater, its provisions are written in a manner that accommodates surface water needs more than groundwater, whose specific characteristics are not considered. Indeed, many of the principles mentioned such as the principle of equitable and reasonable utilization, the duty to not cause significant harm, etc., are geared toward surface water.[64] The importance of the UNWC lies in the fact that a binding international instrument expressly mentioned groundwater. This inclusion meant IWL principles apply to this resource connected to surface water.[65] Moreover, its knowledge remained relatively incomplete when the UNWC was adopted. This stands in contrast to when the Draft Articles were issued.[66]

As a result of these legal developments, confusion has occurred. The UNWC covers some of the aquifers that are dealt with by the Draft Articles. This is likely to increase since the convention uses the term *groundwater* and the Draft Articles *aquifer*.[67] Conflicts have been noted between some of the provisions of both of them.[68] At the time these problems surfaced, the Special Rapporteur suggested the inclusion of an Article in the 2008 mechanism giving primacy to the latter in case both instruments clash. The ILC rejected this suggestion. As such, the final version of the Draft Articles did not include any reference to the UNWC.[69] When the final status of the 2008 mechanism is agreed upon through future negotiations, the scope and substantive provisions can be clarified among states. For the time being, it remains unclear.[70]

It is worth mentioning in this context that the scope of the Draft Articles is considered broader than of the UNWC. This instrument tackles all potential

63 Mechlem, *supra* note 394, at 55–57; Laurence Boisson de Chazournes, Christina Leb & Mara Tignino, *Introduction*, inInternational Law and Freshwater: The Multiple Challenges 1, 3–4 (Laurence Boisson de Chazournes, Christina Leb & Mara Tignino eds., Edward Elgar Publishing 2013).

64 *Id.* at 57–61.

65 *Id.* at 61–62. Christina Leb, *The UN Watercourses Convention: The Eminence Grise behind Cooperation on Transboundary Water Resources*, 38(2) Water International. 146, 146–155 (2013); Owen McIntyre, *Substantive Rules of International Water law*, in Routledge Handbook of Water Law and Policy 234, 234–235 (Alistair Rieu-Clarke, Andrew Allan & Sarah Hendry eds., Routledge 2017); United Nations, United Nations Juridical Yearbook 2008, 185 (United Nations Publications 2010).

66 Bodart, *supra* note 606, at 110.

67 Carlson, *supra* note 14, at 1426–1431.

68 McCaffrey, *supra* note 610, at 132.

69 Rieu-Clarke, *supra* note 592, at 165.

70 Yamada, *supra* note 456, at 15; Brahma Chellaney, Water, Peace, and War: Confronting the Global Water Crisis 257 (Rowman & Littlefield Publishers, Inc 2013).

activities that might affect a TBA,[71] considering the latest developments.[72] In its Article 1, the focus is on *utilization* and not *use*. The rationale behind such an approach is that utilization covers the mechanism and methodology of use. The term *use* includes only the purpose for groundwater extraction. The scope of the Draft Articles also comprises activities that are not only related to the utilization of the resource but may affect the aquifers.[73] It is also important to note that the UNECE Water Convention covered all types of transboundary groundwaters within its scope in contrast to the UNWC,[74] regardless of whether these resources are connected to an international watercourse.[75]

Problems Arising Due to Substantive Norms of the Draft Articles

A Return to the Principle of Absolute Sovereignty

The principle of sovereignty mentioned in Article 3 of the Draft Articles created controversy.[76] It was first established in the 2005 Report of the ILC Working Group. Some states objected to its inclusion while others emphasized the need to strike a balance between the interests and rights of all nations.[77] Before that, sovereignty was discussed in accordance with[78] the definition provided in the UNGA Resolution 1803.[79] Countries that have abundant natural resources must have the ability to use them without interference to protect the

71 McIntyre, *supra* note 411, at 244; Christina Leb & Patricia Wouters, *The Water Security Paradox and International Law: Securitisation as an Obstacle to Achieving Water Security and the Role of Law in Desecuritising the World's Most Precious Resources*, in Water Security: Principles, Perspectives and Practices 26, 30–32 (Bruce Lankford et al eds., Routledge 2013).

72 Owen McIntyre & Mara Tignino, *Reconciling the UN Watercourses Convention with Recent Developments in Customary International Law*, in The UN Watercourses Convention in Force: Strengthening International Law for Transboundary Water Management 286, 286–295 (Flavia Rocha Loures & Alistair Rieu-Clarke eds., Routledge 2013).

73 Draft Articles, *supra* note 515, at Article 1.

74 UNECE Water Convention, *supra* note 431, at Article 1 (1).

75 United Nations-Water, *The United Nations Global Water Conventions: Fostering Sustainable Development and Peace* 16 (UN-Water Policy Brief on the United Nations Global Water Conventions; Geneva, Switzerland, 2020).

76 See in general, Michael A. Greenop, *The United Nations International Law Commission's Draft Articles on Transboundary Aquifers*, 24(1) Max Planck Yearbook of United Nations Law Online. 36, 36–81 (2021).

77 Document A/60/10. Report of the International Law Commission on the Work of its 57th Session (2 May–3 June and 11 July–5 August 2005), p. 15–26.

78 Vick, *supra* note 563, at 1803. See, A. Dan Tarlock, *International Water Law and the Protection of River System Ecosystem Integrity*, 10(2) Brigham Young University Journal of Public Law. 181, 181–211 (1996).

79 General Assembly resolution 1803 (XVII) of 14 December 1962, "Permanent Sovereignty Over Natural Resources". Adopted by the United Nations General Assembly, 14 December, 1962. See, Karol N. Gess, *Permanent Sovereignty over Natural Resources: An Analytical Review of the United Nations Declaration and Its Genesis*, 13(2) The International and Comparative Law Quarterly. 398, 406–408 (1964).

right to economic independence.[80] The concept emerged due to concerns on the national and international level. These worries led to the development of global norms associated with sustainable development and the environment. For this reason, governments advocated for its adoption as a UN Resolution.[81]

This concept has been used to justify a state's unilateral actions affecting a shared water resource in accordance with the Harmon doctrine, which claims that a country possesses sovereignty over international watercourses within its border.[82] The global community has rejected the theory of absolute sovereignty over natural resources in the last century. Instead, it has adopted the concept of a limited territorial one through the UN documents. In these, the principle of permanent sovereignty is not absolute and is subject to legal and economic requirements. Regardless of the opinion of the state taking actions, it must respect the effects of such measures on other nations. Under this, the impact of the activities must be considered since sovereignty is rather limited.[83] Within the framework of IWL, the principle of limited territorial sovereignty has been embraced due to its importance to sharing and protecting transboundary water resources.[84]

Regarding the Draft Articles, the idea of including the principle of absolute sovereignty was to ensure that groundwater was not considered a common good to humankind. Such a definition would have reduced or limited the control of the state owning the shared aquifer.[85] Accordingly, a nation has a sovereign right to the aquifer located within its territory. Under the definitions provided, however, government holds right to the geologic formation,

80 Sangwani Patrick Ng'ambi, *Permanent Sovereignty Over Natural Resources and the Sanctity of Contracts, from the Angle of Lucrum Cessans,*12(2) Loyola University Chicago International Law Review. 153, 154 (2015); Dorothée Cambou & Stefaan Smis, *Permanent Sovereignty Over Natural Resources from a Human Rights Perspective: Natural Resources Exploitation and Indigenous Peoples Rights in the Arctic*, 22(1) Michigan State International Law Review. 347, 348 (2013).

81 Patricia Wouters, *'Dynamic Cooperation' in International Law and the Shadow of State Sovereignty in the Context of Transboundary Waters*, 21(3) Environmental Liability. 88, 91 (2013).

82 Stephen C. McCaffrey, *The Harmon Doctrine One Hundred Years Later: Buried, Not Praised*, 36 Natural Resources Journal. 725, 725–728 (1996).

83 María Augusta León Moreta, The Human Rights Fundaments of Conservation in the Context of the Extraction of Energy Resources 102–105 (Bonn University Press 2015); 10 Malgosia Fitzmaurice, *Natural Resources Management: Protecting Fisheries in the 21st Century*, inNatural Resources and the Green Economy: Redefining the Challenges for People, States and Corporations 191, 195 (Elena Blanco & Jona Razzaque eds., Martinus Nijhoff Publishers 2012). See also on the debate between absolute and limited sovereignty over natural resources, Petra Gumploya, *Sovereignty Over Natural Resources – A Normative Reinterpretation*, 9(1) Global Constitutionalism. 7, 7–37 (2020); Franz Xaver Perrez, *The Relationship Between "Permanent Sovereignty" and the Obligation not to Cause Transboundary Environmental Damage*, 26(4) Environmental Law. 1187, 1187–1212 (1996).

84 Hildering, *supra* note 170, at 99.

85 Castillo-Laborde, *supra* note 346, at 3–4.

but not the water contained within. In fact, states have a right of use that must be realized following the principle of reasonable and equitable utilization. They have the obligation to not cause significant harm toward others.[86] This principle was added to take into account the opinion of the nations claiming permanent sovereignty over natural resources. The Special Rapporteur made it clear that this concept is neither absolute, nor unlimited.[87] The ILC argued that such inclusion was possible since its application would be restricted by the implementation of other substantive principles.[88] Some experts agreed with this interpretation claiming that a balance was established between sovereignty and cooperation among nations.[89] Other nations argued for the limitation of sovereignty and subjecting a TBA to an agreed-upon regulatory framework.[90] The issue of sovereignty was a main reason why several states criticized the UNWC. Sovereignty disputes fueled rejections of the convention due to some nations emphasis on absolute control over natural resources in contrast to the limited sovereignty concept adopted by the ILC.[91]

The principle of absolute sovereignty included in the Draft Articles is considered both a setback and a dynamic for change.[92] The concept is seen as an extreme notion opening the door for states to base their claims on this theory reversing important developments in IWL,[93] and complicating cooperation in good faith.[94] In accordance with this interpretation, nations are not obliged to consider the rights of other states. This principle is startling when considering situations where countries share the same freshwater resource. This also contradicts the concept of equitable and reasonable utilization. Absolute authority will reopen debates about an issue that was initially considered resolved among

86 Quadri, *supra* note 515, at 5.

87 Vick, *supra* note 563, at 1803.

88 Nadia Sanchez Castillo, *Differentiating between Sovereignty over Exclusive and Shared Resources in the Light of Future Discussions on the Law of Transboundary Aquifers*, 24(1) Review of European Community & International Environmental Law. 4, 5 (2015).

89 Michael A Greenop, *The International Law Commission's Draft Articles on Transboundary Aquifers: Striking the Appropriate Balance between Sovereignty and International Cooperation*, 10(20) Cambridge International Law Journal. 229, 229–240 (2021).

90 United Nations General Assembly, International Law Commission, Report of the International Law Commission, 57th Session, p. 29 (2 May–3 June and 11 July–August 2005).

91 Carlson, *supra* note 14, at 1426–1431. For instance, that was one of the main reasons for which China rejected signing the UNWC. See, Hongzhou Zhang & Mingjiang Li, *A Process-Based Framework to Examine China's Approach to Transboundary Water Management*, 34(5) International Journal of Water Resources Development. 705, 706–707 (2018).

92 Tanzi, *supra* note 341, at 200–204.

93 David J. Devlaeminck, *Reassessing the Draft Articles on the Law of Transboundary Aquifers Through the Lens of Reciprocity*, 37(1) International Journal of Water Resources Development. 162, 164–168 (2021).

94 Francesco Sindico, *National Sovereignty Versus Transboundary Water Cooperation: Can You See International Law Reflected in the Water?*, 115 American Journal of International Law. 178, 182 (2021).

scholars.[95] There are clear contradictions between this principle and the one of equitable and reasonable utilization mentioned in the Draft Articles.[96] A state may perceive that it has absolute discretion over the water contained in a TBA that lies within its territory. Likewise, one would wonder how the international community could reconcile the claims of absolute sovereignty made by states sharing groundwater resources.[97]

The only way the ILC could include this concept is by considering the aquifer as subject of regulation since they are an immovable object. Groundwater continually moves from one place to another, though. Thus, this concept cannot govern such a resource. The international community, along with scholars have arrived at a consensus over the idea that states' rights over freshwater could not be determined based on the principle of sovereignty. Even if we agree on the wording of Article 3 which is associated with this notion, it is not clear what implications exist for the definition included.[98] This notion was first adopted by the Commission in 2006.[99] This reflects the opinion of a small number of states looking to secure their interests. According to several scholars, such an opinion should have been disregarded.[100] Others have argued that this concept has limited power given the need to balance it with other substantive principles mainly the one of equitable reasonable utilization, the obligation not to cause significant harm and the concept of cooperation. They claim that critics overexaggerate their arguments.[101] It has been claimed that the inclusion of this principle would facilitate the signature and ratification of the Draft Articles. In particular, hydro-hegemonic states with reluctance to sign an agreement that does not provide them protections for exploiting such a resource.[102] Such an argument would go against the development of

95 McCaffrey, *supra* note 582, at 6–7; MD. FAKRUL ISLAM, WATER USE AND POVERTY REDUCTION 86 (Springer 2016); IBRAHIM KAYA, EQUITABLE UTILIZATION: THE LAW OF NON-NAVIGATIONAL USES OF INTERNATIONAL WATERCOURSES 204 (Ashgate 2003).

96 Eckstein, *supra* note 53, at 566.

97 McCaffrey, *supra* note 582, at 6–7.

98 McCaffrey, *supra* note 463, at 285–292; MYLES FISHER & SIMON COOK, *Introduction: Water, Food and Poverty in River Basins*, in WATER, FOOD AND POVERTY IN RIVER BASINS: DEFINING THE LIMITS 1, 3–4 (Myles J. Fisher & Simon E. Cook eds., Routledge, 2012).

99 Report of the International Law Commission on the work of its 58th session, 1 May–9 June and 3 July–11 August 2006.

100 McCaffrey, *supra* note 463, at 285–292; FISHER & COOK, *supra* note 654, at 3–4.

101 RAYA MARINA STEPHAN & GABRIEL DE LOS COBOS, *State Sovereignty and Transboundary Aquifers*, in A HISTORY OF WATER: SOVEREIGNTY AND INTERNATIONAL WATER LAW 297, 312 (Terje Tvedt et al eds., I.B. Tauris 2015); Article 5(2) of the UNWC states the following: "Watercourse States shall participate in the use, development and protection of an international watercourse in an equitable and reasonable manner. Such participation includes both the right to utilize the watercourse and the duty to cooperate in the protection and development thereof, as provided in the present Convention". UNWC, *supra* note 184, at Article 5(2).

102 James D. Fry & Agnes Chong, *International Water Law and China's Management of its International Rivers*, 39(2) BOSTON COLLEGE INTERNATIONAL & COMPARATIVE LAW REVIEW. 227, 261–262 (2016).

international law where the theory of absolute sovereignty is disregarded and as MEAs and declarations follow this approach.[103] Perhaps the most prominent argument to explain its inclusion is that the text of the article that dealt with this issue is, at best, unclear.[104]

The negative consequences resulting from the adoption of this concept were noted in the 2010 Guarani Aquifer Agreement. The latter defined the aquifer as a transboundary water resource covering the territories of the nations sharing it and who are considered its only owners.[105] The agreement states in Article 2 that each party has control over its portion of the aquifer in accordance with existing legislations and provisions considering international law.[106] Provision 3 of the Draft Articles was incorporated within the Guarani treaty, as the 2008 instrument constituted the basis for the convention.[107]

A Battle for Primacy Between the Principle of Equitable and Reasonable Utilization and the Non-Harm Obligation

Several scholars have stated that the Draft Articles do not need to depart from IWL except for adjustments to the particularities concerning shared aquifers. The main pillars of this framework are mentioned in the 2008 instrument and have been framed using similar language to the UNWC. This language is crafted to consider the specific aspects of aquifers.[108]

The watercourses convention has included the principle of equitable and reasonable utilization in Article 5 which signatories must comply with when utilizing shared waters.[109] A watercourse state must use it considering the interests of the other nations and ensuring its protection. A government accordingly has a right to use the watercourse but also the obligation

103 *Id.* at 254. For instance, Principle 2 of the Rio Declaration states the following: "States have, in accordance with the Charter of the United Nations and the principles of international law, the sovereign right to exploit their own resources pursuant to their own environmental and developmental policies, and the responsibility to ensure that activities within their jurisdiction or control do not cause damage to the environment of other States or of areas beyond the limits of national jurisdiction." Rio Declaration, *supra* note 114, at Principle 2.

104 Dellapenna, *supra* note 449, at 220.

105 Guarani Aquifer Agreement, adopted in 2010, Article 1.

106 *Id.* at Article 2.

107 McIntyre, *supra* note 411, at 251–252. See, Lilian del Castillo-Laborde, *The Guarani Aquifer Framework Agreement (2010)*, in International Law and Freshwater: The Multiple Challenges 196, 205–207 (Laurence Boisson de Chazournes, Christina Leb & Mara Tignino eds., Edward Elgar Publishing 2013). The Guarani aquifer agreement was the first treaty signed between Argentina, Brazil, Paraguay, and Uruguay in 2010 and adopted after the Draft Articles and which was influenced it. See, Francesco Sindico, *The Guarani Aquifer System and the International Law of Transboundary Aquifers*, 13(3) International Community Law Review. 255, 255–260 (2011).

108 Tanzi, *supra* note 341, at 204–206.

109 UNWC, *supra* note 184, at article 5; Traversi, *supra* note 55, at 474–477.

to cooperate for its safeguard and development.[110] The UNECE Water Convention mentioned this principle briefly putting an obligation upon the parties to take all the needed actions to that end. The provision emphasized considering the transboundary character when activities have already or may impact these resources.[111] Through it, it supported this concept incorporated in details in the UNWC[112] without making it a main provision.[113] The 1992 treaty did not list any factor relevant to its implementation and neither offers guidance in this regard. Rather, the guide to implementing the convention points to the UNWC.[114] In fact, the guide considers this concept as one of the most important cornerstones of IWL.[115] Meanwhile, the UNECE Water Convention detailed guidelines clarified substantially general water principles.[116] The Model provisions on transboundary groundwaters adopted by the UNECE reiterates this concept adding the need to consider relevant factors such as those agreed upon by the parties.[117] Hence, this instrument enhances the application of principle of equitable and reasonable utilization mentioned briefly in the UNECE Water Convention to shared groundwater resources.[118]

This principle represents a substantive rule of IWL,[119] which regards the endorsement of equitable solutions for the utilization of shared freshwaters.[120] These interests would be weighted with specific factors included in the instrument or convention to which this concept is added.[121] The Draft Articles ensured that such a notion was not only applicable to the allocation of water, but also to the benefits that could arise from the exploitation of the aquifer. One of the many objectives of the 2008 instrument, as stated through

110 *Id.*

111 UNECE Water Convention, *supra* note 431, at Article 2:2 (c).

112 Chenjun Zheng & Otto Spijkers, *Priority of Uses in International Water Law*, 13 Sustainability. 1, 2 (2021).

113 Rieu-Clarke and Kinna, *supra* note 547, at 20.

114 Philine Wehling, Nile Water Rights: An International Law Perspective 77 (Springer 2020).

115 Owen McIntyre, *The Principle of Equitable and Reasonable Utilization*, in The UNECE Convention on the Protection and Use of Transboundary Watercourses and International Lakes 146, 148 (Attila Tanzi et al eds., Brill 2015).

116 Tanzi, *supra* note 551, at 237.

117 UNECE, *supra* note 554.

118 Paula Hanasz, *Does the Principle of Equitable Utilisation Apply to Transboundary Aquifers?* (Global Water Forum, June 15, 2015), available at https://globalwaterforum.org/2015/06/15/does-the-principle-of-equitable-utilisation-apply-to-transboundary-aquifers/ (last accessed 3 August 2022).

119 Owen McIntyre, *The World Court's Emphasis on Procedural Rules in the Recent Pulp Mills Case: Contributing to the Progressive and Coherent Development of International Water Law*, 4(2) Water Alternatives. 124, 143 (2011).

120 Yaser Khalaileh, *Prospects for Cooperation and Dispute Over Water in the Middle East*, 5(1) Berkeley Journal of Middle Eastern & Islamic Law. 73, 95 (2013).

121 Patricia Wouters, *National and International Water Law: Achieving Equitable and Sustainable Use of Water Resources,* 25(4) Water International. 499, 502 (2000).

Article 4 associated with this principle, was maximizing benefits from the aquifer through comprehensive utilization plans that can be created individually or jointly. The realization of this goal is conditioned on the consideration of current and future water needs as well as alternative water sources. Moreover, the use of shared recharging aquifers must align with a pattern that allows the constant functioning of the latters.[122] Despite all of this, some consider that the explanation of reasonable utilization of a TBA in the 2008 instrument is ambiguous.[123]

In Article 6, the UNWC mentioned factors that must be taken into consideration when determining the equitable and reasonable utilization of an international watercourse. These include those of natural characters such as geographic and hydrological ones; those addressing social and economic needs as well as the population relying on the watercourse; impact occurring on another state from its use etc.[124] This provision has revealed several factors that are relevant to surface water, without providing clear guidance on groundwater. This remains the case since the characteristics of this source are not considered in Article 6. The Draft Articles attempted to rectify this matter.[125] Its Article 5 established a list of non-exhaustive factors through which it was possible to assess whether the actual or potential use of the shared aquifer was reasonable and equitable.[126] This provision added new ones in addition to those that were included in the UNWC. These are: "the natural characteristics of the aquifer or aquifer system"[127]; "the contribution to the formation and recharge of the aquifer or aquifer system";[128] and "the role of the aquifer or aquifer system in the related ecosystem".[129] The other factors reflecting those included in the UNWC focused on TBAs and not international watercourses.[130] They include considering the population relying on the aquifer or aquifer system; the various needs of the aquifer states including social and economic ones; the possible and current ways the aquifers is being used; and its potential impact on the aquifer states.[131] The Draft Articles focused on long-term benefits, rather than utilization. This emphasis allowed a broader consideration of issues that would ensure better exploitation of TBAs.[132] Nonetheless, there were calls for narrowing down their focus while tailoring the list to take into

122 Mechlem, *supra* note 468, at 812; Draft Articles, *supra* note 515, at Article 4 (a); (b); (c) & (d).
123 Margaret J. Vick, *The Law of International Waters: Reasonable Utilization*, 12 Chicago-Kent Journal of International and Comparative Law. 141, 167 (2014).
124 UNWC, *supra* note 184, at article 6.
125 Traversi, *supra* note 55, at 474–477.
126 Mechlem, *supra* note 468, at 812–813.
127 Draft Articles, *supra* note 515, at Article 5: c.
128 *Id.* at Article 5: d.
129 *Id.* at Article 5: i.
130 Traversi, *supra* note 55, at 474–477.
131 Draft Articles, *supra* note 515, at Article 5.
132 McIntyre, *supra* note 411, at 244–245.

account the characteristics of groundwater,[133] as the factors generally provided a holistic approach.[134] It is worth mentioning that their application must consider the circumstances of the basin, governance practices, population, existing frameworks,[135] in addition to other matters.[136]

The second principle is the obligation to not cause significant harm to the aquifer mentioned in Article 6.[137] States sharing freshwater resources must take all the necessary measures to not cause damage to other nations including those with a discharge zone.[138] Unlike the UNWC, this obligation also included activities not related to utilization as a consequence of their inclusion in the scope of the Draft Articles. In that sense, states must guarantee that these activities do not cause significant harm.[139] The obligation mentioned in Article 7 of the UNWC was criticized since the measures that states should take are somewhat vague. Indeed, it did not provide details concerning the actions to be adopted but rather called for eliminating and mitigating the harm as well as discussing potential compensation when needed.[140] The Draft Articles in provision 6 mirrored the same problem. Still, its scope was expanded as aquifer states must take all actions to prevent causing harm to aquifer and non aquifer states that contains a discharge zone. Moreover, the duties were expanded to activities other than utilization of the TBA or the aquifer system that have already or may affect the shared aquifers, the aquifer system or the nations containing a discharge zone— even where those activities are not directly connected to TBAs. And when damage occurs, the states causing it must take all the actions to eliminate and mitigate the harm while consulting the affected state and including potentially the country with a discharge zone if affected.[141]

Regrettably, this provision of the Draft Articles remains vague and applies the same standards mentioned in the UNWC. This is unfortunate because groundwater has different characteristics than surface water. This means that the 2008 instrument no longer complements the UNWC and its consideration of groundwater.[142] Some situations are not included in the scope of the

133 Traversi, *supra* note 55, at 474–477.

134 Samer Talozi et al., *What Constitutes an Equitable Water Share? A Reassessment of Equitable Apportionment in the Jordan–Israel Water Agreement 25 Years Later*, 21 Water Policy. 911, 912 (2019).

135 Zeray Yihdego & Julie Gibson, Implementing International Watercourses Law through the WEF Nexus and SDGs: an Integrated Approach Illustrated in the Zambezi River Basin (Brill 2020).

136 Zheng & Spijkers, *supra* note 668, at 2.

137 Mechlem, *supra* note 468, at 814.

138 Zewdu Mengesha Bashahider, *The Interplay Between the Duty Not to Cause Significant Harm and Equitable and Reasonable Utilization Principle*, 5 Bahir Dar University Journal of Law. 391, 391–396 (2015).

139 Eckstein, *supra* note 460, at 569–576.

140 UNWC, *supra* note 184, at Article 7.

141 Draft Articles, *supra* note 515, article 6.

142 Traversi, *supra* note 55, at 481–486.

Article because the harm did not occur. For instance, contaminants or toxic materials that were buried long ago and are likely to reach shared groundwater resources in the near future are excluded from its scope. Their exclusion is justified since damage has not yet occurred.[143] This concept led to controversies, given that, for a harm to be included in the scope of the Article, it must be significant. There have been calls for lowering this threshold so that aquifers could be better protected, even when damage might not be significant. The concept was ultimately considered as appropriate and flexible by the international community,[144] especially as the latter is currently benefiting from the development of detailed regulations and methodologies concerning the ecosystem and the environment broadly.[145]

The term ***significant harm*** was not used in the UNECE Water Convention but rather the concept of ***transboundary impact***.[146] Nonetheless, this topic has been addressed in details through various provisions given the focus on the protection and use of shared watercourses and international lakes. Indeed, the parties are expected to tackle any transboundary impact by preventing, controlling, or reducing its likelihood. Such measures must not result in the pollution of other parts of the environment and when possible, they must be made at the source of the contamination.[147] The rest of the articles of the treaty provide the means to tackle potential effect through the use of technology for various purposes,[148] the adoption of water-quality objectives and water-quality criteria,[149] research and development,[150] the establishment of agreements and joint bodies,[151] as well as joint monitoring programmes,[152] exchange of data and information, etc.[153]

The 2008 instrument did not include a reference to compensation. In contrast, Article 7 of the UNWC mentioned that states causing significant harm

143 Eckstein, *supra* note 460, at 569–576.

144 Mechlem, *supra* note 468, at 814. A general debate is taking place in international water law with regards to the concept of significant harm. For instance, questions concerning the level of harm to be reached to be considered significant have been made. See, Susanne Schmeier & Joyeeta Gupta, *The Principle of No Signifcant Harm in International Water Law*, 20 International Environmental Agreements: Politics, Law and Economics. 597, 598 (2020).

145 Owen McIntyre, *The Current State of Development of the No Signifcant Harm Principle: How Far Have We Come?*, 20 International Environmental Agreements: Politics, Law and Economics. 601, 616 (2020).

146 Mara Tignino & Christian Bréthaut, *The Role of International Case Law in Implementing the Obligation not to Cause Signifcant Harm*, 20 International Environmental Agreements: Politics, Law and Economics. 631, 632 (2020).

147 UNECE Water Convention, *supra* note 431, at Article 2.

148 *Id.* at Article 3.

149 *Id.* at Article 3 (3).

150 *Id.* at Article 5.

151 *Id.* at Article 9.

152 *Id.* at Article 11.

153 *Id.* at Article 13 & 14.

should provide it to nations whose rights were violated.[154] This duty does not constitute a direct obligation, but is subject to consultation among the countries sharing the freshwater resource.[155] The UNECE Water Convention applied the polluter-pays principle based on which the polluter assumes all the related costs.[156]

Given all the above, the question of whether the principle of equitable and reasonable utilization has priority over the duty not to cause significant harm has been debated.[157] In fact, it is still not clear which principle held primacy in the UNWC. Today, scholars remain divided and arguments for and against each principle have been established.[158] Others argued that the UNWC created a balance between both principles.[159] As the rest of the IWL instruments and conventions, the Draft Articles kept the relationship between both principles vague without indicating priority for each. The issue of compensation was excluded from the provision as international obligations associated with a country's liability or responsibility apply. Analysis of Article 6(3) shows that legislators acknowledged that some harm is acceptable.[160] However, the 2008 instrument failed to solve one of the main dilemmas that faced the UNWC.[161]

The question of primacy has been debated in general by different scholars.[162] The main issue concerns the clash of interests where upstream states favored the principle of equitable and reasonable utilization. This stands in contrast to downstream nations that favored the second principle. These states viewed any potential activities upstream as a limiting factor to their

154 UNWC, *supra* note 184, at Article 7.

155 McIntyre, *supra* note 411, at 247; Esther Schroeder-Wildberg, *The 1997 International Watercourses Convention – Background and Negotiations* 43 (Working Paper on Management in Environmental Planning, 04/2002). The idea of compensation was added to the UNWC as the international community recognized that water is a finite resource. This requires clear protection where economic means can be used to that end. Kai Wegerich & Oliver Olsson, *Late Developers and the Inequity of "Equitable Utilization" and the Harm of "Do No Harm"*, 35(6) WATER INTERNATIONAL. 707, 707–717 (2010). The Draft Articles did not include compensation within Article 6. Compensation was supposed to fall under conventions such as those related to state responsibility. Draft Articles on the Law of Transboundary Aquifers with Commentary 30 (2008).

156 UNECE Water Convention, *supra* note 431, at Article 2:5 (b).

157 McIntyre, *supra* note 411, at 247; Schroeder-Wildberg, *supra* note 711; Wegerich & Olsson, *supra* note 711, at 707–717.

158 Alrbert E. Uton, *Which Rule Should Prevail in International Water Disputes: That of Reasonableness or That of No Harm*, 36(3) NATURAL RESOURCES JOURNAL. 635, 638–641 (1996). See, Bruce Lankford, *Does Article 6 (Factors Relevant to Equitable and Reasonable Utilization) in the UN Watercourses Convention Misdirect Riparian Countries?*, 38(2) WATER INTERNATIONAL. 130, 130–145 (2013).

159 LEB, *supra* note 52, at 102–104.

160 Mechlem, *supra* note 468, at 814–815.

161 Uton, *supra* note 714, at 638–641; Lankford, *supra* note 714, at 130–145.

162 Dellapenna, *supra* note 449, at 278–280; SALMAN M.A. SALMAN & KISHOR UPRETY, CONFLICT AND COOPERATION ON SOUTH ASIA'S INTERNATIONAL RIVERS 27–28 (Kluwer Law International 2002).

hydrological benefits.[163] In practice, harm may occur from downstream countries through the foreclosure of water use and mismanagement by these same nations affecting the ecosystem and environment of the basin as a whole.[164] Broadly, it has been said that the principle of equitable and reasonable utilization enjoys primacy over the non-harm rule. That did not prevent scholars from providing arguments as to why the non-harm rule should have priority. It has been declared that this principle protects weak states from harm that could be inflicted by stronger nations with whom the water is shared. Through this concept, it would be easier to determine the party that caused the damage.[165] Regardless, several experts have argued that both principles are compatible, as they represent two sides of the same coin. Hence, there must be a balanced application of both of them in a given instrument or convention,[166] as they coexist in a harmonious manner in practice.[167]

Moreover, compliance with the two principles is essential to their implementation. Indeed, the clash over these two principles between upstream and downstream nations has been the main cause of water disputes when it comes, for instance, to the Grand Ethiopian Renaissance Dam on the Nile; the conflict between Syria, Turkey, and Iraq concerning Tigris/Euphrates Basins and the clash between China; and Vietnam, Lao Republic, Thailand, and Cambodia regarding the Mekong river basin.[168] When the UNWC was negotiated, state delegations played an important role in the debate by advocating for the principle that best suited their interests,[169] especially as upstream and downstream nations had mainly opposing political and economic interests.[170] This may be

163 Inga M. Jacobs, The Politics of Water in Africa: Norms, Environmental Regions and Transboundary Cooperation in the Orange-Senqu and Nile Rivers 72–75 (Continuum International Publishing Group 2012).

164 Yihdego & Gibson, supra note 691.

165 Dellapenna, *supra* note 449, at 278–280; Salman & Uprety, *supra* note 718, at 27–28; Jerome Delli Priscoli & Aaron T. Wolf, Managing and Transforming Water Conflicts 60 (Cambridge University Press 2010).

166 Stephen C. McCaffrey, The Law of International Watercourses 505–506 (Third Ed., Oxford University Press 2019); Owen McIntyre, Environmental Protection of International Watercourses Under International Law 114–115 (Ashgate 2007); Malcom J. Gander, *International Water Law and Supporting Water Management Principles in the Development of a Model Transboundary Agreement Between Riparians in International River Basins*, 39(3) Water International. 315, 323–324 (2014).

167 Attila M. Tanzi, *The Inter-Relationship Between No Harm, Equitable and Reasonable Utilisation and Cooperation Under International Water Law*, 20 International Environmental Agreements: Politics, Law and Economics. 619, 620 (2020).

168 Salman M.A. Salman, *Equitable and Reasonable Utilization and the Obligation against Causing Significant Harm – Are They Reconcilable?*, 115 American Journal of International Law. 183, 183 (2021).

169 Attila Tanzi, *Codifying the Minimum Standards of the Law of International Watercourses: Remarks on Part One and a Half*, 21(2) Natural Resources Forum. 109, 112–115 (1997).

170 Ute Mager, *International Water Law: Global Developments and Regional Examples* 13–50 (Jedermann-Verlag GmbH, Heidelberg, 2015).

one factor that could delay the adoption of the Draft Articles as a binding instrument. This also delayed the ratification of the UNWC.[171] The inability to solve this controversy presents concerns. IWL does not provide specific guidelines for states, but rather, general principles that would be incorporated in multilateral and bilateral basin water agreements between countries sharing these resources.[172] These principles play an important role in the negotiation process of water agreements.[173] This clash, if not solved, could continue to be one of the weaknesses of the Draft Articles,[174] as it is not clear how both principles can be implemented simultaneously.[175]

Impact of the Contradictory and Flawed Principles on Cooperation

The fact that the international community could not find a compromise between these two principles has negatively affected other concepts in the Draft Articles,[176] mainly the one of cooperation which provides the basis for the implementation of the above-mentioned concepts.[177] It is also included as a substantive norm within this instrument. However, one could question how such cooperation may take place when a clash of interests is taking place between states supporting the above-mentioned notions.[178] The inclusion of absolute sovereignty over natural resources makes this task more difficult. This principle encourages states unilateral actions and limits collaboration.[179] Even if the principle of sovereignty did not exist in the 2008 instrument, international law cannot force states to cooperate. This can only

171 David Devlaeminck, *Revisiting the Substantive Rules of the Law of International Watercourses: An Analysis Through the Lens of Reciprocity and the Interests of China*, 20(2) Water Policy. 323, 323–335 (2017).

172 Shlomi Dinar, International Water Treaties: Negotiation and Cooperation Along Transboundary Rivers 104 (Routledge 2008).

173 Susanne Schmeier, *International Water Law Principles in Negotiations and Water Diplomacy*, 115 American Journal of International Law. 173, 173 (2021).

174 Abdullabi Elmi Mohamed & Hussien M. Iman, *Hydropolitics in the Horn of Africa: Conflicts and Cooperation in the Juba and Shabelle Rivers*, inShared Waters, Shared Opportunities: Hydropolitics in East Africa 37, 41–46 (Bernard Calas & C. A. Mumma Martinon eds., Mkukina Nyota Publishers Limited 2010).

175 *Id.*

176 See also on this matter, Wegerich & Olsson, *supra* note 711, at 707–717.

177 Devlaeminck, *supra* note 727, at 327.

178 *Id.* at 323–335; A. Dan Tarlock, *Four Challenges for International Water Law*, 23(2) Tulane Environmental Law Journal. 369, 369–408 (2010).

179 Richard E. Just & Sinaia Netanyahu, *International Water Resources Conflicts: Experience and Potential*, in Conflict and Cooperation on Trans-Boundary Water Resources 1, 8–9 (Richard E. Just & Sinaia Netanyahu eds., Springer 1998); Ines Dombrowsky, Conflict, Cooperation and Institutions in International Water Management: An Economic Analysis 60–64 (Edward Elgar Publishing 2007); Adams Oloo, *The Nile 'Lone Ranger' in the Nile River Waters Initiative: The Case of Eritrea*, in Cooperative Diplomacy, Regional Stability and National Interests: The Nile and Riparian States 153, 169–171 (Korwa G. Adar & Nicasius A. Check eds., Africa Institute of South Africa 2011).

occur through a relationship based on trust.[180] Diplomatic ties like this run the risk of putting nations in a dangerous and vulnerable position that results from uncertainty regarding a partner's trustworthiness.[181] Cooperation is still vital if states want to implement the substantive principles mentioned above and realize other important objectives. This is why the obligation was expressly included in the UNWC and explicitly recognized as an IWL principle.[182] It seems that nations have much progress to make in understanding its relevance in the management of shared natural resources. Numerous water conflicts have occurred in recent years with many more expected in the near future.[183] Cooperation is necessary for ensuring water security given the need to address the problems facing this resource,[184] through procedural provisions pushing towards such collaboration.[185] This is especially true as growing challenges and uncertainties face its governance.[186] These include increasing water scarcity and disputes among states.[187] Here, experts are calling for the creation of institutional mechanisms that ensure international cooperation.[188]

Generally speaking, this duty in IWL appeared as a result of states collaborating for the management of their shared water resources.[189] Disagreements between scholars emerged over whether the principle constitutes an obligation. It was stated that the concept represents a complex set of duties in the

180 Aaron M. Hoffman, *A Conceptualization of Trust in International Relations*, 8(3) European Journal of International Relations. 375, 375–401 (2002); Clara Weinhardt, *Relational Trust in International Cooperation: The Case of North-South Trade Negotiations*, 5(1) Journal of Trust Research. 27, 27–54 (2015).

181 *Id.* at 27–35; Christoph Elhardt, *The Causal Nexus Between Trust, Institutions and Cooperation in International Relations*, 5(1) Journal of Trust Research. 55, 55–60 (2015).

182 Leb, *supra* note 621, 146–155.

183 John Stuart Gladwell, *International Cooperation in Water Resources Management – Helping Nations to Help Themselves*, 31(4) Hydrological Sciences Journal. 515, 524–526 (1986); Petersen-Perlman, Veilleux & Wolf, *supra* note 186, at 105–110.

184 A. Dan Tarlock, *Toward a More Robust International Water Law of Cooperation to Address Droughts and Ecosystem Conservation*,28 The Georgetown Environmental Law Review. 261, 266–267 (2016).

185 Attila M. Tanzi, *Substantialising the Procedural Obligations of International Water Law Between Compensatory and Distributive Justice*, in A Bridge over Troubled Waters: Dispute Resolution in the Law of International Watercourses and the Law of the Sea 351, 351–355 (Helene Ruiz Fabri et al eds., Brill 2020).

186 Anthony H.J. Dorcey, *The Myth of Interagency Cooperation in Water Resources Management*,12(2) Canadian Water Resources Journal. 17, 18 (1987).

187 Waseem Ahmad Qureshi, *The Indus Basin: Water Cooperation, International Law and the Indus Waters Treaty*, 26(1) Michigan State International Law Review. 43, 46–47 (2017).

188 Asit K. Biswas, *Institutional Arrangements for International Cooperation in Water Resources*, 11(2) International Journal of Water Resources Development. 139, 139–145 (1995).

189 Christina Leb, *One Step at a Time: International Law and the Duty to Cooperate in the Management of Shared Water Resources*, 40(1) Water International. 21, 22–32 (2015).

general framework of customary international law.[190] The notion has been evolving over the years, in parallel with the development of water regulations. Different binding and non-binding legal instruments were adopted for this purpose by the ILC and the ILA mainly the water conventions previously mentioned, the Resolutions on the HRWS as well as regional and basin specific water agreements.[191] Moreover, the International Court of Justice (ICJ) has confirmed the existence of a general customary international law duty to cooperate between nations sharing a watercourse in the Gabcikovo-Nagymaros dispute.[192] In fact, the ICJ in the various cases concerning shared freshwater resources has aimed to foster cooperation.[193] A similar approach was adopted by arbitration courts.[194] The UN reflected the importance of this duty through its designation of the year 2013 as the International Year of Water Cooperation.[195] It is also seen in the targets of Sustainable Development Goal (SDG) 6 of Agenda 2030 which supports the implementation of provisions related to collaboration within water conventions and instruments.[196] Target 6.5 focuses on the adequate use of transboundary cooperation to achieve integrated water resources management and the expansion of global collaboration for helping developing nations in the activities and programs related to water and sanitation.[197]

Provision 7 of the Draft Articles covers the general obligation to cooperate to ensure the equitable and reasonable utilization as well as the protection of the aquifer. It mentions that states should establish joint mechanisms for

190 Owen McIntyre, *International Water Resources Law*, 38(3) ENVIRONMENTAL POLICY AND LAW. 131, 134 (2008).

191 Patricia Wouters, *International Law – Facilitating Transboundary Water Cooperation* 14–15 (Global Water Partnership, Technical Committee (TEC); TEC Background Paper No. 17, 2013).

192 McIntyre, *supra* note 746, at 134. The case concerned the "implementation and the termination of the Budapest Treaty of 16 September 1977 on the Construction and Operation of the Gabčíkovo-Nagymaros Barrage System and on the construction and operation of the 'provisional solution'". International Court of Justice, Gabčíkovo-Nagymaros Project (Hungary/Slovakia): Overview of the Case, available at https://www.icj-cij.org/en/case/92 (last accessed 3 August 2022).

193 International Water Law Project, International Court of Justice – International Water Law Cases, available at https://www.internationalwaterlaw.org/cases/icj.html (last accessed 3 August 2022).

194 International Water Law Project, Other Tribunals – International Water Law Cases, available at https://www.internationalwaterlaw.org/cases/othertribunals.html (last accessed 3 August 2022).

195 Yong Zhong et al, *Rivers and Reciprocity: Perceptions and Policy on International Watercourses*, 18(4) WATER POLICY. 803, 806 (2016).

196 Otto Spijkers, *The Cross-Fertilization Between the Sustainable Development Goals and International Water Law*,25(1) REVIEW OF EUROPEAN, COMPARATIVE & INTERNATIONAL ENVIRONMENTAL LAW. 39, 46 (2016).

197 United Nations Department of Economic and Social Affairs, *Goals 6: Ensure Availability and Sustainable Management of Water and Sanitation for All. Targets and Indicators*, available at https://sdgs.un.org/goals/goal6 (last accessed 3 August 2022).

collaboration based on specific requirements.[198] The UNWC provided further details concerning these mechanisms, which may take the form of commissions. They can be created when needed benefiting from experiences taking place through existing mechanisms in various places.[199] Cooperation was listed in several provisions of the Draft Articles and could be used as a compromise to reconcile competing principles. Some elements of the provisions related to it could be viewed as progressive.[200] States having a recharge or discharge zone without being aquifer nations must cooperate with aquifer states to safeguard the aquifer and its ecosystem.[201] An obligation of technical collaboration with developing countries is included covering scientific, educational, and legal issues in addition to other types directly or through an international organization.[202] Cooperation is expected in emergency situations where the government having the emergency must collaborate with the rest of the affected nations and with potentially global organizations. Cooperation in this context includes the provision of various types of supports such as scientific, technical, and logistical ones.[203] Finally, states must cooperate in the provision, when possible, of data and information related to national defence and security.[204]

The Draft Articles mentioned some procedural obligations in Part Three in relation to protection, preservation, and management covering ecosystems, recharge and discharge zones, prevention, reduction and control of pollution, monitoring, management, and planned activities.[205] Such obligations are much more detailed in the UNWC. Part III of the convention covering Articles 11–19 are crafted to specifically address solely planned measures.[206] Meanwhile Part IV tackles protection, preservation, and management.[207] These duties have incremental importance in the context of the general duty of cooperation. Although aquifer states must establish joint mechanisms to

198 Draft Articles, *supra* note 515, at Article 7(1) & (2).
199 UNWC, *supra* note 184, at Article 8.
200 Mechlem, *supra* note 468, at 815–817.
201 Draft Articles, *supra* note 515, at Article 11(2).
202 *Id.* at Article 16.
203 *Id.* at Article 17.
204 *Id.* at Article 19.
205 *Id.* at Articles 10–15.
206 UNWC, *supra* note 184, at Articles 11–19. These provisions cover information concerning planned measures; notification concerning planned measures with possible adverse effects; period for reply to notification; obligations of the notifying State during the period for reply; reply to notification; absence of reply to notification; consultations and negotiations concerning planned measures; procedures in the absence of notification and urgent implementation of planned measures.
207 *Id.* at Articles 20–26. These provisions cover protection and preservation of ecosystems; prevention, reduction, and control of pollution; introduction of alien or new species; protection and preservation of the marine environment; management; regulation and installations.

that end following Article 7(2) of the Draft Articles, the inclusion of further provisions in the 2008 instrument could have helped its realization.[208]

The UNWC made cooperation a duty through Article 8 to ensure the adequate use and protection of an international watercourse.[209] The earliest instruments adopted by organizations like the ILA described the importance of the concept in detail – even though they did not explicitly state the existence of such a duty. It was not until the 1970s that the association recognized the principle as an obligation. Similarly, at the beginning of the drafting process of the UNWC in the 1970s, this notion was not mentioned. The situation changed in the 1980s.[210] Since then, the Special Rapporteurs have gradually developed the concept.[211] The need to cooperate for the protection of surface water remained a forefront issue in the ILC's efforts to prepare the UNWC.[212] This culminated in the adoption of it as a provision within the convention.[213] According to Article 8, cooperation should take place while respecting the principles of sovereign equality, territorial integrity, mutual benefit, and good faith.[214] It is also mentioned in Article 5(2), according to which states must collaborate for the protection and development of the international watercourse.[215]

Among the many issues that should be the subject of cooperation, one could mention concerns related to hydrology and ecology.[216] The conditions related to this duty are very important. For instance, the condition of cooperating in good faith prevents the occurrence of superficial collaboration where one party has no intention of signing the agreement. This is included within provision 7 of the Draft Articles among many others.[217] International organizations like

208 McIntyre, *supra* note 411, at 246.

209 UNWC, *supra* note 184, at Article 8; Muhammad Mizanur Rahaman, *Principles of Transboundary Water Resources Management and Ganges Treaties: An Analysis*, 25(1) INTERNATIONAL JOURNAL OF WATER RESOURCES DEVELOPMENT. 159, 162–63 (2009); Dante A. Caponera, *Patterns of Cooperation in International Water Law: Principles and Institutions*, 25(3) NATURAL RESOURCES JOURNAL. 563, 569–571 (1985).

210 Leb, *supra* note 621, at 148–150.

211 *Id.*

212 Lazerwitz, *supra* note 197, at 248.

213 Leb, *supra* note 621, at 148–150.

214 UNWC, *supra* note 184, at Article 8; MARIA MANUELA FARRAJOTA, *International Cooperation on Water Resources*, in THE EVOLUTION OF THE LAW AND POLITICS OF WATER 337, 339 (Joseph W. Dellapenna & Joyeeta Gupta eds., Springer 2009).

215 *Id.* at Article 5(2).

216 Farnaz Shirani, *Cooperation in International Water Law and, States Human Rights Obligation to Fulfill the Human Right to Water*, 5(1) GLOBAL JOURNAL OF POLITICS AND LAW RESEARCH. 50, 63 (2017).

217 Draft Articles, *supra* note 515, at Article 7; GABRIEL ECKSTEIN, *Transboundary Legal Perspective: International Water Law*, in HYDRODIPLOMACY, LEGAL AND INSTITUTIONAL ASPECTS OF WATER RESOURCES GOVERNANCE: FROM THE INTERNATIONAL TO THE DOMESTIC PERSPECTIVE 28, 35 (International Hydrological Programme & the United Nations Educational, Scientific and Cultural Organization, UNESCO 2016).

the World Bank endorsed this principle after the adoption of the UNWC.[218] The UNECE Water Convention contains several provisions related to it. The latter is mentioned several times in the Preamble. Article 9 focuses in details on bilateral and multilateral cooperation in the context of existing or future agreements and providing guidelines for protecting and tackling transboundary harm as well as establishing joint bodies that stipulate the tasks that shall be completed.[219] Examples of the responsibilities include the collection and compilation of data to figure out possible pollution sources, the establishment of joint of monitoring programmes in relation to water quantity and quality and the promotion of data concerning technologies and collaborating in scientific research.[220] This provision even addresses the potential impact on coastal states which can then be involved in the joint bodies and the interplay between different joint bodies in this case between those established by nations sharing freshwater and the ones created by the coastal states.[221] Cooperation is mentioned within the articles concerning consultations; joint monitoring and assessment; common research and development; and exchange of information between riparian parties.[222]

Cooperation over transboundary water resources is a must if one wishes to avoid the occurrence of disputes and the development of friendly relations among states[223] sharing freshwater resources that are vital to civilization.[224] In the absence of international or bilateral rules, nations are more inclined to take unilateral measures without being concerned by their negative impacts.[225] It is worth mentioning in this context that collaboration also occurs without having legal mechanisms through the daily interaction between water managers of different countries.[226]

218 Qureshi, *supra* note 743, at 64.

219 UNECE Water Convention, *supra* note 431, at Article 9. Other Articles that are also associated with the duty to cooperate are provisions 10; 11; 12; 13; 14; 15; & 16.

220 *Id.* at Article 9 (a); (b); & (i).

221 *Id.* at Article 9: 3, 4, 5.

222 *Id.* at Articles 9–13.

223 Nkechinyelu Patricia Oranye & Abimbola W. Aremu, *The Duty to Cooperate in State Interactions for the Sustainable Use of International Watercourses*, 2 Discover Sustainability. 1, 1–4 (2021).

224 Petersen-Perlman, Veilleux & Wolf, *supra* note 186, at105–120; Enamul Choudhury & Shafiqul Islam, *Nature of Transboundary Water Conflicts: Issues of Complexity and the Enabling Conditions for Negotiated Cooperation*, 155(1) Journal of Contemporary Water Research & Education. 43, 43–52 (2015).

225 Green & Perrings, *supra* note 306, at 178–179.

226 Christina Leb, *Implementation of the General Duty to Cooperate*, in Research Handbook on International Water Law 95, 107 (Stephen C. McCaffrey, Christina Leb, and Riley T. Denoon eds., Edward Elgar Publishing 2019).

Environmental Matters as a Secondary Concern

Concerns on groundwater were mentioned in the first freshwater conference and its instruments[227] as well as international conferences like the 1972 Stockholm one. There were calls for the adoption of measures for the protection of this resource, in particular, as some of the principles of the issued declarations and documents addressed shared groundwater indirectly.[228] Other conferences and mechanisms included provisions and principles that are relevant to the management of TBAs.[229] One must keep in mind that IEL evolved independently from IWL,[230] as the latter is a sub-set of the former.[231] Indeed, water principles applicable to watercourses have evolved simultaneously to IEL.[232] The inclusion of environmental provisions within water agreements is the result of a gradual progress.[233] From an environmental perspective, concerns about escalating disputes over shared freshwater constitute an important element of the growing scarcity of natural resources that might fuel conflicts[234] that will further worsen as a result of climate change.[235]

IEL influenced the drafting of the third part of the Draft Articles related to protection, preservation, and management.[236] The instrument did not place the same emphasis on the safeguard of the environment when compared for instance with the issue of equitable and reasonable utilization. It is clear from its provisions that this topic was not the main emphasis of the ILC.[237] Nonetheless, it is one of the most urgent issues that must be dealt with since

227 Mar Del Plata Conference, *supra* note 374.

228 The principles of the Stockholm Declaration that are relevant in the context of TBAs were mentioned in the second chapter of this book. Villar, *supra* note 26, at 7. Robert D. Hayton, *International Aquifers and International Law*, 6(4) Water International. 158, 162 (1981).

229 These were also tackled in the previous chapter. Asit K. Biswas, *Management of International Waters: Problems and Perspective*, 9(2) International Journal of Water Resources Development. 167, 174–177 (1993).

230 Joyeeta Gupta & Kirstin Conti, *Global Climate Change and Global Groundwater Law: Their Independent and Pluralistic Evolution and Potential Challenges*, 42(6) Water International. 741, 741–756 (2017).

231 Aaron Tesfaye, *Environmental Security, Regime Building and International Law in the Nile Basin*, 46(2) Canadian Journal of African Studies. 271, 276 (2012).

232 J. Owen Saunders, *The Legal Dimension of Interjurisdictional Water Management*, 17(2) Canadian Water Resources Journal. 161, 167 (1992).

233 Francisco Nunes Correia & Joaquim Evaristo da Silva, *International Framework for the Management of Transboundary Water Resources*,24(2) Water International. 86, 90 (1999).

234 Tesfaye, *supra* note 787, at 276.

235 Global Water Partnership, *Climate Change One of the Biggest Challenges in International Water Law* (22 April 2021), available at https://www.gwp.org/en/About/more/news/2021/climate-change-one-of-the-biggest-challenges-in-international-water-law/ (last accessed 3 August 2022).

236 Mechlem, *supra* note 362, at 220–221.

237 Draft Articles, *supra* note 515, at Articles 10–15; Mechlem, *supra* note 468, at 817–818.

water constitutes an environmental necessity.[238] Although, groundwater is considered an extremely vulnerable resource that could easily be subject to pollution, protections for it are lacking. Guarding it is vital as it is difficult to clean it up after pollution[239] and neglecting the environment and ecosystem may lead to this resource's replenishment.[240]

The UNWC has included several environmental provisions such as the ones related to the protection, preservation, and management of ecosystems, the management of emergency situations, etc. Despite the problems witnessed in this convention, it is considered a great contribution to IEL. This has been stated given the existence of multiple provisions dealing with environmental protection such as Articles 20, 21, 22, 23, and 24.[241] It is important to acknowledge that states disagreed over the wording of these provisions.[242] Even though the UNWC was used as a model for preparing the Draft Articles, this instrument included fewer principles that address the environment.[243] This is considered a blow to the ILC's efforts, given its role in the progressive codification of IWL. IEL is very important to freshwaters including groundwater. It is unfortunate that the Draft Articles has not made this topic a priority.[244] In particular, there is a need to balance the use of freshwater resources for the development of current societies and environmental protection.[245] Moreover, the principle of sustainable development does not represent a priority in the 2008 instrument even though it was mentioned in the preamble and Article

238 Yamada, *supra* note 456, at 9–15; Philippe Sands, *Water and International Law*, 44 (1/20) Environmental Policy and Law. 188, 196–197 (2014). See, Kuokkanen, *supra* note 201, at 4.

239 Dwain K. Butler, *Groundwater Resource Assessments*, 7(3) International Journal of Sustainable Development & World Ecology. 173, 173–180 (2000); David E. Burmaster, *Groundwater: Saving the Unseen Resource,* 28(1) Environment: Science and Policy for Sustainable Development. 25, 25–26 (1986).

240 Jacob D. Petersen-Perlman & Eran Feitelson, *The Environment Comes Later: When and How are Environmental Considerations Included in Transboundary Water Agreements*, Water International. 1, 2 (2022).

241 UNWC, *supra* note 184, at Part IV; Luis Barrionuevo Arevalo, *The Work of the International Law Commission in the Field of International Environmental Law*, 32(3) Boston College Environmental Affairs Law Review. 493, 498–501 (2005); Musa Mohammed Abseno, *Role and Relevance of the 1997 UN Watercourses Convention in Resolving Transboundary Water Disputes in the Nile,* 11(2) International Journal of River Basin Management. 193, 199 (2013).

242 Yu Su, *Contemporary Legal Analysis of China's Transboundary Water Regimes: International Law in Practice,* 39(5) Water International. 705, 710–711 (2014).

243 Leslie-Anne Duvic-Paoli, The Prevention Principle in International Environmental Law 105–106 (Cambridge University Press 2018).

244 Nanda & Pring, *supra* note 478, at 329–330; A. Nollkaemper, *The Contribution of the International Law Commission to International Water Law: Does it Reverse the Flight from Substance?*,27 Netherlands Yearbook of International Law. 39, 49-55 (1996).

245 Wouters, *supra* note 188, at 204.

7(1).[246] This rationale was explained by the Special Rapporteur Yamada, who claimed that a strict application of it would prohibit the use of groundwater by aquifer states.[247]

When compared to the UNWC, the provisions related to protection, preservation, prevention, reduction, and control of pollution are somewhat vague and less detailed.[248] The obligations stated in Article 10 have been included as a general duty for the safeguard of the environment. The primary objective is to benefit humankind.[249] These provisions not only call for taking all the necessary measures for the protection of freshwater ecosystems, but also the recharge and discharge zones included in Article 11.[250] One can notice how the provisions of the Draft Articles related to environmental protection have been intentionally altered to be less strict. For example, according to Article 12, states are required to take precautionary measures to address TBA's susceptibility to pollution considering existing uncertainties.[251] More specifically, the ILC decided to use the term *Precautionary Approach* instead of *Precautionary Principle* to avoid further discussions that might be related to the substantive nature of the Article or the procedures.[252] The precautionary approach would likely be based on the precautionary principle mentioned in Principle 15 of the Rio Declaration.[253] The focus of the Draft Articles remains on economic concerns, rather than environmental ones. This results from the classification of water resources as property in accordance with the principle of absolute sovereignty.[254]

The Draft Articles did not establish many provisions that develop specific procedures for planned measures. Mainly Article 15 mentions this matter.[255] The UNWC includes much more details on this subject.[256] This approach goes against the general idea of ensuring that IWL takes into consideration the norms of IEL so that environmental damages could be addressed appropri-

246 Draft Articles, *supra* note 515, at Preamble & Article 7(1); Allan, Tignino & Loures, *supra* note 12, at 235–237.

247 C. Yamada, 3rd Report on Shared Natural Resources: Transboundary Groundwaters, U.N. Doc. A/cn.4/551 (2005), p. 9 ("Yamada 2005").

248 Draft Articles, *supra* note 515, at Articles 10 & 12; Mechlem, *supra* note 468, at 817-818; Mechlem, *supra* note 362, at 220–221; McIntyre, supra note 411, at 247.

249 Draft Articles, *supra* note 515, at Articles 10; Eckstein, *supra* note 460, at 584.

250 *Id.* at Article 11. Quadri, *supra* note 515, at 10–11.

251 *Id.* at Article 12.

252 *Id.*

253 McCaffrey, *supra* note 463, at 278; Principle 15 of the Rio Declaration states the following: "In order to protect the environment, the precautionary approach shall be widely applied by States according to their capabilities. Where there are threats of serious or irreversible damage, lack of full scientific certainty shall not be used as a reason for postponing cost-effective measures to prevalent environmental degradation". See Rio Declaration, *supra* note 114.

254 McIntyre, *supra* note 411, at 247.

255 Draft Articles, *supra* note 515, at Article 15.

256 UNWC, *supra* note 184, at Part III: Planned Measures.

ately.[257] The provisions related to planned activities were more detailed in the UNWC because of the various water projects and disputes revolving around international watercourses.[258] To the credit of the Draft Articles, Article 15 mentions that not only aquifer states, but also non-aquifer states must assess the adverse effect of any measure taken within its territory.[259] One also has to acknowledge that unlike the UNWC, it required states to establish monitoring activities that would provide further environmental protection to shared groundwater. This is justified by the lack of information on TBAs in the international sphere when compared to surface water.[260] In that sense, environmental principles are fundamental to groundwater protections because this resource is more susceptible to pollution than surface water.[261]

It is worth mentioning that the UNECE Water Convention paid great attention to the environment in its provisions especially as the UNECE focused a lot on protecting[262] and tackling environmental disputes.[263] The 1992 treaty focused on taking adequate measures for safeguarding the environment[264] be it the one of the shared resource or influenced by it and making sure that this treaty does not further deteriorate the ecosystem.[265] It obliges the use of environmental practices, the conduct of EIAs,[266] the development of appropriate knowledge, the deployment of environmentally sound technologies, and sound methods to eliminate risky materials.[267] States for instance are expected to exchange data and information on environmental conditions.[268] In fact, guidelines for developing best environmental practices have been created in Annex II.[269]

257 McIntyre, *supra* note 411, at 247.
258 Eckstein, *supra* note 460, at 594.
259 *Id.* at 594–595.
260 Draft Articles, *supra* note 515, at Article 13; Allan, Loures & Tignino, *supra* note 12, at 243–246.
261 Traversi, *supra* note 55, at 477.
262 Ruby Moynihan, Transboundary Freshwater Ecosystems in International Law: The Role and Impact of the UNECE Environmental Regime 16–50 (Cambridge University Press 2021); Swedish Environmental Protection Agency, *UNECE Fortifies Environmental Management*, available at https://www.naturvardsverket.se/en/environmental-work/international-cooperation/multilateral-cooperation/unece/ (last accessed 3 August 2022).
263 Branko Bosnjakovic, *The UNECE Environmental Conventions: Their Role and Potential to Promote Conflict Prevention and Settlement of Disputes in Transboundary Environmental Issues*, in Responding to Environmental Conflicts: Implications for Theory and Practice 263, 263–270 (Eileen Petzold-Bradley, Alexander Carius & Arpád Vincze eds., Springer 2001).
264 UNECE Water Convention, *supra* note 431, at Article 2(2) (b).
265 *Id.* at Article 2 (6) & (7).
266 *Id.* at Article 3 (1) (g) & (h).
267 *Id.* at Article 5.
268 *Id.* at Article 13(1) (a).
269 *Id.* at Annex II.

A Need to Create Synergies with the UNECE Water Convention as well as the UNWC

Given the constant development of the scientific understanding of water, the emergence of new technologies changing the way this field is managed, and the occurrence of unexpected events over the years, fragmentation was inevitable.[270] Despite the importance of the UNECE Water Convention as a treaty, and the many added values it brings, its adoption was not made with the thought that one day it would become a global agreement.[271] It was only through amendments to its Articles 25 and 26 in 2003[272] that states not located in the region covered by it were given the right to become parties to it.[273] These amendments became enforceable in 2013,[274] granting the treaty global outreach. UN states had the ability to accede to it by 2016.[275] The Draft Articles were adopted to fill gaps in the UNWC and did not consider the UNECE Water Convention.[276]

The UNECE Water Convention was developed as a regional agreement between member states and holds many purposes ranging from cultural and political to economic ones. The agreement targeted a region with much rainfall and abundant watercourses. As such, all these factors were taken into consideration when drafting it where states were required, in accordance with the treaty, to cooperate and realize its objectives. It has the goal of preventing water pollution and ensuring environmental protection as the region did not suffer from a shortage of water. For this reason, it focused on avoiding

270 See for instance, Ludwik A. Teclaf, *Fiat or Custom: The Checkered Development of International Water Law*, 31 Natural Resources Forum. 45, 45–73 (1991); Maryam Jafroudi, *Enhancing Climate Resilience of Transboundary Water Allocation Agreements: The Impact of Shortening the Agreement's Lifetime on Cooperation Stability*, 18 International Environmental Agreements: Politics, Law and Economics 707, 707–722 (2018); Imad Antoine Ibrahim, *Legal Implications of the Use of Big Data in the Transboundary Water Context*, 34 Water Resources Management. 1139, 1139–1153 (2020).

271 Zeitoun, *supra* note 200, at 949–960.

272 United Nations Economic and Social Council, Economic Commission for Europe, *Meeting of the Parties to the Convention on the Protection and Use of Transboundary Watercourses and International Lakes* (ECE/MP.WAT/14 12 January 2004).

273 Patricia Wouters & Dinara Ziganshina, *Tackling the Global Water Crisis: Unlocking International Law as Fundamental to the Peaceful Management of the World's Shared Transboundary Waters – Introducing the H2O Paradigm*, in Water Resouces Planning and Management 175, 220 (R. Quentin Grafton & Karen Hussey eds, Cambridge University Press 2011).

274 UNECE, *Introduction: About the Water Convention*, available at https://unece.org/environment-policy/water/about-the-convention/introduction (last accessed 3 August 2022).

275 Bo Libert, *The UNECE Water Convention and the Development of Transboundary Cooperation in the Chu-Talas, Kura, Drin and Dniester River Basins*, 40(1) Water International. 168, 169 (2015); Maria E. Milanes-Murcia, *Cannabis and Water Management: International Regulation and the Legal Framework of the European Union*, 49 The University of Pacific Law Review. 117, 129–130 (2017).

276 Zeitoun, *supra* note 200, at 949–960.

pollution and transboundary harm. It dealt with problems that are very specific, since the states memberswere suffering from similar issues.[277] At the time the decision was made to amend the UNECE Water Convention, the rationale was that it could serve as an international water instrument. This argument emerged because, in 2003, there were only 11 ratifications of the UNWC, but 35 ratifications are required for its entry into force.[278] Indeed, even by 2012 when the UNWC was still not in force, a mechanism to foster and enhance realization and compliance with the UNECE Water Convention was adopted along with an implementation committee.[279] Its purpose is fostering application and compliance in an objective manner.[280] This treaty represents a forum for negotiating water-related matters given the important results it has achieved throughout the years.[281] Indeed, it contributed to the development of several agreements for the management of a shared basin in places like the Danube and the Rhine.[282]

In this context, the Draft Articles were adopted to fill gaps in the UNWC and did not consider the UNECE Water Convention.[283] The treatment of groundwater in the latter is different from that in the 1997 treaty. The 1992 agreement applies to all kinds of transboundary groundwaters. In contrast, the UNWC applies only to specific ones connected to surface water and flowing into a common terminus.[284] Article 1, Paragraph 1 of the UNECE Water Convention expressly states that waters covered through it are all types of

277 UNECE Water Convention, *supra* note 431, at Articles 2 & 3; McCaffrey, *supra* note 463, at 12–13. ALISTAIR RIEU-CLARKE, *Remarks on the Drafting History of the Convention*, in THE UNECE CONVENTION ON THE PROTECTION AND USE OF TRANSBOUNDARY WATERCOURSES AND INTERNATIONAL LAKES 1, 1–14 (Attila Tanzi et al eds, Brill 2015); Jonathan Verschuuren, *The Case of Transboundary Wetlands under the Ramsar Convention: Keep the Lawyers Out!*, 19(1) COLORADO JOURNAL OF INTERNATIONAL ENVIRONMENTAL LAW AND POLICY. 49, 52 (2008); BOSNJAKOVIC, *supra* note 816, at 266–268.

278 Stephen C. McCaffrey, *The Convention Enters into Force*, 44(4) ENVIRONMENTAL POLICY AND LAW. 351, 355 (2014).

279 Decision VI/1: Support to Implementation and Compliance; ECE/MP.WAT/37/Add.2. Johan G. Lammers, *Helsinki Water Convention: A New Implementation Mechanism and Committee*, 44 (1/2) ENVIRONMENTAL POLICY AND LAW. 117, 117–120 (2014).

280 UNECE, *Implementation Committee: Background*, available at https://unece.org/environment-policy/water/about-the-convention/convention-bodies/implementation committee#:~:text=The%20Implementation%20Committee%20under%20the,WAT%2F37%2FAdd (last accessed 3 August 2022).

281 Laurence Boisson de Chazournes, *International Institutions, Fresh Water and the Environment: Mutual Incentives*, 44 (1/2) ENVIRONMENTAL POLICY AND LAW. 172, 173 (2014).

282 HODL, *supra* note 437, at 328.

283 Zeitoun, *supra* note 200, at 949–960.

284 UNWC, *supra* note 184, Article 2(a); Rieu-Clarke & Kinna, *supra* note 547, at 20. Generally speaking, it has been stated that the UNECE Water Convention and the UNWC are compatible under international water law. Though, several differences between both conventions exist. Stephanie Biggs, *Water Management on the Brahmaputra and the Applicability of the UNECE Water Convention*, 51 VANDERBILT JOURNAL OF TRANSNATIONAL LAW. 555, 564–566 (2018).

shared surface water and groundwaters.[285] The UNECE treaty did not adopt rules that specifically tackle matters particular to transboundary groundwater resources.[286] The latter and the Draft Articles have several provisions in common. For instance, both mention the principle of equitable and reasonable utilization explicitly.[287] This principle is not central to the UNECE Water Convention as it is mainly focusing on taking actions to prohibit, tackle, and reduce any effect in the transboundary context.[288] This is precisely why the duty of preventing significant harm was not explicitly mentioned in the UNECE Water Convention, even though the provisions of the instrument dealt with this matter.[289] The latter did not clarify the relationship between the principle of equitable and reasonable utilization and the above mentioned obligation.[290] When reading its provisions, it is clear that the convention embraces the concept of limited territorial sovereignty. This stands in contrast to the Draft Articles.[291]

Unlike the 2008 instrument, the UNECE Water Convention obliges states to revise and adapt existing agreements and eliminate contradictions where basic principles should be incorporated. The convention requires that nations enter into bilateral and multilateral treaties when they are lacking. Countries must establish joint management mechanisms that shall perform a non-exhaustive list of functions.[292] The UNECE Water Convention has more procedural requirements compared with the Draft Articles that are used to deal with transboundary impacts where measures should be taken for instance for ensuring sustainable management and preventing groundwater contamination.[293] The provisions related to monitoring do not include any element that address the specifics of groundwaters.[294] The convention tackles the issue of transboundary waters broadly where surface water rules included in it also apply to TBAs. Even then, these provisions are more progressive than those in the Draft Articles. For example, states are required to jointly monitor

285 Report of the UN/ECE Task Force on Legal and Administrative Aspects, *The Relationship between the 1992 UNECE Convention on the Protection and Use of Transboundary Watercourses and International Lakes and the 1997 UN Convention on the Law of the Non Navigational Uses of International Watercourses*, Drawn by Professor Attila Tanzi, Geneva, Feb. 2000.

286 Allan, Loures & Tignino, *supra* note 12, at 234.

287 UNECE Water Convention, *supra* note 431, at Article 2 (2) (c); Draft Articles, *supra* note 515, at Article 4; Zeitoun, *supra* note 200, at 949–960.

288 Rieu-Clarke & Kinna, *supra* note 547, at 20–21.

289 Zeitoun, *supra* note 200, at 959–960.

290 McCaffrey, *supra* note 463, at 12–13.

291 UNECE Water Convention, *supra* note 431, at Article 2, Paragraph 6.

292 *Id.* at Article 9; Rieu-Clarke & Kinna, *supra* note 547, at 21.

293 See for instance Article 3(h) & (k) of the UNECE Water Convention, *supra* note 431.

294 *Id.* at Articles 3 (1) (b); 4; 9 (2) (b); 11; 13 (1) (c) & 16 (1) (c).

activities. The 2008 instrument only requires such joint monitoring wherever possible.[295]

The application of the UNECE Water Convention to all types of TBAs is the most significant difference compared with the UNWC. Its guidelines on monitoring and assessment of transboundary groundwaters and the guide to implementation of the convention confirm this approach.[296] The former were adopted in 2000 to provide guidance in the establishment of rules and systems for groundwater resources.[297] The latter was created for facilitating the use of the convention to ensure the protection and good management of transboundary freshwaters. This includes groundwater resources.[298] The UNECE adopted a document entitled *Model Provisions on Transboundary Groundwaters* in 2014. Its provisions set forth guidelines that would facilitate the implementation of the convention in a transboundary groundwater context.[299] The model provisions are not binding. Some of them replicate those in the Draft Articles such as the principle of equitable and reasonable utilization and the obligation to not cause significant harm. It applies substantive norms as well as some of the procedural rules like the exchange of data and information. They also require the establishment of a joint institutional mechanism, which stands in contrast to the Draft Articles. They mandate the sustainable use of transboundary groundwater while embracing the integrated management concept of surface and groundwater.[300]

The importance of the UNECE Water Convention lies within some of its provisions that are more progressive than those of the UNWC and the Draft Articles. For instance, Article 3(1), requires the parties to conduct an EIA and use any means necessary to ensure the prevention, control, or reduction of transboundary harm. Both the UNWC and the Draft Articles only suggest that an EIA be conducted.[301] International lawyers will have to create synergies between the Draft Articles and UNECE Water Convention. This would depend on the fate of the 2008 instrument and whether it would be amended or adopted as a convention. There are already many discussions taking place as to whether the UNWC and the UNECE Water Convention have overlapping

295 *Id.* at Article 11; Draft Articles, *supra* note 515, at Article 13; Raya Maria Stephan, *Groundwater Monitoring in International Conventions and Agreements, in* Groundwater Monitoring 13, 16 (Anne Marie Fouillacet al. eds., Wiley 2009); Tanzi, *supra* note 551, at 234–237.

296 Tanzi, *supra* note 551, at 236. See, Razzaque, *supra* note 436, at 132.

297 UN/ECE Task Force on Monitoring & Assessment, *Guidelines on Monitoring and Assessment of Transboundary Groundwaters* 7 (Work Programme 1996-1999; Lelystad, Mar. 2000).

298 United Nations Economic Commission for Europe, *Guide to Implementing the Water Convention* V (United Nations; New York & Geneva, 2013).

299 UNECE, *supra* note 554. See, Pateiro, *supra* note 525.

300 *Id.* at Model Provision 1; 6; 9 and others; Eckstein, *supra* note 19.

301 UNECE Water Convention, *supra* note 431, at Article 3 (1) (h) & Article 9 (2) (j); UNWC, *supra* note 184, at Article 12; Draft Articles, *supra* note 515, at Article 15 (2) & Article 16 (f); McIntyre, *supra* note 671, at 74–78.

or contradicting provisions, and how the international community should create synergies between both treaties. The same discussion concerning the relationship between the 1992 agreement and the Draft Articles must take place, especially as the latter was initially drafted to complete the codification of IWL after the adoption of the UNWC and not the UNECE Water Convention.[302] This discussion will occur in the context of fragmentation of IWL.[303]

In Summary

This chapter examined the different legal challenges that emerged in the wake of the adoption of the Draft Articles and have not yet been resolved. They hold relevance, not only in the context of the UNWC, but also for the UNECE Water Convention. This, however, received less focus from water lawyers.[304] Despite the many problems of the UNWC, the UNECE Water Convention, and the Draft Articles, these instruments still represent the most sophisticated attempt for the codification of IWL and constitute guiding mechanisms for states.[305]

The Draft Articles have the potential of making great contributions to the development and progressive codification of IGL especially as they incorporate several general principles of international law. They can provide much-needed assistance to countries looking to establish multilateral and bilateral agreements to manage their shared resources.[306] The Draft Articles have already influenced for instance the adoption of treaties such as the Guarani Aquifer

302 Stoa, *supra* note 529, at 1333–1353.

303 See for instance, Philippe Quevauviller et al., Groundwater Monitoring 14 (Wiley 2009); Tanzi, *supra* note 551, at 240; Francesco Sindico & Laura Movilla Pateiro, *The Interplay Between the UN Watercourses Convention and the Law on Transboundary Aquifers*, in The UN Convention on the Law of the Non-Navigational Uses of International Watercourses: A Commentary 383, 405–406 (Laurence Boisson de Chazournes et al eds., Oxford University Press 2018).

304 Vick, *supra* note 563, at 198–200.

305 See, Peter Beaumont, *The 1997 UN Convention on the Law of Non-Navigational Uses of International Watercourses: Its Strengths and Weaknesses from a Water Management Perspective and the Need for New Workable Guidelines*, 16(4) International Journal of Water Resources Development. 475, 475 (2000); Laurence Boisson de Chazournes, Christina Leb & Mara Tignino, *The UNECE Water Convention and Multilateral Environmental Agreements*, in The UNECE Convention on the Protection and Use of Transboundary Watercourses and International Lakes: Its Contribution to International Water Cooperation 60, 60–72 (Attila Tanzi et al eds., Brill 2015); Jacques Ganoulis & Jean Fried, Transboundary Hydro-Governance: From Conflict to Shared Management 23–24 (Springer 2018).

306 McCaffrey, *supra* note 463, at 292; Atul Alexander & Anushna Mishra, *Contribution of General Principles of International Law in Progressive Development of Transboundary Aquifers*,8(2) Groningen Journal of International Law. 183, 183–190 (2021).

Agreement in 2010[307] and the 2014 Memorandum of Understanding for the Establishment of a Consultation Mechanism for the Integrated Management of the Water Resources of the Iullemeden, Taoudeni/Tanezrouft Aquifer System.[308]

The Draft Articles managed to incorporate the scientific realities of TBAs by taking into consideration their particularities. The substantive provisions focus more on ensuring cooperation among states sharing an aquifer than preventing harm from occurring.[309] There is no clear direction as to whether this instrument will become enforceable, even though the ILC advocated for its adoption as a convention at a later stage.[310] The Draft Articles will have to answer the same controversial questions that faced the international community during the drafting of the UNWC. Namely, it must consider issues related to dispute settlement and the relationship between the Convention and other treaties.[311] Even if it is adopted as a treaty, it would have to deal with the lack of support and small amount of state ratification. These factors are currently preventing an efficient application of the UNWC. This highlights that states do not agree with the substantive rules of IWL, as laid down within the UNWC as well as other disagreements over the main principles.[312] All

307 Guarani Aquifer Agreement, *supra* note 661.

308 Food and Agricultural Organization of the United Nations, Memorandum of Understanding for the Establishment of a Consultation Mechanism for the Integrated Management of the Water Resources of the Iullemeden, Taoudeni/Tanezrouft Aquifer Systems (ITAS), available at https://www.fao.org/faolex/results/details/en/c/LEX-FAOC135180/ (last accessed 3 August 2022).

309 Frink, *supra* note 602, at 518–520.

310 2 Ryan Stoa, *Harmonizing International Water Law: Current Challenges and Future Prospects*, in Legal Instruments for the Implementation of Sustainable Development (Instrumentos Jurídicos Para a Implementação do Desenvolvimento Sustentável) 533, 540–544 (Carina Costa de Oliveira & Rômulo Silveira da Rocha Sampaio eds., FGV, Direito Rio, Programa em Direito e Meio Ambiente 2012).

311 Mechlem, *supra* note 466, at 819–820; The Draft Articles lacks the establishment of dispute settlement provisions. This is in contrast to both the UNWC and the UNECE Water Convention. The provisions related to the settlement of disputes in both conventions are similar in that they both instruct the parties to seek solutions via negotiations or other means. In the case of failure to reach the desired outcome, arbitration and/or adjudication are seen as potential ways to solve the disputes. This holds as long as the parties explicitly consent to the use of these mechanisms. The UNWC also includes an option for the establishment of a "fact finding commission" tasked with the collection of any information that is relevant to the dispute. Its recommendations are not binding. The UNECE Convention does not contain a similar provision. Yet, an implementation committee was set up in recent years by the parties to the convention and which could take on similar tasks. UNWC, *supra* note 184, at Article 33; UNECE Water Convention, *supra* note 431, at Article 22. See, Rieu-Clarke & Kinna, *supra* note 544, at 21–22. Also see, Attila Tanzi & Enrico Milano, *Article 33 of the UN Watercourses Convention: A Step Forward for Dispute Settlement?*,38(2) Water International. 166, 167–168 (2013).

312 Stoa, *supra* note 526, at 1333–1353.

the issues mentioned in this chapter created the necessary situation for water lawyers and experts to provide suggestions and proposals for solving these matters, resulting in the emergence of a plethora of articles examining these dilemmas.[313]

313 The research conducted in this book benefited significantly from these studies. Numerous articles have been used for conducting the necessary analysis. The latters assessed the provisions of the Draft Articles, per se, by comparing them to other international water instruments and agreements, mainly the UNWC and the Berlin Rules.

4 The Legal Classification of Transboundary Aquifers

In parallel with the discussion concerning IWL and TBAs and their development challenges, the international community has engaged in a debate related to water as a resource. Matters concerning the latter have been dealt with through three different means: via the principles of IWL, as well as economic and human rights approaches.[1] Shared groundwaters are being extracted for direct consumption by the user, for cleaning, cooking, agriculture, livestock use, etc.[2] Draining it has resulted in several risks, namely depletion and pollution.[3] Given the UN Resolutions on the HRWS adopted in 2010, this chapter is dedicated to discussing whether TBAs should be dealt with from a human rights perspective among many others. Generally speaking, the state decides how the HRWS can be realized at the domestic level through national and local rules that may be adopted.[4] The choice of governance model is extremely important because the lack of access to adequate water is perceived as a management problem.[5] The following sections will examine the different categories that may apply to shared groundwaters, which will then be analyzed from

1 Joyeeta Gupta, Rhodante Ahlers, Lawal Ahmed, *The Human Right to Water: Moving Towards Consensus in a Fragmented World*, 19(3) Review of European, Comparative & International Environmental Law. 294, 295 (2010).

2 Arjen Y. Hoekstra, Ashok K. Chapagain, Maite M. Aldaya, Mesfin M. Mekonnen, The Water Footprint Assessment Manual: Setting the Global Standard (Earthscan 2011); Venkatesh Uddameri, Danny Reible, *Food-Energy-Water Nexus to Mitigate Sustainability Challenges in a Groundwater Reliant Agriculturally Dominant Environment (GRADE)*, 37(1) Environmental Progress & Sustainable Energy. 21, 21–36 (2018).

3 Michael N. Fienen & Muhammad Arshad, *The International Scale of Groundwater Issues*, in Integrated Groundwater Management: Concepts, Approaches, and Challenges 21, 21–25 (Anthony J. Jakeman, Olivier Barreteau, Randall J. Hunt, Jean-Daniel Rinaudo & Andrew Ross eds., Springer 2016).

4 Pedi Obani & Joyeeta Gupta, *Inclusive Development as an Imperative to Realizing the Human Right to Water and Sanitation*, 8(2) Journal of Sustainable Development Law and Policy. 67, 75–76 (2017).

5 Anna FS Russell, *Incorporating Social Rights in Development: Transnational Corporations and the Right to Water*, 7(1) International Journal of Law in Context. 1, 9 (2011).

DOI: 10.4324/9781003537724-5

a human rights perspective. It is worth mentioning that many of the arguments and claims made apply to water in general and not solely groundwater.

Transboundary Groundwater as a Common Good

Shared groundwater is an extremely complex resource requiring joint management to ensure its good governance and sustainable use.[6] Pressures resulting from the conflict between its exploitation and conservation can lead to tragedy in the absence of adequate management practices.[7] Due to its asymmetric availability and the drive of states and consumers to over-consume,[8] the creation and implementation of agreements are needed. Ideally, this would occur through the adoption of collective solutions.[9] The alternative to this is its unilateral exploitation.[10] The nature of groundwater as a common resource pool makes it difficult to exclude people and states from using it. It is considered an open-access good that must be regulated by the state[11] since it represents 97% of existing freshwater resources despite being hidden,[12] and as water generally is essential for life.[13] Yet, technical knowledge is required to exploit

6 Robert V. Dodge, Schelling's Game Theory: How to Make Decisions 189 (Oxford University Press 2012). The debate over the concept of common goods in the general sense is beyond the scope of this book. On this issue see, for instance, Saki Bailey & Ugo Mattei, *Social Movements as Constituent Power: The Italian Struggle for the Commons*, 20(2) Indiana Journal of Global Legal Studies. 965, 965–1013 (2013); Stefano Rodota, *The Role of Common Goods in Fostering Shared Responsibility, Linking Sustainable Social Cohesion to the Reduction of Inequalities* 2–11 (IUC Research Commons, International University College of Turin, 2011); Mark Hoipkemier, *Critical Realism and Common Goods*, 15(1) Journal of Critical Realism. 53, 53–71 (2016); Ellen Hazelkorn & Andrew Gibson, *Public Goods and Public Policy: What is Public Good, and Who and What Decides?* (Center for Global Higher Education working paper series no. 18; May 2017).

7 David N. Cassuto & Romulo S.R. Sampaio, *Keeping it Legal: Transboundary Management Challenges Facing Brazil and the Guarani*, 36(5) Water International. 661, 667 (2011).

8 Jennifer Jacquet, David Frank, & Christopher Schlottmann, *Asymmetrical Contributions to the Tragedy of the Commons and Some Implications for Conservation*, 5(3) Sustainability. 1036, 1036–1038 (2013).

9 Elizabeth Kahn, *The Tragedy of the Commons as an Essentially Aggregative Harm*, 31(3) Journal of Applied Philosophy. 223, 224 (2014).

10 Rouba Al-Fattal, *The Tragedy of the Commons: Institutions and Fisheries Management at the Local and EU Levels*, 21(4) Review of Political Economy. 537, 537 (2009).

11 Charalambous, *supra* note 340, at 73; Shammy Puri, Alice Aureli & Raya M. Stephan, *Shared Groundwater Resources: Global Significance for Social and Environmental Sustainability*, in Overexploitation and Contamination of Shared Groundwater Resources 3, 19 (Christophe J. G. Darnault ed., Springer 2008).

12 Astrid Hillers, *Water Underground: Why Protecting What's Hidden Matters to our Health and for the Planet* (GEF, Mar. 21, 2022), available at https://www.thegef.org/newsroom/blog/water-underground-why-protecting-whats-hidden-matters-our-health-and-planet (last accessed 3 August 2022).

13 M. Gassiot I Matas, A. Florensa & R. Gonzalez-Olmos, *Water, a Common Good to Share*, (10) Ramon Llull Journal of Applied Ethics. 201, 203 (2019).

it[14] and conserve it, especially during extreme events such as droughts.[15] Legislations are very important,[16] however; over-regulation can hinder its use and conservation.[17]

Classifying shared groundwater as a common good requires the establishment of the necessary legal and institutional mechanisms to guarantee cooperation among the different nations.[18] This is especially true considering that water matters are associated with a plethora of other socioeconomic issues such as poverty, climate change, and health.[19] At the international level, the rules that govern this resource in the transboundary context have been contested. This further complicates the task before the global community,[20] even though its appropriate management is still based on interstate cooperation necessary to ensure its protection and long-term sustainable use.[21] Given its non-excludability, nations must avoid damaging it by participating in joint efforts to mitigate harm and cooperate at the various levels.[22] Nonetheless, its classification as a common pool resource creates several challenges. The Food and Agriculture Organization (FAO) has summarized the latter, which include inter alia: depletion, pollution, and salinization; degradation of the environment and the ecosystem; negative consequences of human activities; inefficient groundwater use across sectors; etc.[23]

Several factors complicate the efficient management of TBAs, resulting in the abovementioned issues. These include the current state of IGL, which was examined in the previous chapter, highlighting, among many things, a shortage in the number of bilateral or multilateral agreements between nations sharing groundwater. The existence of institutional problems, the need for political tradeoffs, and the adoption of short-term perspectives that maximize profits

14 Emmanuelle Hellier, *Commodity towards Common Good. The Users and NGO's Involvement in Water Utilities in European Union (Study cases in France, Italy, Romania)* 4 (7th CIRIEC International Research Conference on Social Economy – Social and Solidarity Economy: Moving Towards a New Economic System, Jun 2019, Romania).

15 See Janine M. Stone & Patrick S. Johnson, *Conserving for the Common Good: Preferences for Water Conservation Policies during a Severe Drought in Northern California,* 37 Water Resources and Economics. 1, 1 (2022).

16 Solanes, *supra* note 315, at 86.

17 Cassuto & Sampaio, *supra* note 876, at 667.

18 Vanessa Vaessen et al., *Training Manual: Integration of Groundwater Management into Transboundary Basin Organization in Africa,* 4 (Africa Groundwater Network (AGW-Net), 2014).

19 Mallory Orme et al., *Good Transboundary Water Governance in the 2015 Sustainable Development Goals: A Legal Perspective,* 40(7) Water International. 969, 976 (2015).

20 Zewdineh Beyene & Ian Wadley, *Common Goods and the Common Good: Transboundary Natural Resources, Principled Cooperation, and the Nile Basin Initiative,* 1 (UC Berkeley: Center for African Studies, 2004).

21 Dimkic et al., *supra* note 339, at 45.

22 Elena Lopez-Gunn, *Governing Shared Groundwater: The Controversy over Private Regulation,* 175(1) The Geographical Journal. 39, 41–42 (2009).

23 Team Specialists, *Global Framework for Action to Achieve the Vision on Groundwater Governance,* 23–25 (Food and Agriculture Organization, March 2016).

and resource use further complicate this resource's governance.[24] Additionally, scientific uncertainty arises due to the lack of proper information and technical expertise, the high costs associated with data collection, and the need to cover information spread across several countries. This creates a situation where nations sharing an aquifer have different or asymmetric information impacting their interpretation of matters related to its management, such as its availability, use, and recharge.[25] These challenges are easier to detect and deal with at the local level.[26] Regardless, it is very hard to track the individual use of aquifers at the state level, as domestically, users aim to exploit the resource to its maximum. They do this without considering the consequences. It is even harder to pin accountability in a transboundary context.[27]

Like other common goods, the sustainable management of TBAs is at risk. This is because of the unilateral focus on classifying water for human use instead of adopting an ecosystem approach.[28] Rather than concentrating solely on balancing the interests of different users (states), ecological interests must be considered. The former approach is based on respecting territorial sovereignty and does not contribute to cooperation with common environmental interests.[29] To prevent the tragedy of the commons, several governance elements must exist, mainly efficient institutions; access to reliable information; and strong civil society, as well as economic and legal regimes.[30] Moreover,

24 Marc F. Muller, Michele C. Muller-Itten, & Steven M. Gorelick, *How Jordan and Saudi Arabia are Avoiding a Tragedy of the Commons Over Shared Groundwater*, 53(7) WATER RESOURCES RESEARCH. 5451, 5451–5452 (2017); ELENA LOPEZ-GUNN & DOMINIC STUCKER, *Introduction to Adaptation to Climate Change through Water Resources Management: A Systems Approach*, in ADAPTATION TO CLIMATE CHANGE THROUGH WATER RESOURCES MANAGEMENT: CAPACITY, EQUITY AND SUSTAINABILITY 1, 1–17 (Dominic Stucker, Elena Lopez-Gunn eds., Routledge 2015).

25 Anita Milman & Isha Ray, *Interpreting the Unknown: Uncertainty and the Management of Transboundary Groundwater*, 36(5) WATER INTERNATIONAL. 631, 632 (2011).

26 PURI, AURELI & STEPHAN, *supra* note 880, at 19.

27 Steven M. Gorelick & Chunmiao Zheng, *Global Change and the Groundwater Management Challenge*, 51(5) WATER RESOURCES RESEARCH. 3031, 3031–3032 (2015).

28 PURI, AURELI & STEPHAN, *supra* note 880, at 19. There are other challenges or conceptions of reality concerning the concept of common goods which are beyond the scope of this section. See, for instance, Ugo Mattei, *Protecting the Commons: Water, Culture, and Nature: The Commons Movement in the Italian Struggle against Neoliberal Governance*, 112(2) SOUTH ATLANTIC QUARTERLY. 366, 366–376 (2013); SAKI BAILEY, GILDA FARRELL, UGO MATTEI EDS., PROTECTING FUTURE GENERATIONS THROUGH COMMONS (Trends in Social Cohesion, No. 26; Council of Europe Publishing, 2013); Fulvio Cortese, *What Are "Common Goods" (beni comuni)? Pictures from the Italian Debate,* 11(2) Polemos. (2017).

29 Owen McIntyre, *The Emergence of an 'Ecosystem Approach' to the Protection of International Watercourses under International Law*, 13(1) REVIEW OF EUROPEAN COMMUNITY AND INTERNATIONAL ENVIRONMENTAL LAW. 1, 1 (2004).

30 Tamee R. Albrecht et al., *Governing a Shared Hidden Resource: A Review of Governance Mechanisms for Transboundary Groundwater Security,* 2 WATER SECURITY. 43, 50 (2017).

the decision-making process must include science to ensure sound management.[31] This task is extremely complex as it involves stakeholders at various levels such as governments, companies, and civil society working jointly toward shared goals.[32] These actors must coordinate their efforts to guarantee the sustainable management of this resource considering all types of human activities.[33] Building trust among the parties sharing the aquifer is of outmost importance,[34] to mitigate the risk of a conflict.[35]

Transboundary Groundwater as an Economic Good

The private sector has been suggested as a solution for the management of shared groundwater. The water crisis is ongoing and has not been solved by public actors. Privatization transfers responsibility from authorities to private entities[36] and converts a good or service into a strictly market commodity.[37] Involvement of this sector began in the 1970s after the negative consequences of public management practices were noted. Among those included were a lack of recovery, high costs of implementation with low profits, inadequate productivity,[38] and the absence of efficient billing and collection practices.[39] It promised to address all these issues and provide additional advantages compared to government involvement.[40] The result was the creation of public-private partnerships.[41]

The main reason for considering this resource an economic good was that the amount of high-quality water for drinking, cooking, and cleaning purposes was limited. The demand for it, however, was high. The latter in this case is considered a quasi-commodity and does not satisfy all the criteria to be

31 Robert T. Caccese & Lara B. Fowler, *Reasonable Use?: The Challenges of Transboundary Groundwater Regulation in the Eastern United States,* 56(3) Journal of the American Water Resources Association. 379, 379 (2020).

32 Sisira Withanachchi, *The Study of Transboundary Groundwater Governance in the Notion of Governmentality: In the Case of Guaraní Aquifer*, AQUA Mundi. 9, 10 (2012).

33 Golovina et al., *supra* note 605, at 1.

34 Brooks & Linton, *supra* note 24, at 456–458.

35 Pateiro, *supra* note 525, at 851.

36 Sarah I. Hale, *Water Privatization in the Philippines: The Need to Implement the Human Right to Water*, 15(3) Pacific Rim Law & Policy Journal. 765, 766 (2006).

37 Peter H. Gleick, Gary Wolff, Elizabeth L. Chalecki & Rachel Reyes, *The New Economy of Water: The Risks and Benefits of Globalization and Privatization of Fresh Water*, 9 (Pacific Institute, Feb. 2002).

38 Asanga Gunawansa & Sonia Ferdous Hoque, *Right to Water versus Water Pricing: Challenges in Developing Countries*, 12 (Lee Kuan Yew School of Public Policy Working Paper Series, January 10, 2012).

39 *Id.* at 13.

40 Vanessa Casado Perez, *Whose Water? Corporatization of a Common Good*, in Environmental Law, Disrupted 79, 84 (Keith Hirokawa & Jessica Owley eds., Environmental Law Institute 2021).

41 Gunawansa & Hoque, *supra* note 907, at 13.

perceived as a full commodity.[42] In fact, the cost of improving this resource's quality, supplying it through proper infrastructures, and transporting it make it connected to capitalist market principles.[43] This argument is supported by current realities in developing countries. For instance, in Yemen, water is considered a free resource. However, funds are necessary to provide the service and maintain infrastructure.[44] This situation has further worsened with the ongoing armed conflict.[45] If water was supplied at an extremely low cost, users would not be motivated to conserve it. Meanwhile, charges associated with maintaining supplies need to be covered, but not at the expense of low-income citizens. Governments must balance water use and consumption with environmental protection as it is important to ensure ecosystem sustainability.[46] Some claim that water should always be available for free because it is vital to the realization of other human rights. Even in the framework of HRWS, water cannot be supplied in an unlimited quantity and without interruption. On the contrary, considering this resource an economic good could force users to consume it in a responsible manner.[47] Privatization must take place because of the lack of available capital. This is among the many obstacles encountered when public utilities attempt to provide this service. Corruption is another major element. At the very least, privatizing water solves the problem of a state's incapacity to produce and distribute it via their institutions. Hence, the private sector will fulfill the needs of the consumers better than the government as it possesses the capital required for making the necessary installations and maintaining services. Thus, it is easier to mobilize capital for this purpose. Given the existing monetary incentive dictated by the market, private companies have no choice but to be efficient to remain competitive.[48] Many economists support this approach.[49]

42 Wouter Vandenhole & Tamara Wielders, *Water as a Human Right – Water as an Essential Service: Does It Matter*, 26(3) Netherlands Quarterly of Human Rights. 391, 403 (2017).

43 Catarina De Albuquerque, Inga T. Winkler, *Neither Friend nor Foe: Why the Commercialization of Water and Sanitation Services is not the Main Issue in the Realization of Human Rights*, 17(1) Brown Journal of World Affairs. 167, 168 (2010).

44 Daphina Misiedjan & H.F.M.W. Van Rijswick, *A Human Right to Water While the Wells Run Dry: Analyzing the Legal and Regulatory Framework of Yemen Water Law*, 24(5/6) Journal of Water Law. 199, 199–206 (2015).

45 Mohammad Al-Saidi, Emma Lauren Roach, & Bilal Ahmed Hassen Al-Saeedi, *Conflict Resilience of Water and Energy Supply Infrastructure: Insights from Yemen*, 12 Water. 1, 1 (2020).

46 Swechhya Sangroula, *A Right to Water in International Human Rights Law: Flow from Implicit to Explicit Right*, 5(2) Kathmandu School of Law Review. 156, 156 (2017).

47 Derrick Howard, *A Modest Proposal: A Dialogue to Implement the Human Right to Water*, 1(1) Seattle Journal of Environmental Law. 123, 128 (2011).

48 Russell Rutherford, *An International Human Right to Water: How to Secure the Place of People Ahead of Profits in the Struggle for Water Access*, 62(4) Alabama Law Review. 857, 862–863 (2011).

49 William Blomquist, *Beneath the Surface: Complexities and Groundwater Policy-Making*, 36(1) Oxford Review of Economic Policy. 154, 154 (2020).

In this context, one would wonder whether TBAs serve as a good economic lead for transboundary water governance via adequate market based mechanisms,[50] given the existing numerous obstacles?[51] It is not easy to answer this question as there are no established rules that define the role of stakeholders. This responsibility would be divided among governments and other actors playing a role in the management of shared aquifers.[52] Still, many have attempted to address this matter, suggesting economic models for the optimal use of such an aquifer,[53] and examining the financial approaches of the institutions managing it.[54] Groundwater is scarce and valuable,[55] and not readily accessible to the public since many costs are incurred before the supply is reached.[56] Yet, these factors are not considered when it is being managed and used.[57] For exploiting it, economic actors must determine several elements. Among these are the capital investment required and the amount of water withdrawn.[58] Positive and negative externalities must always be taken into account as well,[59] while legislations regulate corporations activities.[60]

The emergence of private actors tackling water issues has benefited from the development of a global civil society allowing transnational debates where new players besides the states are relevant.[61] This is currently taking place in the context of an ideological conflict between a rights-based approach versus privatization.[62] According to GC 15, water is not mainly an economic good but rather a social and cultural one.[63] Its economic nature was not ignored,

50 Orme et al., *supra* note 888, at 972–973.
51 Zachary P. Sugg, Robert G. Varady, Andrea K. Gerlak, Rafael de Grenade, *Transboundary Groundwater Governance in the Guarani Aquifer System: Reflections from a Survey of Global and Regional Experts*, 40(3) WATER INTERNATIONAL. 377, 380 (2015); Mangala Subramaniam & Beth Williford, *Contesting Water Rights: Collective Ownership and Struggles against Privatization*, 6(5) SOCIOLOGY COMPASS. 413, 414 (2012).
52 MICHAEL E. CAMPANA ET AL., *Dynamics of Transboundary Groundwater Management: Lessons from North America*, in GOVERNANCE AS A TRIALOGUE: GOVERNMENT-SOCIETY-SCIENCE IN TRANSITION 167, 192 (Anthony R. Turton et al. eds., Springer 2017).
53 Janie M. Chermak, Robert H. Patrick & David S. Brookshire, *Economics of Transboundary Aquifer Management*, 43(5) GROUNDWATER. 731, 731 (2005).
54 Eric C. Edwards & Todd Guilfoos, *The Economics of Groundwater Governance Institutions Across the Globe* (Center for Environmental and Resource Economic Policy; Working Paper Series: No. 20-001, May 2020).
55 Zack Donohew, *Markets and Private Property Rights to Groundwater*, 15–17 (Conservation Leadership Council, 2012).
56 JOB, *supra* note 341, at 304.
57 Donohew, *supra* note 924, at 15–17.
58 *Id.* J Pasqual & I Rocabert, *Consumption of Groundwater as a Private or a Public Good*, 39 DEVELOPMENTS IN WATER SCIENCE, 423, 423 (1989).
59 *Id.* at 424.
60 R Quentin Grafton, Long Chu & Paul Wyrwoll, *The Paradox of Water Pricing: Dichotomies, Dilemmas, and Decisions*, 36(1) OXFORD REVIEW OF ECONOMIC POLICY. 86, 95 (2020).
61 Lopez-Gunn, *supra* note 891, at 45–47.
62 *Id.* at 47.
63 General comment 15, *supra* note 472; Sangroula, *supra* note 915, at 56.

but was not given equal classification as a social good. One may suggest that treating water as an economic good for guaranteeing access can work as long as the purpose is the realization of the HRWS.[64] There are global pressures to privatize this resource through the marketization of its reserves, which include a number of implications on water services such as their liberalization.[65] These pressures are supported by the existence of a *financial casino* in the global economy. This concept encompasses investors who are seeking to make money out of the classification of water as a market commodity.[66] Advocates of such privatization claim that the objective is the long-term sustainable management of freshwater resources through corporations and the global market, which make decisions concerning their use.[67] The rationale behind this approach is that considering water an expensive commodity discourages wasting, which normally occurs if no price is set.[68] Technological developments are being used as a justification, since private companies are capable of collecting data at a lower cost than governments.[69] This argument is supported by the incapacity of states to provide freshwaters in the South.[70]

The international community is developing global regulatory frameworks for TBAs and is not following a market-enabling environment.[71] Still, the question of whether such a resource should be free due to its importance or expensive since it's valuable remains without a clear answer.[72] The emergence of private environmental governance has been both a challenge and an opportunity. Private actors are replacing states due to their incapacity to implement or enforce rules, which will ultimately affect the relationship between nations sharing aquifers. Moreover, the appearance of a network of actors governing TBAs may lead to the dilution of the idea of state sovereignty. This would result from the important role that other stakeholders, such as the private sector and civil society, would play.[73] All of these claims have been criticized to some degree. Meanwhile, the appearance of new stakeholders was welcomed,

64 *Id.*
65 Lopez-Gunn, *supra* note 891, at 47.
66 Kristin L. Retherford, *Regulating the Corporate Tap: Applying Global Administrative Law Principles to Achieve the Human Right to Water*, 88 Indiana Law Journal. 811, 816 (2013).
67 Hilal Elver, *International Environmental Law, Water and the Future*, 27(5) Third World Quarterly. 885, 893 (2006).
68 Erik B. Bluemel, *The Implications of Formulating a Human Right to Water*, 31(4) Ecology Law Quarterly. 957, 963 (2004).
69 *Id.* at 894.
70 *Id.* at 895.
71 Lopez-Gunn, *supra* note 891, at 45.
72 Bruce Pardy, *The Dark Irony of International Water Rights*, 28(3) Pace Environmental Law Review. 907, 917 (2011).
73 Lopez-Gunn, *supra* note 891, at 45.

especially with globalization,[74] as the economic benefits of groundwater use are immense.[75]

Transboundary Goundwater as a Public Good

A public good can be defined as one in which its use does not lead to clashes among people since everyone can equally benefit from it.[76] It may produce externalities, such as encouraging the unsustainable consumption of the resource.[77] Water was considered a public good in the past, for instance, under Roman and Islamic Law.[78] It is still conceived as being so, whether it is a domestic or transboundary source,[79] but a very complex one.[80] Despite that, many countries lack effective control over it. Regions in the Middle East are a good example of this.[81] Water, in essence, is a public good. Private companies cannot simply own it because the government has a responsibility to ensure and protect access to it for all types of uses. This responsibility does not mean that authorities must provide water services for free.[82] Public utilities are delegated to provide access to it or sanitation. Likewise, such tasks can be given to private entities. In contrast, when water is seen as an economic good, markets develop within a system. This allows the recovery of the costs of the operations, which may exclude the part of the population unable to pay for water use.[83] Still, the market may fail to deliver an appropriate supply. This means

74 Retherford, *supra* note 935, at 818–819.

75 UNESCO, *New Report: Is the Solution to Water Crises Hiding Right under our Feet?* (Press Release, 21 April 2022), available at https://www.unesco.org/en/articles/new-report-solution-water-crises-hiding-right-under-our-feet (last accessed 3 August 2022).

76 Anders Jägerskog et al., *Transboundary Water Management as a Regional Public Good. Financing Development – An Example from the Nile Basin*, 7 (Report Nr. 20. SIWI, Stockholm, 2007).

77 W. Douglass Shaw, Water Resource Economics and Policy: An Introduction, 16 (Edward Elgar Publishing 2005).

78 Stephen C. McCaffrey, *The Human Right to Water: A False Promise?*, 47 The University of the Pacific Law Review. 221, 223 (2016).

79 Joakim Ojendal, Anton Earle & Anders Jagerskog, *Towards a Conceptual Framework for Transboundary Water Management*, in Transboundary Water Management: Principles and Practice 237, 244 (Anton Earle ed., Earthscan 2010).

80 Sanjeev Vidyarthi & Charles Hoch, *Learning from Groundwater: Pragmatic Compromise Planning Common Goods*, 36(4) Environment and Planning C: Politics and Space. 629, 629 (2018).

81 William M. Alley & Rosemarie Alley, High and Dry: Meeting the Challenges of the World's Growing Dependence on Groundwater, 102 (Yale University Press 2017).

82 Hubert H.G. Savenije, *Why Water is not an Ordinary Economic Good, or Why the Girl is Special*, 27(11/22) Physics and Chemistry of the Earth, Parts A/B/C, 741, 743 (2002).

83 Obani & Gupta, *supra* note 873, at 75–76. Cooperation between private companies and the public sector is also viewed as beneficial. Instead of focusing on one of the two sectors, the creation of synergies between the two is much more beneficial in the long-term. Food and Agriculture Organization of the United Nations, *Global Diagnostic on Groundwater Governance*, 134 (Groundwater Governance: A Global Framework for Action, March 2016). The differ-

that giving private companies a license to provide water does not, per se, lead to better results.[84] In fact, the risk of privatization revolves around the loss of control of governments, which must then use the law to guarantee that citizens have access to it.[85] This has been proven to be the case during the Covid-19 pandemic where increased insecurity was noticed due to lacking sufficient water for households.[86]

Even in cases where the state regulates water services, new problems have emerged. Namely, these include the lack of competition and the inability of residents to negotiate the terms related, for instance to quantity, quality, and price. It is important to note here that monopolies do not satisfy citizens needs.[87] When water is treated as a private good, non-economic matters such as social responsibility are excluded unless they can contribute to making profits. As in many cases, water problems have increased after the private sector took charge. For instance, Chile considered water a commodity in 1981, affecting the poor who could not afford to buy it. This situation forced the government to change its attitude and obliged companies to take the public interest into consideration. Nations elsewhere have failed to make the necessary reforms in their legal systems once water was considered a commodity. This led to severe water crises for several reasons, including corruption, poor management, and lack of efficient regulations. In some places, the price of water became higher than of food.[88] This is not to say that the fees associated with this resource cannot increase when it is provided as a public good. This has been the case in 2018 in Cape Town, South Africa, due to extreme droughts,[89] highlighting once more that the provision of public goods can be inadequate regardless of the circumstances.[90]

Water is a vital resource for survival, which is why it should be treated as a *public social good*. Here, institutions not seeking profits take charge.[91]

---

ence between a public good and a common good is that a public good is "non-excludable and non-rival". In other words, a person using that good does not affect another person's ability to enjoy that same good. In contrast, a common good is "non-excludable, but rival". This means that its use by one person affects the ability of others to use that same good. See Public and Common Goods, *Econ 102: Introduction to Microeconomics*, pp. 2, available at https://murraylax.org/e102/spring2009/publicgoods_print.pdf (last accessed 3 August 2022).

84 Savenije, *supra* note 951, at 743.

85 Melina Williams, *Privatization and the Human Right to Water: Challenges for the New Century*, 28(2) Michigan Journal of International Law. 469, 493–494 (2007).

86 Emily Kumpel et al., *Water Use Behaviors and Water Access in Intermittent and Continuous Water Supply Areas during the COVID-19 Pandemic*, 20(1) Journal of Water & Health. 139, 139–140 (2022).

87 Pardy, *supra* note 941, at 918.

88 Rutherford, *supra* note 917, at 863–864.

89 David Zetland, *The Role of Prices in Managing Water Scarcity*, 12 Water Security. 1, 2 (2021).

90 Laura Grant & Christian Langpap, *Private Provision of Public Goods by Environmental Groups*, 116(12) PNAS. 5334, 5335 (2019).

91 Retherford, *supra* note 935, at 816.

Groundwater, in particular, is of great importance because of the needs that it fulfills.[92] This importance highlights its significance given its wide use. This is why the protection of aquifers has received great attention from governments, especially because of growing public concerns.[93] Authorities usually try to control groundwater by declaring it a public resource to tackle the fears of its citizens,[94] since privatization models are flawed as corporations focus on profit maximization,[95] and as multiple socioeconomic factors limit accessibility.[96] Global governance of the water sector in this context is essential to control transnational companies, which are not accountable to the public, and also to states where they are extremely powerful.[97] In such a case, water is considered a global public good when it can benefit multiple nations, citizens, and generations.[98]

Considering transboundary groundwater as a public good will not, per se, improve its management unless the state possesses the capacity to understand matters pertaining to law and policy as well as the science related to it.[99] Policy decisions in relation to water governance occur on an hourly to decades long basis considering various elements such as planning, finance, and operations. This is just at the local and national level before even considering the complexities when this resource crosses political borders.[100] Authorities must possess the expertise and competencies to provide water as a public good.[101] Nations sharing, for instance, the Guarani Aquifer (Argentina, Brazil, Paraguay, and Uruguay) are expected to expand their water usage for a variety of purposes. These decisions are made by the states that have control over their portion.[102] But, is the groundwater contained within the aquifer protected when

92 Milan Dimkic & Ph. Quevauviller, *Concluding Remarks, in* Groundwater Management in Large River Basins 117, 117 (Milan Dimkic, Heinz-Jurgen Brauch & Michael Kavanaugh eds., IWA Publishing 2008).

93 Enzo Funari & Marco Vighi, Pesticide Risk in Groundwater 259 (CRC Press 1995).

94 Insa Theesfeld, *Institutional Challenges for National Groundwater Governance: Policies and Issues*, 48(1) Groundwater. 131, 134 (2010).

95 Retherford, *supra* note 935, at 829.

96 Andrea K. Gerlak, *Review: Human Rights and Privatization of Water in the European Union and Beyond*, 13(3) International Studies Review. 529, 529–531 (2011).

97 Retherford, *supra* note 935, at 829–830.

98 Kalomoira Zisopoulou, Dimitris Zisopoulos, & Dionysia Panagoulia, *Water Economics: An In-Depth Analysis of the Connection of Blue Water with Some Primary Level Aspects of Economic Theory I*, 14 Water. 1, 6 (2022).

99 Eckstein & Eckstein, *supra* note 1, at 687–688.

100 Jay R. Lund, *Integrating Social and Physical Sciences in Water Management*, 51(8) Water Resources Research. 5905, 5905 (2015).

101 Marina Povitkina & Ketevan Bolkvadze, *Fresh Pipes with Dirty Water: How Quality of Government Shapes the Provision of Public Goods in Democracies*, 58(4) European Journal of Political Research. 1191, 1191 (2019).

102 Jacob D. Petersen-Perlman & Aaron T. Wolf, *Getting to the First Handshake: Enhancing Security by Initiating Cooperation in Transboundary River Basins*, 51(6) Journal of the American Water Resources Association. 1688, 1696 (2015).

extracted for public water supply or for other reasons? The evidence from the Disi Aquifer, shared between Saudi Arabia and Jordan, suggests otherwise. Even though both governments agreed on a set of measures to protect it, the agreement is not sufficient to prevent its depletion. Considering transboundary groundwater as a public and social good did not, in this case, lead to its proper management.[103] Such classification does not automatically lead to the protection of aquifers, as states may still may overuse water out of ignorance or to secure economic interests.[104] Nations must analyze the different competing uses (e.g., consumption, food production, and industrial operations) and potential conflicts and crises that may occur,[105] constantly adapt rules to changes, and make compromises.[106]

While considering groundwater a public good, the government must focus on tackling the challenges of its effective administration through several means. These include establishing the necessary governance mechanisms as its proper use requires the efforts of all nations sharing it.[107] This is called *Collaborative Governance* and is seen as more appropriate for dealing with uncertainty and the fast developments that occur. This creates benefits from the constant generation of knowledge, new ideas, and opinions.[108] Governance of this public good must take into account the socioeconomic as well as hydrological dimensions formed by local management regimes as domestic needs must be satisfied.[109] These regimes may differ as some of them have advanced national legal frameworks and policies.[110] This constituted one of the many reasons that some nations justified their desire to keep the existing status quo at the international level. They argue that local elements allow for the adoption of a tailored approach for the management of TBAs.[111] Nonetheless, a national approach to this matter does not result in the appropriate governance of this shared public good.[112]

103 Müller, Müller-Itten & Gorelick, *supra* note 893, at 5452–5453.

104 Marty Rowland, *A Framework for Resolving the Transboundary Water Allocation Conflict Conundrum*, 43(5) GROUNDWATER. 700, 701 (2005).

105 Gorelick & Zheng, *supra* note 896, at 3031.

106 Mark Zeitoun, Marisa Goulden, & David Tickner, *Current and Future Challenges Facing Transboundary River Basin Management*, 4(5) WIREs CLIMATE CHANGE. 331, 332 (2013).

107 Deborah L. Hathaway, *Transboundary Groundwater Policy: Developing Approaches in the Western and Southwestern United States*, 47(1) JOURNAL OF THE AMERICAN WATER RESOURCES ASSOCIATION. 103, 112 (2011).

108 Andrea K. Gerlak, *Resistance and Reform: Transboundary Water Governance in the Colorado River Delta*, 32(1) REVIEW OF POLICY RESEARCH. 100, 102 (2015).

109 Rosario Sanchez & Gabriel Eckstein, *Aquifers Shared Between Mexico and the United States: Management Perspectives and Their Transboundary Nature*, 55(4) GROUNDWATER. 495, 503 (2017).

110 DE CHAISEMARTIN et al, *supra* note 1, at 218–219.

111 Eckstein & Sindico, *supra* note 56, at 38.

112 Jägerskog, *supra* note 945, at 7.

Transboundary Groundwater as a Human Right

This section examines the HRWS and the duties arising from it. It discusses its application to shared groundwaters and the limits of such an approach.

A Brief Historical Overview of the Adoption of the HRWS

Discussions from the 1950s through the 1970s led to the indirect recognition of a HRW. Yet, the adopted mechanisms did not expressly mention such a right.[113] Neither Article 25 UDHR (adopted in 1948), nor Articles 11 and 12 ICESCR (adopted in 1966), mention water.[114] Article 25 UDHR provides a list of non-exhaustive rights excluding the HRW, which has been considered by many as implicitly included.[115] The UDHR is non-binding and has only moral weight.[116] Water as a human rights issue was left out of the debate until the 1970s, when the Mar del Plata Action Plan declared that everyone has a right to water access considering their basic needs.[117] It was the first to explicitly recognize its existence.[118] Before the 1990s, several conventions acknowledged the HRW that was applicable to the persons who were covered under these treaties.[119] Reference to ensuring equal access to clean water services was mentioned in Article 28 of the Convention on the Rights of Persons with Disabilities[120] and to adequate sanitary installations within Article 5 of the ILO's Convention No. 161 of 1985 on Occupational Health Services.[121] Soft law instruments mention the HRW.[122] These include the Standard Minimum Rules for the Treatment of Prisoners of 1955 in the context of personal

113 Brett A. Miller, *Navigating the Confluence: Sources of Reconciliation Flowing Between the Human Right to Water and Economic Efficiency*, 28 Duke Environmental Law & Policy Forum. 105, 139 (2017).

114 Mathias Risse, *The Human Right to Water and Common Ownership of the Earth* 3 (HKS Working Paper No. RWP13-003, Mar. 20, 2013).

115 Universal Declaration of Human Rights, adopted by the United Nations General Assembly at its 183rd session on 10 December 1948 as Resolution 217 at the Palais de Chaillot in Paris, France, Article 25(1).

116 *Id.*

117 Adele J. Kirchner, *The Human Right to Water and Sanitation*, 15(1) Max Planck Yearbook of United Nations Law. 445, 449–450 (2011). Mar Del Plata Action Plan, United Nations Water Conference, Mar Del Plata, Argentina, 14–15 March 1977, p. 63.

118 Miller, *supra* note 982, at 139.

119 Jootaek Lee & Maraya Best, *Attempting to Define the Human Right to Water with an Annotated Bibliography & Recommendations for Practitioners*, 30 The Georgetown Environmental Law Journal. 75, 88 (2017).

120 United Nations, Convention on the Rights of Persons with Disabilities, adopted on 13 December 2006, Article 28, 2 (a).

121 C161 – Occupational Health Services Convention, 1985 (No. 161), Article 5 (b).

122 Surabhi Chopra, *The Rights to Food and Water: Dependencies and Dilemmas* 7 (Institute for Human Rights and Business, Jan. 2011).

hygiene and for drinking purposes[123] as well as the Vancouver Declaration from the UN Conference on Human Settlements of 1976, which emphasized the importance of water as a human need and right.[124]

Since the 1990s, statements, declarations, and mechanisms addressing this resource have been made given the great recognition of the lack of water access.[125] These include the Rules for the Protection of Juveniles Deprived of their Liberty of 1990, mentioning the need to provide clean drinking water,[126] Agenda 21, which cited this resource several times as highlighted previously[127] and the Dublin Statement on Water and Sustainable Development.[128] In fact, the Statement expressly declared in its guiding principles the relevance of ensuring clean access to water and sanitation for everyone in exchange for a reasonable fee. This stands in contrast to the 1992 Rio Declaration and Agenda 21, which failed to address this matter.[129] The Dublin Statement somehow managed to recognize the economic value of water. This was when this resource was considered an economic good. It recognized the existence of a HRW. Chapter 18 of Agenda 21 considered water an economic and social good.[130] The International Conference on Population and Development of 1994 made a reference to water and sanitation as part of an individual's right to an adequate standard of living.[131] In 1999, a UN Resolution expressed the importance of the right to clean water within the right to development and the obligation of protecting it.[132] Several soft law measures have been adopted since the 2000s to address the question of water access, including the

123 Standard Minimum Rules for the Treatment of Prisoners. Adopted by the First United Nations Congress on the Prevention of Crime and the Treatment of Offenders, held in Geneva in 1955, and approved by the Economic and Social Council by its resolutions 663 C (XXIV) of 31 July 1957 and 2076 (LXII) of 13 May 1977.

124 The Vancouver Declaration on Human Settlements, from the report of Habitat: United Nations Conference on Human Settlements, Vancouver, Canada, 31 May to 11 June 1976. Habitat: United Nations Conference on Human Settlements; George S. McGraw, *Defining and Defending the Right to Water and Its Minimum Core: Legal Construction and the Role of National Jurisprudence*, 8(2) Loyola University Chicago International Law Review. 127, 140–141 (2011).

125 Lee & Best, *supra* note 988, at 89.

126 United Nations Rules for the Protection of Juveniles Deprived of their Liberty. Adopted by General Assembly resolution 45/113 of 14 December 1990.

127 Agenda 21, *supra* note 114, at chapter 18.

128 Lee & Best, *supra* note 988, at 89.

129 Kirchner, *supra* note 986, at 451.

130 Dublin statement, *supra* note 426, at principle 1–4; Agenda 21, *supra* note 114, at chapter 18; Lee & Best, *supra* note 988, at 89.

131 Program of Action adopted at the International Conference on Population and Development; Cairo, 5–13 September 1994; 20th Anniversary Edition, Principle 2, p. 11. Kirchner, *supra* note 986, at 451.

132 United Nations General Assembly, 54th session; Agenda item 116 (b); Resolution adopted by the General Assembly [on the report of the Third Committee (A/54/605/Add.2)] 54/175. The right to development; *Id.* at 452.

Ministerial Declaration of the Hague on Water Security in the 21st Century[133] and the United Nations Millennium Declaration in 2000 that focused on ensuring safe drinking water for those lacking it and tackling unsustainable management practices.[134]

The recognition of the HRW is the result of a long historical struggle that began after World War II. This emerged with the foundation of human rights parameters in the UN system.[135] All the efforts that were made after the 1990s led to the adoption of GC 15 in 2002. It considered Article 11 of the ICESCR as including an HRW essential for guaranteeing an adequate standard of living[136] since the list of rights mentioned there is not exclusive.[137] Article 12(1) of this convention imposes an obligation upon states to guarantee the highest attainable standard of physical and mental health. This right is connected to access to safe and adequate water for drinking and sanitation according to GC 15.[138] It is associated with other rights within the context of Articles 11(1) and 12(1) of the ICESCR. This is the case even though it was not explicitly mentioned in these provisions.[139] It is linked to the right to work under Article 6(1) and the right to take part in cultural life under Article 15(1) of the same treaty.[140] The relevance of GC 15, despite its non-legally binding nature, was that it provided an authoritative interpretation of the HRW for the first time.[141] The importance of water to the realization of other rights under ICESCR constituted the basis for the explicit recognition of an HRW in this comment.[142] Yet, its soft nature meant that more developments needed

133 Ministerial Declaration of the Hague on Water Security in the 21st Century. Agreed to on Wednesday, 22 March 2000, in The Hague, The Netherlands.

134 United Nations General Assembly, 55th session; Agenda item 60 (b), Resolution adopted by the General Assembly [without reference to a Main Committee (A/55/L.2)] 55/2. United Nations Millennium Declaration. 18 September 2000.

135 Pedi Obani & Joyeeta Gupta, *The Evolution of the Right to Water and Sanitation: Differentiating the Implications*, 24(1) Review of European Community & International Environmental Law. 27, 27–30 (2015). This was among the many shortcomings of the ICESCR, which faced severe criticism as a result by many scholars. See, Audrey R. Chapman, *A "Violation Approach" for Monitoring the International Covenant on Economic, Social and Cultural Rights*, 18(1) Human Rights Quarterly. 23, 23–24 (1996).

136 ICESCR, *supra* note 218, at Article 11 (1).

137 *Id*; Lee & Best, *supra* note 988, at 90.

138 ESCR Committee, General Comment No. 14, UN DOC.E/C.12/2000/4, paras 4, 11 (emphasis added), pp.195–198.

139 Ling-Yee Huang, *Not Just Another Drop in the Human Rights Bucket: The Legal Significance of a Codified Human Right to Water*, 20 Florida Journal of International Law. 353, 357 (2008).

140 ICESCR, *supra* note 218, at Article 6(1) & Article 15(1).

141 Malcolm Langford, *The United Nations Concept of Water as a Human Right: A New Paradigm for Old Problems?*, 21(2) International Journal Water Resources Development. 273, 275 (2005).

142 Huang, *supra* note 1008, at 353 & 357.

to be taken afterward to ensure the adoption of legally binding instruments.[143] New soft measures were adopted. These include the UNGA Resolution 58/217 of 2003, the International Decade for Action, *"Water for Life"* (Dec. 23, 2003) that began from 2005 to 2015,[144] various guidelines, studies, and reports;[145] 2008 HRC Resolution 7/22[146] and 2009 HRC Resolution 12/8[147] where both addressed Human Rights and Access to Safe Drinking Water and Sanitation. Recent documents include the 2016 UNGA Resolution 71/222, International Decade for Action "Water for Sustainable Development, 2018–2028[148] and 2015 UNGA Resolution 70/169 on the Human Rights to Safe Drinking Water and Sanitation.[149]

In 2010, the UNGA adopted Resolution A/64/292 – the HRWS, through which safe, clean, and accessible drinking water was recognized as a fundamental right essential for the realization of other ones.[150] Through it, water as a human right was explicitly acknowledged by the international community.[151] The 2010 Resolution was perceived as a shock for many countries. 41 abstained from voting, and 122 supported its creation.[152] States that were in favor wished that it was established via consensus, instead of voting, due to the importance of having it.[153] In the same year, the UNHRC adopted

143 *Dinara Ziganshina, Rethinking the Concept of the Human Right to Water*, 6 Santa Clara Journal of International Law, 113, 116 (2008).

144 United Nations General Assembly, 58th session; Agenda item 95, Resolution adopted by the General Assembly [on the report of the Second Committee (A/58/485)] 58/217. International Decade for Action, "Water for Life", 2005–2015, 23 December 2003.

145 Kirchner, *supra* note 986, at 453.

146 Human Rights Council, Resolution 7/22. *Human Rights and Access to Safe Drinking Water and Sanitation*. 41st Meeting; 28 March 2008. Adopted without a vote.

147 United Nations General Assembly, Human Rights Council, 12th session; Agenda item 3: Promotion and Protection of all Human Rights, Civil, Political, Economic, Social and Cultural Rights, including the Right to Development. Resolution adopted by the Human Rights Council. 12/8. Human rights and access to safe drinking water and sanitation, A/HRC/RES/12/8; 12 October 2009.

148 United Nations General Assembly, 71st session; Agenda item 19 (a); Resolution adopted by the General Assembly on 21 December 2016 [on the report of the Second Committee (A/71/463/Add.1)] 71/222. International Decade for Action, "Water for Sustainable Development", 2018–2028. Distr.: General. 7 February 2017.

149 United Nations General Assembly, 70th session, Agenda item 72 (b), Resolution adopted by the General Assembly on 17 December 2015 [on the report of the Third Committee (A/70/489/Add.2)] 70/169. The human rights to safe drinking water and sanitation. Distr.: General; 22 February 2016. Lee & Best, *supra* note 988, at 90–97.

150 United Nations General Assembly, 64th session, Agenda item 48, Resolution adopted by the General Assembly on 28 July 2010. 64/292. The human right to water and sanitation. A/RES/64/292, Distr.: General, 3 August 2010.

151 Ewelina Cala-Wacinkiweicz, *Right to Water – Considerations in the Context of International Protection of Human Rights*, 11 US-China Law Review. 1302, 1304 (2014).

152 Miller, *supra* note 982, at 145–146.

153 Gonzalo Aguilar Cavallo, *The Human Right to Water and Sanitation: From Political Commitments to Customary Rule*, 3(5) Pace International Law Review Online Companion. 136, 168–169 (2012).

another resolution recognizing the existence of a human right to access safe drinking water and sanitation.[154] The HRC noted that the HRWS go hand in hand where the GA Resolution constituted the basis for such adoption.[155] The HRC Resolution listed state responsibilities in detail. The latter further strengthened Resolution 64/292 and the HRWS.[156] Since then, several have been adopted reaffirming the existence of the HRWS, such as the 2011 World Health Organization (WHO) Resolution in 2011[157] and the HRC Resolution 24/18 of 2013.[158] In 2015, a new one was adopted by UNGA separating the HRW from the right to sanitation. This differentiation was made because the right to sanitation is often neglected and needs to be considered separately.[159] The recognition of the HRWS is a considerable step forward. This is especially true since this right has legal foundations in international law through both hard and soft instruments.[160] One has to point out that some states had already advanced legislations concerning this matter within their constitutions, domestic regulations, and other documents.[161] These resolutions are still non-binding in nature.[162]

Most literature focused on the HRW, despite the importance the lack of sanitation carries. This is a global concern affecting billions of people. For example, around a billion people practice open defecation. Sanitation depends

154 United Nations, Human Rights Council, 15th Session, Agenda Item 3, Promotion and Protection of All Human Rights, Civil, Political, Economic, Social, and Cultural Rights, Including the Right to Development. 15/... Human Rights and Access to Safe Drinking Water and Sanitation. A/HRC/15/L.14. Distr.: Limited. 24 September 2010. SAUL, KINLEY, & MOWBRAY, *supra* note 31, at 909–910.

155 Cala-Wacinskiweicz, *supra* note 1020, at 1307.

156 Lori Beail-Farkas, *The Human Right to Water and Sanitation: Context, Contours and Enforcement*, 30(4) WISCONSIN INTERNATIONAL LAW JOURNAL. 761, 786 (2013).

157 64th World Health Assembly, Agenda item 13.15, Drinking Water, Sanitation and Health (WHA64.24, 24 May 2011).

158 United Nations General Assembly, Human Rights Council, 24th session, Agenda item 3: Promotion and Protection of all Human rights, Civil, Political, Economic, Social, and Cultural Rights, Including the Right to Development. Resolution Adopted by the Human Rights Council, 24/18: The Human Right to Safe Drinking Water and Sanitation. Distr.: General; 8 October 2013; Lee & Best, *supra* note 988.

159 According to the resolution: "The rights to safe drinking water and sanitation are closely related, but have distinct features which warrant their separate treatment in order to address specific challenges in their implementation and that sanitation too often remains neglected, if not addressed as a separate right, while being a component of the right to an adequate standard of living". United Nations General Assembly, 70th session; Third Committee Agenda item 72 (b) Promotion and protection of human rights: human rights questions, including alternative approaches for improving the effective enjoyment of human rights and fundamental freedoms; The human rights to safe drinking water and sanitation, p. 4 (A/C.3/70/L.55/Rev.1; Distr.: Limited; 18 November 2015).

160 INGA WINKLER, THE HUMAN RIGHT TO WATER: SIGNIFICANCE, LEGAL STATUS, AND IMPLICATIONS FOR WATER ALLOCATIONS, 95–99 (Hart Publishing 2012).

161 MALCOLM LANGFORD, *The Right to Water in National Law: A Review*, in THE HUMAN RIGHT TO WATER 115, 115 (Eibe H. Riedel et al eds., Berliner Wissenschafts-Verlag 2006).

162 Cavallo, *supra* note 1022, at 190.

not only on the presence of a toilet or latrine but includes a multi-step system to ensure proper disposal and treatment.[163] This right is derived from the one related to an adequate standard of living. This is mentioned within the ICESCR, which considers the improvement of living conditions an element of enhancing the quality of life.[164] National and international donors, however, have invested more in water than sanitation.[165] The latter was not even included in the original version of the Millennium Development Goals and was added later on in 2002 during the World Summit on Sustainable Development in its plan of implementation and in many other documents issued.[166] The main problem threatening to stop concrete efforts toward universal sanitation is that this topic is still considered taboo in many places globally. This is why existing challenges are not being addressed.[167] Progress was initially slow and only gained traction when GC 15 was drafted. Further developments and political declarations followed.[168] Several debates occurred during the drafting of GC 15. The main question concerned whether water should be connected to sanitation. The committee that drafted the comment was not ready to address this topic from a holistic approach, which is why sanitation was only mentioned marginally a few times where terms such as adequate, personal, and basic were used when referring to it. Nonetheless, it provided a strong push toward addressing this issue as a human right through different reports and recommendations.[169] The first time sanitation was granted separate attention from water was in 2008, which was declared the International Year of Sanitation.[170] The Sustainable Development Goals (SDGs) summit in 2015 resulted in the adoption of SDG 6 related to ensuring access to water and sanitation for all.[171] The latter was mentioned expressly in three of the targets associated with this goal, where target 6.2 focuses on realizing equal access to appropriate and equitable sanitation and hygiene and the elimination of

163 Human Rights Watch, *Introduction: Sanitation as a Human Right* (19 April 2017), available at https://www.hrw.org/report/2017/04/19/going-toilet-when-you-want/sanitation-human-right_(last accessed 3 August 2022).

164 ICESCR, *supra* note 218, at Article 11 (1).

165 Human Rights Watch, *supra* note 1032.

166 Inga T. Winkler, *The Human Right to Sanitation*, 37(4) University of Pennsylvania Journal of International Law. 1331, 1347 (2016). United Nations, Report of the World Summit on Sustainable Development, Johannesburg, South Africa, 26 August–4 September 2002.

167 *Id.* at 1348; Kathleen Naday, *Toilet Taboo Keeps us from Discussing Real Impact of Sanitation Failures* (Global Times, 18/11/2015), available at https://www.globaltimes.cn/content/953458.shtml (last accessed 3 August 2022).

168 Winkler, *supra* note 1032, at 1350. The right to sanitation was mentioned in the context of other rights such as the right to health and the right to housing. *Id.* at 1352–1354.

169 *Id.* at 1354–1356. General Comment 15, *supra* note 472.

170 *Id.* at 1349; UN Water, *Tackling a Global Crisis: International Year of Sanitation 2008* (2008).

171 United Nations Sustainable Development Goals, *Goal 6: Ensure Access to Water and Sanitation for All*, available at https://www.un.org/sustainabledevelopment/water-and-sanitation/ (last accessed 3 August 2022).

open defecation by 2030. Particular focus on women and girls in vulnerable contexts is emphasized.[172]

Duties Arising from the HRWS

Scholars advocating for the classification of water as a human right do so under the framework of human dignity. This would ensure access to an adequate quantity of high-quality water. Their argument is based on the idea that a HRWS would allow individuals and states alike to use the human rights regime to seek judicial enforcement, which could occur at either the international or domestic level.[173] Proponents advocating for water as a human right hoped to initially use the ICCPR and, in particular, Article 6 as a basis.[174] Scholars have tried to expand the interpretation of this provision to include an obligation for states to take actions to ensure that citizens have access to resources, including water. This article proposes positive and negative rights.[175] It provides civil rights in the sense that it prevents governments from killing their citizens but does not address other causes like famine or water shortage.[176] Recent developments concerning Article 6, coupled with the adoption of GA 36 related to this provision, have not changed much in this regard. Water was mentioned only for ensuring the existence of adequate conditions for the protection of the right to life.[177] Those supporting an HRWS are seeking to ensure that states are held accountable for providing citizens with basic necessities.[178] Nations accordingly have a responsibility and must take action.[179] The recognition of this right creates obligations on states to provide the necessary elements that help citizens realize it. This is required even in situations where the population cannot meet their basic needs such as during natural disasters or poverty.[180]

GC 15, for instance, mentions the essential elements for the realization of the HRW,[181] including physical accessibility, acceptable quality, location,

172 *Id.*

173 Lee & Best, *supra* note 988, at 85.

174 Rutherford, *supra* note 917, at 873. Article 6 states that everyone has a right to life protected by regulations. This right cannot be taken away arbitrarily. ICCPR, *supra* note 219.

175 Thorsten Kiefer, *Beyond State Sovereignty: The Human Right to Water*, 5 Non-State Actors and International Law. 183, 187–190 (2005).

176 Rutherford, *supra* note 917, at 873.

177 General comment No. 36 (2018) on article 6 of the International Covenant on Civil and Political Rights, on the right to life, pp. 6, Distr.: General, 30 October 2018.

178 Villar, *supra* note 6, at 85.

179 Salman MA Salman & Siobhan Mcinerney-Lankford, *The Human Right to Water: Legal and Policy Dimensions*, 65 (World Bank 2004).

180 Valentina Cornea, *Content and Effects of Recognition of the Right to Water*, 1 Cross-Border Journal of International Studies. 49, 54 (2016).

181 General Comment 15, *supra* note 472; Chopra, *supra* note 991, at 8.

and price affordability.[182] It adds further requirements related to water use for domestic and personal purposes and confirms that this right is essential to the achievement of other ones such as those to health and adequate food.[183] This right cannot be realized without ensuring access to water policies, rules, and measures.[184] In terms of normative content, there are freedoms and entitlements. The former comprises being free from interference and maintaining access to water supplies. Water must be adequate considering various elements, mainly its availability, quality, and accessibility. The latter contains physical, economic, and information accessibility on a non-discriminatory basis. In fact, the principles of non-discrimination and equality are emphasized concerning different categories of people such as children, women, and refugees.[185] There are general, immediate, specific, and core obligations arising.[186] The immediate ones that must be fulfilled include principally tackling discriminatory practices related to water access and working towards the realization of this right. Three specific duties must also be realized: the responsibility to respect others, to protect resources, and to fulfill obligations. These are considered positive duties.[187]

The obligation to respect asserts that states must not intervene directly or indirectly with the enjoyment of this right by, for instance denying water access. The duty to protect exists where governments must shield citizens from third-party interference. These include individuals, groups, corporations, etc. [188] They have a responsibility toward their own companies operating in international waters or abroad.[189] The implementation of the first two obligations is less complicated than the third one, given their strict definitions.[190] States must, according to the last duty, facilitate the capacity of citizens and communities to enjoy it through positive measures. Nations are expected to also promote this right through various means. They must fulfill it for those not possessing the capacity to do so due to uncontrollable circumstances.[191]

In terms of obligations, states are expected to acknowledge the role of international cooperation and assistance and adopt joint and separate actions to achieve this right. Nations must respect the need to enjoy it in another country

182 *Id*; O. Gbadamosi, *Progressive Realization of the Right to Safe Water and Adequate Sanitation*, 12 UNIVERSITY OF BOTSWANA LAW JOURNAL 53, 55 (2011).
183 General Comment 15, *supra* note 472; Gbadamosi, *supra* note 1051, at 57.
184 Chopra, *supra* note 991, at 8.
185 General Comment 15, *supra* note 472, at 6–7.
186 Ramin Pejan, *The Right to Water: The Road to Justiciability*, 36 GEORGE WASHINGTON INTERNATIONAL LAW REVIEW. 1181, 1186 (2004).
187 *Id.* at 1187.
188 General Comment 15, *supra* note 472, at 8–9.
189 *Id.*; Jimena Murillo Chavarro, *Extraterritorial Obligations to Ensure the Enjoyment of the Human Right to Water in a Transboundary Context*, 9(1) HUMAN RIGHTS AND INTERNATIONAL LEGAL DISCOURSE. 90, 96–98 (2015).
190 Pejan, *supra* note 1055, at 1187
191 General Comment 15, *supra* note 472, at 9–10.

and refrain from taking various measures potentially affecting its implementation. They must prevent their citizens and companies from breaching the rights of individuals and communities elsewhere and facilitate the achievement of this right considering water availability. Governments must guarantee that this right is incorporated within agreements and the development of new legal instruments to that end at the various levels. They should consider this right when acting as members of international organizations.[192]

Finally, several core obligations that must be immediately realized are mentioned. Examples of these include guaranteeing minimum access to water for personal and domestic use; ensuring access includes reasonable physical access on a non discriminatory basis and the equitable distribution of this resource to facilities and services.[193] It is worth mentioning that IHRL recognizes that the available resources of the state must be taken into consideration to ensure the progressive realization of different rights.[194] GC 15 covers specific requirements that nations must fulfilll to implement and monitor compliance.[195] These include reviewing and amending existing legislation, strategies, and policies when needed; the adoption of a national strategy or plan of action based on specific principles; the creation of coordination between the different authorities tackling this topic; and the identification of challenges facing the realization of this right when monitoring progress.[196]

The 2010 UNGA Resolution recognizing HRWS included few obligations upon states and international organizations to provide the needed finances, capacity-building, and technology transfer via global assistance and cooperation.[197] It was the 2010 HRC Resolution in relation to this right that imposed detailed obligations. These comprise inter alia the establishment of various tools (legal, economic…); guaranteeing transparency in the planning and implementation process; considering vulnerable and marginalized groups; the creation and realization of efficient legislation and effective monitoring of the latter, and the adoption of effective remedies. The Resolution imposed duties on non-state service providers, mainly the realization of their human rights responsibilities when conducting their operations; contributing to the provision of adequate water supply and sanitation services, and considering rights within the impact assessments.[198]

192 *Id.* at 10–12.
193 *Id.* at 12–13.
194 Chopra, *supra* note 991, at 13–14.
195 General Comment 15, *supra* note 472; Pejan, *supra* note 1055, at 1189–1190.
196 Chopra, *supra* note 991, at 14–16.
197 Resolution 64/292, *supra* note 1019, at 3.
198 Human Rights Council 15th Session, Agenda item 3: Promotion and Protection of all Human Rights, Civil, Political, Economic, Social, and Cultural Rights, Including the Right to Development. Resolution Adopted by the Human Rights Council, 15/9: Human Rights and Access to Safe Drinking Water and Sanitation.

Transboundary Groundwater as a Human Right

There is an overall consensus at the international level that TBAs are increasingly relied upon for the satisfaction of human needs.[199] Indeed, this resource is the most extracted worldwide for various purposes including drinking, cooking, and hygiene. In many places, mainly arid and semi-arid areas, it even constitutes the only or primary means for satisfying these needs. For instance, the Nubian Sandstone Aquifer, shared between Libya, Chad, Egypt, and Sudan, provides the majority of freshwater used in Libya. Moreover, several communities residing near the US-Mexican border have relied on TBA exploitation for decades.[200] The HRWS, in this context, is relevant given the existence of hydrologic interdependence. In that sense, the rights to groundwater held by citizens residing in one state are affected by the way a TBA is being exploited by another nation.[201] Meanwhile, the presence of physical systems that are related to the hydrological cycle, such as soil, ecosystems, and atmosphere, further complicates its management.[202] The HRWS impacts the way in which groundwater is being governed. It can create tensions as countries have to navigate between ensuring its sustainability and guaranteeing economic development where it plays a role.[203] It mainly emphasizes the necessity to govern groundwater resources in an equitable manner and that its use for fulfilling the HRW is prioritized in water allocation.[204] This means that principles such as accountability, transparency, and non-discrimination must apply. Policymakers face multiple challenges when attempting to draft policies and rules concerning TBAs,[205] especially as it has global political implications.[206] Unfortunately, there are insufficient legal frameworks that take these matters

199 Eran Feitelson, *Impediments to the Management of Shared Aquifers: A Political Economy Perspective*, 14(3) Hydrology Journal. 319, 319–320 (2006).

200 Gabriel Eckstein, *International Law for Transboundary Aquifers: A Challenge for Our Times*, 115 American Journal of International Law. 201, 202 (2021).

201 Christina Leb, *The Right to Water in a Transboundary Context: Emergence of Seminal Trends*, 37(6) Water International. 640, 641 (2012).

202 Marian J. Neal et al., *The Social-Environmental Justice of Groundwater Governance*, in Integrated Groundwater Management: Concepts, Approaches And Challenges 253, 254 (Anthony J. Jakeman et al eds., Springer 2016).

203 Sean G. Furey, *Groundwater Governance for Poverty Eradication, Social Equity and Health*, in Advances in Groundwater Governance (Karen G. Villhoth et al. eds., CRC Press, 2018).

204 Jenny Gronwall, *World Water Day 2022: Groundwater and Water-Related Human Rights* (SIWI; Mar. 17, 2022), available at https://siwi.org/latest/world-water-day-2022-groundwater-and-water-related-human-rights/ (last accessed 3 August 2022).

205 Shammy Puri, *Aquifers Know No Boundaries … But Farmers Do! So, Who Should Care?!*, in The Dilemma of Boundaries: Toward a New Concept of Catchment 221, 231 (Makoto Taniguchi & Takayuki Shiraiwa eds., Springer 2012).

206 Yanme He, *China's Transboundary Groundwater Cooperation in the Context of Emerging Transboundary Aquifer Law*, 55(3) Ground Water. 489, 489 (2017).

into consideration[207] where for instance nonbinding instruments such as the Berlin rules were impacted by specific rights within IHRL.[208]

Historically, TBAs were not taken into consideration in treaties.[209] Policymakers neglected them even though they play a significant role in human development.[210] The majority of existing non-renewable aquifers are transboundary ones.[211] In many places, the lack of technological capacities among the nations sharing one may lead to its unfair and uneven utilization. This affects the populations of the states that lack water access, and thus prevents them from satisfying existing needs,[212] which constitutes an urgent matter.[213] Nations may try to exploit an aquifer without considering other countries.[214] This is why questions surrounding the rights and obligations of states sharing these resources have been raised,[215] where a human rights approach can provide a further push towards realizing states' duties in the context of groundwater.[216] The latter is being extensively used,[217] as cheaper and more advanced technologies are available,[218] and since nations are increasingly seeing this shared resource as a new means to reach their goals and interests in terms of development.[219]

Transboundary groundwater resources allow the human population to satisfy its requirements for freshwater for direct and indirect consumption. In many regions, such as the Middle East or North Africa, TBAs represent

207 Conti & Gupta, *supra* note 376, at 850.

208 Joseph W. Dellapenna, *The Work of International Legal Expert Bodies*, in Research Handbook on International Water Law 26, 41 (Stephen C. McCaffrey, Christina Leb & Riley T. Denoon eds., Edward Elgar Publishing 2019).

209 Eckstein, *supra* note 460, at 526.

210 S. Puri & A. Aureli, *Transboundary Aquifers: A Global Program to Assess, Evaluate, and Develop Policy*, 43(5) Ground Water. 661, 661 (2005).

211 Mateljan, *supra* note 355, at 181.

212 Carlson, *supra* note 14, at 1418.

213 W. Todd Jarvis, *Strategies for Groundwater Resources Conflict Resolution and Management*, in Overexploitation and Contamination of Shared Groundwater Resources 393, 394 (Christophe J. G. Darnault ed., Springer 2008).

214 Traversi, *supra* note 55, at 456.

215 Alice Aureli & Gabriel Eckstein, *Strengthening Cooperation on Transboundary Groundwater Resources*, 36(5) Water International. 549, 549 (2011).

216 Naho Mirumachi et al., *The Human Right to Drinking Water: Impact of Large-Scale Agriculture and Industry*, 33 (European Parliament; Directorate-General For External Policies; Policy Department; European Union, 2021).

217 Shammy Puri & Hazim El-Naser, *Intensive Use of Groundwater in Transboundary Aquifers*, in Intensive Use of Groundwater: Challenges and Opportunities 415, 415 (Ramon Llamas & Emilio Custodio eds., Swets & Zeitlinger B. V., 2003).

218 Jenny Grönwall & Kerstin Danert, *Regarding Groundwater and Drinking Water Access through a Human Rights Lens: Self-Supply as a Norm*, 12(2) Water. 1, 1 (2020).

219 Gabriel E. Eckstein, *Managing Hidden Treasures Across Frontiers: The International Law of Transboundary Aquifers*, 1–2 (International Conference "Transboundary Aquifers: Challenges and New Directions," ISARM, 2010).

either the primary or only source.[220] In this context, it has been said that the HRW enhances management practices to guarantee good water quality and quantity.[221] This argument is supported by skeptics who question the ability of nations to manage shared groundwater since, in many cases, one might wonder whether the policies and rules adopted are indeed in the interest of the population. This situation has been documented as, in several instances, citizens have been subject to criticism as ethnic minorities in fragile or rogue states are viewed as the enemy. Public interest is not taken into consideration when water is used to bargain at the international level where it can play a role in reaching a compromise and strengthening the position of a particular state regarding other global matters.[222] This is unfortunate as the protection of this resource is a must for the further enhancement of human life,[223] through the creation of preservation zones in the most vulnerable parts of the aquifers.[224]

Unlike transboundary surface waters, shared aquifers did not witness debates with similar intensity in the past. This was the case despite the fact that they possess the quantities necessary to fulfill citizens' essentials for decades.[225] However, TBAs have been recognized as vital for human development since the 1990s. This classification has led to the emergence of debates concerning this issue.[226] Groundwater is considered ideal for the satisfaction of the HRWS because of its superior quality in comparison to surface water,[227] and as it requires minimum treatment to become drinkable in contrast to surface water.[228] Moreover, the conditions in which it is located make it less likely to be polluted in comparison to surface water.[229] Having a superior quality of water, or one that requires little treatment is very important because of the daily need for this resource.[230] Nevertheless, groundwater is subject to uncertainties

220 Eckstein & Sindico, *supra* note 56, at 32.

221 Villar, *supra* note 6, at 94.

222 Lopez-Gunn, *supra* note 891, at 43.

223 Raya Marina Stephan, ed., *Transboundary Aquifers: Managing a Vital Resource. The UNILC Draft Articles on the Law of Transboundary Aquifers*, 4 (United Nations Educational, Scientific and Cultural Organization, 2009).

224 Elisa Morgera et al., *The Right to Water for Food and Agriculture*, 67 (Food and Agriculture Organization of the United Nations; FAO Legislative Study 113; 2020).

225 Puri, Aureli & Stephan, *supra* note 880, at 12.

226 J. E. Cobbing et al, *A Critical Overview of Transboundary Aquifers Shared by South Africa*, 16(6) Hydrogeology Journal. 1207, 1208 (2008).

227 Kerstin Mechlem, *Groundwater Governance: The Role of Legal Frameworks at the Local and National Level – Established Practice and Emerging Trends*, 8(8) Water. 347, 348 (2016).

228 G Howard et al., *Groundwater and Public Health: Managing the Quality of Drinking-Water Sources*, in Protecting Groundwater for Health: Managing the Quality of Drinking-Water 1, 4 (Oliver Schmoll et al. eds., IWA Publishing 2006).

229 Vincent W. Uhl et al., *Groundwater Development: Basic Concepts for Expanding CRS Water Programs*, 4 (Technical paper, Catholic Relief Services, July 2009).

230 Risse, *supra* note 983, at 2.

related to scientific, chemical, and biological processes.[231] Pollution prevention and monitoring are much more difficult in this case because of its hidden nature. Cleaning potential pollutants and determining their impacts is thus more difficult.[232] Moreover, its quality varies from one aquifer to another.[233]

Embracing the HRWS within groundwater regulations helps to protect this resource and ensures sustainable use and management.[234] This right would push towards the realization of water access globally through the use of aquifers.[235] This reasoning follows the current paradigm shift in international law towards considering water a human right. This is expected to affect the interstate rules applicable to TBAs.[236] One has to keep in mind that the implementation of this right and its relationship to transboundary groundwater resources will bring new challenges into practice regarding the way it can be imposed,[237] as various factors must be considered together, such as the impact of climate change on the realization of the HRWS broadly.[238] This is due to the absence of concrete measures within IHRL as to the means on the basis of which HRWS obligations to protect, respect, and fulfil can be achieved, including in the context of TBAs.[239]

The Limits of a Human Rights Approach

There is no customary HRW that forms a compulsory duty upon states for the time being.[240] Resolutions, as well as the publications and reports by the UN, do not constitute normative obligations. Examples include GC 15 that mentions Articles 11 and 12 ICESCR. Its non-binding nature derives from the idea that this right is sourced from other ones within the convention. The situation is worse for the right to sanitation since there is no consensus, description, or definition of the term. In fact, there is no treaty instrument expressly mentioning the HRW. The latter, for the moment, is not considered

231 Jacques Ganoulis, *A Risk-based Integrated Approach for Managing Transboundary Groundwater Resources*, in Overexploitation and Contamination of Shared Groundwater Resources 355, 357–358 (Christophe J. G. Darnault ed., Springer 2008).

232 Philippe Quevauviller, *General Introduction: The Need to Protect Groundwater*, in Groundwater Science and Policy: An International Overview 1, 4 (Philippe Quevauviller ed., RSC Publishing 2008).

233 Grönwall & Danert, supra note 1087, at 9.

234 Mechlem, *supra* note 1096, at 348.

235 Villar, *supra* note 6, at 96.

236 Catherine Brolmann, *Transboundary Aquifers as a Concern of the International Community*, 13(3) International Community Law Review, 189, 189 (2011).

237 Nelson & Quevauviller, *supra* note 303, at 184; Furey, *supra* note 1072.

238 United Nations, Human Rights Office of the High Commissioner, *Special Thematic Report on Climate Change and the Human Rights to Water and Sanitation* (Jan. 28, 2022), available at https://www.ohchr.org/en/documents/thematic-reports/special-thematic-report-climate-change-and-human-rights-water-and (last accessed 3 August 2022).

239 Grönwall & Danert, *supra* note 1087, at 15.

240 Greco, *supra* note 47, at 35.

part of customary international law.[241] Several states have abstained from voting for numerous reasons.[242] Nations that disagreed with the adoption of the HRW declared that the UN is actually still debating this issue. Moreover, they argued that the opinions and sovereignty of nations are not taken into consideration.[243] The 2010 Resolution on the HRWS is not legally binding, and the international recognition of such a right is meaningless if governments do not implement it.[244] There is no global instrument in the form of a convention that directly recognizes its existence. In that sense, no obligation currently takes place for its protection, which can originate from a treaty and not a resolution that has a lower status. This is why these are considered by many scholars as soft law instruments, rather than mechanisms capable of imposing duties on states. This is the case despite the existence of mechanisms to deal with human rights violations.[245] In general, states have a difficult time approving control mechanisms, and in particular, concerning human rights.[246]

In fact, the Committee on Economic, Social and Cultural Rights (CESCR), long before the adoption of HRWS and GC 15, criticized many states for their incapacity to implement it on the domestic level. This criticism resulted from an examination of reports submitted by nations which remained silent despite the fact that the ICESCR does not contain explicit reference to this right. This means that they recognize its existence.[247] In this context, some have argued that the HRWS is unique[248] because of the absence of its direct mention within

241 Owen McIntyre, *The Human Right to Water as a Creature of Global Administrative Law*, 37(6) Water International. 654, 660–661 (2012).

242 Cristy Clark, *Of What Use is a Deradicalized Human Right to Water?*, 17(2) Human Rights Law Review. 231, 244 (2017).

243 Howard, *supra* note 916, at 130.

244 Rutherford, *supra* note 917, at 876–877.

245 Cala-Wacinskiweicz, *supra* note 1020, at 1309. One of the main challenges of the human right to water is identifying violations. Nations must show that they have taken all necessary measures for its realization, even in the context of limited resources. Human rights agreements create domestic obligations, not interstate ones. Other countries can provide reports on the human rights situation in a given state. In the case of a breach of the right to water, citizens are entitled to reparations stemming from national and international tribunals. Huang, supra note 762, at 361–363. Globally, monitoring mechanisms established are of two types. On one hand, there are the treaty-based bodies comprised of committees to monitor the realization of human rights treaties. On the other hand, there are the charter-based bodies which contain the HRC, special procedures, the universal periodic review, and independent investigations. United Nations Human Rights Office of the High Commissioner, *Instruments & Mechanisms*, available at https://www.ohchr.org/en/instruments-and-mechanisms (last accessed 3 August 2022).

246 Ziganshina, *supra* note 1012, at 116.

247 Takele Soboka Bulto, *The Emergence of the Human Right to Water in International Human Rights Law: Invention or Discovery?*, 12(2) Melbourne Journal of International Law. 305, 305–307 (2011).

248 Pierre Thielbörger, The Right(s) to Water: The Multi-Level Governance of a Unique Human Right, Abstract (Springer 2014).

human rights agreements.[249] This status is the result of the need to clarify the relationship between this right and other ones such as those related to health or food.[250] The entire discussion over its existence, value, and pertinence means nothing if it cannot be implemented in practice.[251] It is not sufficient to simply make statements recognizing its importance, in particular, to poor communities.[252] Rather, there is a need for a continuous examination of the ways it can be realized.[253] For instance, what is the amount of water that must be provided to each citizen on a daily basis? The answer will depend on elements such as culture and lifestyle. Should these elements be taken into consideration, or should citizens worldwide have access to the same amount of water equally? Another question is related to its quality. Humans had, and still have, access to this resource. Without this, they could not survive. Even though the mainstream discussion revolves around this subject, this is not the main problem faced. The issue is the lack of safe drinking water or one of high quality,[254] the main matters that experts examined after adopting the HRWS its practical implementation and consequences. It was also stated that the proponents of this right must consider all the actors at the national level, such as NGOs, unions, and citizens.[255] Many scholars questioned the capacity to fulfill it. Conducting an economic analysis, Jeffords and Shah noted that its realization is extremely difficult.[256] Brunner et al. noted that the HRWS has faced numerous challenges, including discrepancies in water-governance.[257] According to Pardy, this right does not lead to the protection of freshwater resources or the provisions of clean water as it does not deal with water threats.[258] The latter, among many others, have not been given

249 Amanda Cahill, *'The Human Right to Water – A Right of Unique Status': The Legal Status and Normative Content of the Right to Water*, 9(3) Water International. 389, 404 (2005).

250 *Id.* at 404.

251 Peter Gleick, *Implementing the Human Right to Water, in* The Human Right to Water 143, 146 (Eibe H. Riedel & Peter Rothen eds., Berliner Wissenschafts-Verlag 2006).

252 Damon Barrett & Vinodh Jaichand, *The Right to Water, Privatized Water and Access to Justice: Tackling United Kingdom Water Companies' Practices in Developing Countries*, 23(3) South African Journal on Human Rights. 543, 561 (2007).

253 Leila M. Harris, Lucy Rodina & Cynthia Morinville, *Revisiting the Human Right to Water from an Environmental Justice Lens,* 3(4) Politics, Groups, and Identities. 660–665 (2015).

254 Cecilia Tortajada & Asit K. Biswas, *Water as a Human Right*, 33(4) International Journal of Water Resources Development, 509, 510 (2017).

255 Langford, *supra* note 1010, at 280; Erik Gawel & Wolfgang Bretschneider, *Specification of a Human Right to Water: A Sustainability Assessment of Access Hurdles*, 42(5) Water International 505, 505–506 (2017).

256 Christopher Jeffords & Farhed Shah, *On the Natural and Economic Difficulties to Fulfilling the Human Right to Water Within a Neoclassical Economics Framework*, 71(1) Review of Social Economy. 65, 88 (2013).

257 Norbert Brunner et al., *The Human Right to Water in Law and Implementation*, 4(3) Laws. 413, 413 (2015).

258 Pardy, *supra* note 941, at 908.

sufficient attention.[259] Other studies have shown that even when funding is available and proper infrastructure is built, factors such as having clean and adequate toilets affect citizens' access, particularly women.[260]

To their credit, many proponents have begun suggesting a shift in the focus to national courts that are perceived as institutions that can protect this right.[261] Still, achieving it is not that simple. Even if many states have taken steps to implement it through national legislation, shortfalls persist.[262] There is an assumption that somehow recognizing its existence by a state can immediately lead to satisfying the needs of the population lacking water without considering the capabilities of that nation.[263] Such acknowledgment cannot lead to substantial changes without having the means to implement it or to provide ways to deal with breaches that occur. This right must be executed at the national and domestic levels where state consent and capacity determine whether this is possible. Despite its presence in several constitutions, it is still not clear how it has altered the obligations of governments. Problems related to access to water in developing countries were not solved just because of the adoption of HRWS. In the South, issues related to the quality of water persist. All the while, efforts to ensure access to quality water continue.[264] Indeed, there are plenty of practical matters that face its effective implementation, including legal and political ambiguities as well as insufficient human and financial resources.[265]

Each body of the legal system's structure plays an important role in complicating or facilitating the implementation of the HRWS.[266] Regimes and doctrines must be adjusted to take this right into consideration. Meanwhile, the question of water privatization remains far from a solid solution.[267] States are using several elements that were mentioned in GC 15 or that are included in IHRL as an excuse to reduce the pressure of the international community for the realization of their obligations. For instance, the fact that they must fulfill this right in accordance with their available financial resources does not

259 Asit K. Biswas, *Water as a Human Right in the MENA Region: Challenges and Opportunities*, 23(2) International Journal of Water Resources Development, 209, 215 (2007).

260 Édila Dalmaso Coswosk et al., *Having a Toilet is not Enough: The Limitations in Fulfilling the Human Rights to Water and Sanitation in a Municipal School in Bahia, Brazil*, 19(137) BMC Public Health. 1, 1–5 (2019).

261 M. Belén Olmos Giupponi & Martha C. Paz, *The Implementation of the Human Right to Water in Argentina and Colombia*, 15(1) Anuario Mexicano de Derecho Internacional. 323, 350–351 (2015).

262 Thielbörger, *supra* note 1117, at 40.

263 McCaffrey, *supra* note 947, at 230.

264 Kirsten Snell, *Can Water Be a Human Right?*, 19(1) Appeal: Review of Current Law and Law Reform. 131, 132–139 (2014).

265 Kirchner, *supra* note 986, at 478–480.

266 Rhett B. Larson, *The New Right in Water*, 70 (4) Washington and Lee Review. 2181, 2209–2230 (2013).

267 Howard, *supra* note 916, at 124.

take into consideration their priorities.[268] According to the Organization for Economic Cooperation and Development, seven categories affect a state's ability when it comes to HRWS implementation. These are (1) administrative, (2) policy, (3) information, (4) capacity, (5) funding, (6) objective, and (7) accountability.[269] This is why suggestions to strengthen realization are made, such as increasing awareness of the different domestic stakeholders of state obligations and the promotion of constructive dialogue between governments and civil society organizations.[270] Hence, there are many challenges and factors that must be considered if a human rights approach is used for the classification of TBAs. Previous research on the HRWS must be taken as a basis[271] especially the work of experts with practical expertise[272] to strike a balance between different competing values, mainly the use of groundwater for satisfying human needs and its protection as part of an ecosystem.

Water as a Quasi-Commodity: A Compromise Between Two Ideological Approaches

The debate concerning whether water should be classified as a private or a public good is far from over. The constant increase in the need for this resource fuels this discussion.[273] It has a value that cannot be monetarily quantified since it is absolutely necessary for well-being and health.[274] Its management requires collaborative solutions where regulations play a vital role in preventing its depletion.[275] Water for drinking and sanitation is important, but it is not the only matter being examined in this context. Numerous other uses are being impacted, such as its use for food production, its role in megacities, and flood management.[276] These issues go beyond its classic consideration

268 Salman M.A. Salman, *The Human Right to Water and Sanitation: Is the Obligation Deliverable?*, 39(7) Water International. 969, 977 (2014);

269 org. For econ. cooperation and dev., *Water and Sustainable Development – from Vision to Action: Governance Challenges and Suggested Tools for the Implementation of the Water-Related Sustainable Development Goals*, 1–3 (2015).

270 Louisa Gosling et al., *Analysis of Experience Using Human Rights to Accelerate WASH Access in Four Countries*, 5(2) H2 Open Journal. 234, 234–236 (2022).

271 Christopher Michael Faulkner et al., *The Human Right to Water and Sanitation: Using Natural Language Processing to Uncover Patterns in Academic Publishing*, 13 Water. 1, 1–5 (2021).

272 See, for instance, the most recent work of the previous special rapporteur Leo Heller, "The Human Rights to Water and Sanitation" (Cambridge University Press 2022).

273 Cory Fletcher, Anja van Heelsum, & Conny Roggeband, *Water Privatization, Hegemony, and Civil Society: What Motivates Individuals to Protest about Water Privatization?*, 14(3) Journal of Civil Society. 241, 241 (2018).

274 Savenije, *supra* note 951, at 743.

275 Philip Mader, *Attempting the Production of Public Goods through Microfinance: The Case of Water and Sanitation*, 25(1) Economic Research-Ekonomska Istraživanja. 190, 197 (2012).

276 Savenije, *supra* note 951, at 744.

as an economic and a public good, or a human right. In fact, this resource is unique, which prohibits the use of market concepts and theories for its management.[277] It has more value than diamonds and even air.[278] Therefore, it encompasses elements beyond its economic nature, including cultural and emotional ones.[279]

Despite the focus on water as a commodity, classifying it as such will lead to a situation where the poor will not have access to it. Considering the latter a human right will result in a similar situation.[280] Analysis conducted on data from several countries shows that access to water for the poor has improved when related to the HRWS. Other states witnessed little progress, while some without formal recognition of this right have shown significant increases in the percentage of the population having access to water. The analysis highlighted the ineffectiveness of this right in nations suffering from bad governance practices.[281] Considering water a commodity has worked in several developed and developing countries. The UK, Singapore, and the Philippines are good examples here.[282] It has failed to reach its stated objectives in other places.[283] Perhaps, given this reality, it is time to look at both approaches differently.[284] The discussion over its classification should not be the main concern. What is crucial is whether access to water of high quality can be provided to citizens without interruption. This task cannot be solved by simply considering it a human right, a public good, or a commodity.[285]

Recognizing the existing risks associated with the classification of water and acknowledging the failure of the public sector to deliver it efficiently, semi-privatization was proposed as a compromise.[286] As such, one would wonder whether this resource can be considered a proponent of human rights and a commodity at the same time. Can the existence of different legal regimes (human rights and international economic law) strengthen the efforts made for

277 *Id.* at 744.

278 *Note, What Price for the Priceless?: Implementing the Justiciability of the Right*, 120(4) Harvard Law Review, 1067, 1068 (2007).

279 United Nations Educational Scientific and Cultural Organization (UNESCO) – *World Water Assessment Program (WWAP) (2006) Water, a Shared Responsibility*, 403–405 (The United Nations World Water Report 2. Paris and New York: UNESCO and Berghahn Books).

280 P. B. Anand, *Right to Water and Access to Water: An Assessment*, 19(4) Journal of International Development. 511, 520 (2007).

281 *Id.* at 524.

282 Gunawansa & Hoque, *supra* note 907, at 16.

283 *Id.*

284 David Zetland, The End of Abundance: Economic Solutions to Water Scarcity 81 (Aguanomics Press 2011).

285 David B. Brooks, *Human Rights to Water in North Africa and the Middle East: What is New and What is Not; What is Important and What is Not*, 23(2) International Journal of Water Resources Development. 227, 230 (2007).

286 Jernej Letnar Cernic, *Corporate Obligations under the Human Right to Water*, 39(2) Denver Journal of International Law and Policy. 303, 306 (2011).

ensuring access to and protection of freshwater simultaneously?[287] One cannot deny the economic value of this resource since it has a cost. Yet, it cannot be defined using the traditional definition of a commodity.[288] It is considered a quasi-commodity because of its role in satisfying basic human needs, environmental maintenance, and economic development.[289] In that sense, consumers of freshwater shall be treated as customers rather than citizens.[290] Once water is conceived as a quasi-commodity, there will be a need for a reevaluation of the relationship between the environment and those who utilize it.[291] Under such a system, water is seen as a specific type of public good where the rules of the free market economy partially apply.[292]

Some argue that water is an economic good and a human right. Here, the state has the role of regulating the activities of the private sector that are responsible for providing water of high quality. Scholars maintain that such provision does not exempt the country from its obligations in protecting the HRWS. The government must regulate the provision of water services through agreements with the private sector. This is especially true where human rights norms are considered. Such a role falls under the duty to protect, as states must prevent third parties from affecting the provision of safe and acceptable water, among many other things.[293] To ensure that this resource is not merely a commodity, companies that take charge or are given authorization from the state to supply it are expected to comply with regulations guaranteeing that these corporations respect and implement human rights requirements.[294] In this case, the responsibility to protect includes the monitoring and penalization of violators.[295]

When a state regulates the water system, even if it is being supplied by a private company, the question of whether this resource is a human right or a

287 Marie Cuq, *Water: Human Right or Commodity? Reflections on the Effectiveness of a Human Right to Water*, 1–10 (Human Rights Abuses in the Contemporary World: Legal approaches 6. – 9. September 2011; Human Rights and a Globalized Economy – Areas of conflict?).

288 A commodity can be defined as "a standardized good or service, with interchangeable units, sold at a price determined through market exchange". KAREN BAKKER, *Neoliberalizing Nature? Market Environmentalism in Water Supply in England and Wales*, in NEOLIBERAL ENVIRONMENTS: FALSE PROMISES AND UNNATURAL CONSEQUENCES 101, 107 (Nik Heynen, James McCarthy, Scott Prudham & Paul Robbins eds., Routledge 2007).

289 Douglas Donoho, *Some Critical Thinking about a Human Right to Water*, 19 ILSA JOURNAL OF INTERNATIONAL & COMPARATIVE LAW. 91, 112 (2012).

290 KAREN BAKKER, *The Business of Water*, *in* THE OXFORD HANDBOOK OF WATER POLITICS AND POLICY 407, 415 (Ken Conca & Erika Weinthal eds., Oxford University Press 2018).

291 KAREN BAKKER, PRIVATIZING WATER: GOVERNANCE FAILURE AND THE WORLD'S URBAN WATER CRISIS 37–38 (Cornell University Press 2010).

292 DAVID MCDONALD & GREG RUITERS, THE AGE OF COMMODITY: WATER PRIVATIZATION IN SOUTHERN AFRICA 20 (EarthScan 2005).

293 Khulekani Moyo, *Privatization of the Commons: Water as a Right; Water as a Commodity*, 22(3) STELLENBOSCH LAW REVIEW. 804, 815 (2011).

294 Howard, *supra* note 916, 138.

295 *Id.* at 483.

commodity is irrelevant. This is the case because the government decides the degree to which water is classified as such, as water is no longer subject to market forces.[296] This approach addresses many of the shortcomings of classifying it as a private good. This includes the inability of the private sector to supply poor communities or citizens. The state can set the degree to which water is a human right and provide subsidies to these companies.[297] The combination of effective government regulations with the privatization of water services can balance the need for a sustainable supply.[298] This proposal is an opportunity to reconcile both approaches. Considering the end goal, which is the provision of access to high-quality water for citizens, this seems to satisfy those ends.[299] The efficiency of the private sector is used to the benefit of society through proper regulations that tackle the negative consequences of classifying water only as a commodity.[300]

The existence of general obligations under the HRW to respect, protect, and fulfill has been interpreted as indirectly providing a door for private sector involvement given the need of the states to satisfy these obligations. Paragraph 27 of GC 15 explicitly makes reference to third parties while stating that equity must apply when fees are paid in exchange for water services, regardless of the party providing it, considering disadvantaged groups.[301] Paragraph 41 of the GA expressly provides room for the private sector in case of state incapacity to fulfill its obligations.[302] Paragraph 50 obliges the adoption of rules for the implementation of the HRW while collaborating with many stakeholders, including the private sector.[303] Moreover, Clause 7 of Resolution 15/9 concerning the HRWS adopted by the HRC in 2010 acknowledges states' right to allow non-state actors the provision of water services on the basis of transparency, non-discrimination, and accountability.[304]

Implications of Considering Water a Quasi-Commodity for TBAs

The problems of water management at the national and international levels are not going to be solved by declaring water a human right. The issue is, rather,

296 Brooks, *supra* note 1154, at 230.

297 Diana Mitlin & Anna Walnycki, *Informality as Experimentation: Water Utilities Strategies for Cost Recovery and Their Consequences for Universal Access*, 56(2) The Journal of Development Studies. 259, 259–277 (2019).

298 Naren Prasad, *Privatization of Water: A Historical Perspective*, 3(2) Law, Environment and Development Journal. 217, 233 (2007).

299 Brooks, *supra* note 1154, at 230.

300 Naren Prasad, *Social Policies and Water Sector Reform*, 21 (United Nations Research Institute for Social Development (UNRISD) Program Paper, September 2007).

301 General Comment 15, *supra* note 472, at Paragraph 27.

302 *Id.* at Paragraph 41.

303 *Id.* at Paragraph 50.

304 Resolution 15/9, *supra* note 1067, at 3.

one of bad governance.[305] In the transboundary context, this is often the result of ineffective and inefficient unilateral actions. In many instances, this harms other nations and creates tensions.[306] This situation has begun to shift as countries are increasingly acknowledging the benefits of cooperation. This is due to the negative consequences of individual measures that emerged over time.[307] These are some of the problems associated with the management of shared freshwaters. Addressing the specifics of aquifers is much more difficult.[308] The discussion of whether this resource constitutes a human right or a private good cannot be separated from the debate related to their governance.[309] There is an extremely long list of questions that requires answers beyond the ideological dilemmas,[310] as the value of this resource cannot be the main subject.[311] Perhaps instead, it is better to discuss mutual interests of nations: protection and sustainable use of freshwaters, including shared aquifers.[312]

The nature of this resource is closer to the classification of a global public good rather than a human right or private good, given the need to consider the interests of other nations while ensuring its efficient and sustainable use.[313] This approach has been criticized by opponents of this classification.[314] They question the ability of international frameworks to protect and deal with such global public goods and whether such a strategy will actually lead to the claimed benefits.[315] In that sense, how can water be considered a global public good when negative consequences are witnessed at the regional and local level[316], and where nations have different levels of knowledge and institutional

305 Arjun Kumar Khadka, *The Emergence of Water as a 'Human Right' on the World Stage: Challenges and Opportunities*, 26(1) International Journal of Water Resources Development. 37, 49 (2010); Larry Swatuk, Meghan McMorris, Charmaine Leung & Yuyan Zu, *Seeing "Invisible Water": Challenging Conceptions of Water for Agriculture, Food, and Human Security*, 36(1) Canadian Journal of Development Studies. 24, 24 (2015).

306 Erik Mostert, *Conflict and Co-operation in International Freshwater Management: A Global Review*, 1(3) International Journal of River Basin Management. 267–278 (2003).

307 *Id.*

308 Howard et al., *supra* note 1097, at 4; Quevauviller, *supra* note 1101, at 4.

309 Linton & Brooks, *supra* note 23, at 606–618; Gorelick & Zheng, *supra* note 896, at 3031–3051.

310 Neelke Doorn, *Water and Justice: Towards an Ethics of Water Governance*, 5(1) Public Reason. 97, 103 (2013).

311 *Id.* at 98.

312 Monika Ambrus, Herman Kasper Gilissen & Jasper J.H. van Kempen, *Public Values in Water Law: A Case of Substantive Fragmentation?* 10(2) Utrecht Law Review. 8, 12 (2014).

313 Daniel Augenstein, *To Whom It May Concern: International Human Rights Law and Global Public Goods*, 21 (Berlin Social Science Center, SP IV 2015-809, October 2015).

314 Gonzalo Aguilar Cavallo, *The Human Right to Water and Sanitation: Going Beyond Corporate Social Responsibility*, 29(76) Utrecht Journal of International and European Law. 39, 64 (2013).

315 *Keeping Up with the Fashion: Human Rights and Global Public Goods*, 16 International Journal on Minority and Group Rights. 165, 176–179 (2009).

316 Newig & Challies, *supra* note 599, at 446.

capacity[317] while many possess weak and poor legal frameworks.[318] In fact, the complex nature of shared groundwater, where several authorities have to agree on a common management strategy[319] does not leave much space for any other approach. Only through a global perspective can good governance occur,[320] as the number of TBAs increase.[321] Complex management structures that consider their unique specificities are needed.[322] Whatever regime is enacted must to be tailored to the particular circumstances of each aquifer, given the different circumstances and geopolitical situations.[323]

This reality has been widely recognized. A global regime for the governance of TBAs has been emerging for quite some time to ensure the sustainable use of groundwater resources[324] in the general context of promoting sustainable development. International intervention is seen as a way to improve the management of shared water resources and support governments in reaching their objectives.[325] Several factors must be considered. The latter is not related to the legal classification of TBAs, in particular, whether its governance should take a human right or a private good approach. They include, inter alia: the sharing of benefits between states; the need to protect the ecosystem; tackling the different competing water needs; enhancing integrated water resources management; and developing the knowledge for proper governance and conflict avoidance.[326]

As one can notice, ensuring access to water is one of the many components of this resource's sustainable management. However, it is not the only one as other factors are equally important.[327] One may wonder whether a global regime for the governance of TBAs can navigate the different legal classifications that were given to freshwater resources, including the HRWS. So far, this book has provided the legal basis for the management of shared aquifers and highlighted the various categorizations that can apply to them. The following chapter will examine the interplay between IWL and IHRL considering TBAs. It will also assess the extra-territorial application of the HRWS.

317 Puri, Aureli & Stephan, *supra* note 880, at 3.

318 Alice Aureli, *The UNESCO IHP's Shared Aquifer Resources Management Global Project*, AQUAmundi. 1, 2 (2010).

319 Marwan Haddad, Eran Feitelson & Shaul Arlosoroff, *The Management of Shared Aquifers: Principles and Challenges*, in Management of Shared Groundwater Resources: The Israeli-Palestinian Case with an International Perspective 3, 21–22 (Eran Feitelson & Marwan Haddad eds., Springer 2001).

320 Newig & Challies, *supra* note 599, at 446.

321 Nanda & Pring, *supra* note 478, at 325.

322 E. Feitelson, *The Upcoming Challenge: Transboundary Management of the Hydraulic Cycle*, 123 Water, Air, and Soil Pollution. 533, 534–535 (2000).

323 Lopez-Gunn, *supra* note 891, at 48.

324 Conti & Gupta, *supra* note 375, at 849–850.

325 Anton Earle & Marian J. Neal, *Inclusive Transboundary Water Governance*, in Freshwater Governance for the 21st Century 145, 156 (Eiman Karar ed., Springer 2017).

326 P. K. Parhi & R. N. Sankhua, *Beyond the Transboundary River: Issues of Riparian Responsibilities*, 94(4) Journal of the Institution of Engineers (India): Series A. 257, 257–258 (2014).

327 *Id.*

5 The Interplay Between International Water Law and Human Rights Agreements

Transboundary freshwaters, including groundwaters in particular, are necessary to satisfy basic human needs. States sharing them, however, are experiencing difficulties meeting growing demands. This is making it harder to consider the interests of other nations.[1] This is the main dilemma in water governance. IWL and human rights agreements have been the largest proponents of these developments. Here, the focus remains on regulating shared freshwaters or ensuring access to water and sanitation in the transboundary context.[2] This chapter will examine the interplay between these legal regimes to study whether synergies can be established. If so, is there room for harmonization, or is it better to keep these frameworks independent? It is important to mention here that an analysis concerning the broad issue of human rights is beyond the scope of this book. Instead, it focuses on the interplay between IWL and the HRWS. It is worth noting the existence of an entire body of literature that addresses a wide range of aspects related to IHRL considering legal and philosophical approaches. These pieces can aid in addressing the interplay between human rights and other fields that question this concept and its relevance.[3]

1 See, for instance, Knut Bourquain, Freshwater Access from a Human Rights Perspective: A Challenge to International Water and Human Rights Law 48–49 (Brill / Nijhoff 2008).

2 See Anna FS Russell, *The Human Right to Water in a Transboundary Context, in* Research Handbook on International Water Law 255, 255–270 (Stephen C. McCaffrey, Christina Leb & Riley T.Denoon eds., Edward Elgar Publishing 2019).

3 Fernando Suárez Müller, *The Hierarchy of Human Rights and the Transcendental System of Right*, 20 Human Rights Review. 47, 47–66 (2019); Steven Wheatley, The Idea of International Human Rights Law (Oxford University Press 2019); Mark Lattimer, *Two Concepts of Human Rights*, 40(2) Human Rights Quarterly. 406, 406–419 (2018); Pablo Gilabert, Human Dignity and Human Rights (Oxford University Press 2018); Pavel Ondřejek, *A Structural Approach to the Effects of Fundamental Rights on Legal Transactions in Private Law*, 13(2) European Constitutional Law Review. 281, 281–304 (2017); Jane Kotzmann & Cassandra Seery, *Dignity in International Human Rights Law: Potential Applicability in Relation to International Recognition of Animal Rights*, 26(1) Michigan State International Law Review. 1, 1–42 (2017); Hurst Hannum, *Reinvigorating Human Rights for the Twenty-First Century*, 16(3) Human Rights Law Review. 409, 409–451 (2016); Laksshini Sundaramoorthy, *Is the*

DOI: 10.4324/9781003537724-6

The Extraterritorial Nature of Human Rights Obligations

Human rights have created a vertical relationship between states and individuals. The objective is to protect the population of a particular nation. It is now, however, beginning to develop a horizontal connection. This is due to the existence of extraterritorial obligations of one state towards the citizens of another.[4] Owing to a variety of factors, some countries have not been able to fulfill human rights commitments. Meanwhile, global organizations have intervened to fill the gaps where necessary to satisfy existing duties. States may be affected by the actions of other nations who act outside of their boundaries,[5] or impact the territory of different countries by causing harm.[6] Here, the concept of extraterritorial obligations emerged. Within this, several terminologies were used to refer to the same notion of international responsibilities,[7] including those related to protecting individuals and groups located beyond a state's jurisdiction.[8]

Extraterritorial obligations can be defined as duties of states to act or refrain from acting within or outside their territory, which impacts human

Idea of Human Rights a Universal Concept?, 2 MERICI. 23, 23–29 (2016); ANDREW CLAPHAM, HUMAN RIGHTS: A VERY SHORT INTRODUCTION (2d ed. Oxford University Press 2015); Julio César Montero, *Human Rights, International Human Rights, and Sovereign Political Authority: A Draft Model for Understanding Contemporary Human Rights*, 7(4) ETHICS & GLOBAL POLITICS. 143, 143–162 (2014); PETER DE BOLLA, THE ARCHITECTURE OF CONCEPTS: THE HISTORICAL FORMATION OF HUMAN RIGHTS (Fordham University Press 2013); MICHAEL FREEMAN, HUMAN RIGHTS: AN INTERDISCIPLINARY APPROACH (Polity Press 2011); JOHANNES MORSINK, INHERENT HUMAN RIGHTS: PHILOSOPHICAL ROOTS OF THE UNIVERSAL DECLARATION (University of Pennsylvania Press 2009); Gianluigi Palombella, *From Human Rights to Fundamental Rights: Consequences of a Conceptual Distinction*, 93(3) ARCHIVES FOR PHILOSOPHY OF LAW AND SOCIAL PHILOSOPHY. 396, 396–426 (2007); ARVIND SHARMA, ARE HUMAN RIGHTS WESTERN?: A CONTRIBUTION TO THE DIALOGUE OF CIVILIZATIONS (Oxford University Press 2006); JACK DONNELLY, UNIVERSAL HUMAN RIGHTS IN THEORY AND PRACTICE (Cornell University Press 2003); BRIAN OREND, HUMAN RIGHTS: CONCEPT AND CONTEXT (Broadview Press 2002); JANUSZ SYMONIDES, HUMAN RIGHTS: CONCEPT AND STANDARDS (Ashgate 2000); Sompong Sucharitkul, *Multi-Dimensional Concept of Human Rights in International Law*, 62(3) NOTRE DAME LAW REVIEW. 305, 305–317 (1987); JAMES W. NICKEL, MAKING SENSE OF HUMAN RIGHTS: PHILOSOPHICAL REFLECTIONS ON THE UNIVERSAL DECLARATION OF HUMAN RIGHTS (University of California Press 1987).

4 Chavarro, *supra* note 1058, at 92.

5 Wouter Vandenhole, *Beyond Territoriality: The Maastricht Principles on Extra-Territorial Obligations in the Area of Economic, Social, and Cultural Rights*, 29(4) NETHERLANDS QUARTERLY OF HUMAN RIGHTS. 429, 430 (2011).

6 John H. Knox, *Climate Change and Human Rights Law*, 50(1) VIRGINIA JOURNAL OF INTERNATIONAL LAW. 163, 200 (2009–2010).

7 ROLF KUNNEMANN & SANDRA RATJEN, *Extraterritorial Obligations: A Response to Globalization*, in GLOBAL OBLIGATIONS FOR THE RIGHT TO FOOD 33, 38 (George Kent ed., Rowman & Littlefield Publishers, 2008).

8 Leb, *supra* note 1070, at 644.

rights beyond its jurisdictions.[9] These are conceived as responsibilities towards the international community, focusing on the protection of noncitizens,[10] and holding actors at the global level accountable.[11] The term acknowledges that the relationship between a country and noncitizens located outside its territory is not the same as the one with the population and migrants subject to its rules.[12] Nations have negative duties that may prevent them from violating the rights of individuals directly. They also possess positive ones related to the realization of ESC rights.[13] Other positive responsibilities stem from the extraterritorial application of human rights, such as assistance and cooperation. Many theorists argue that negative commitments are better established at the international level than positive ones.[14] It seems that there is an emerging consensus over the existence of a customary negative extraterritorial obligation. The latter is imposed on all nations and promotes the protection of ESC rights. This is applicable to state actions that have an impact outside their territory. It is difficult to confirm the existence of a similar positive duty given the absence of a consensus on what establishes this when states have the capacity to assist.[15] Cooperation aiming towards the realization of basic human rights can be found in Article 1(3) of the UN Charter.[16] Articles 55 and 56 state that

9 Cedric Ryngaert, *EU Trade Agreements and Human Rights: From Extraterritorial to Territorial Obligations*, 20(3–4) International Community Law Review. 374, 378 (2018).

10 María José Añón, *Human Rights Obligations, Especially in Times of Crisis*, 17 The Age of Human Rights Journal. 1, 1–20 (2021).

11 Elena Pribytkova, *What Global Human Rights Obligations Do We Have?*, 20(2) Chicago Journal of International Law. 384, 386 (2020).

12 Kunnemann & Ratjen, *supra* note 1203, at 38.

13 Fons Coomans, *The Extraterritorial Scope of the International Covenant on Economic, Social, and Cultural Rights in the Work of the United Nations Committee on Economic, Social, and Cultural Rights*, 11(1) Human Rights Law Review. 1, 6 (2011).

14 Tahmina Karimova, Human Rights and Development in International Law 151 (Routledge 2016).

15 Malcolm Langford, Fons Coomans & Felipe Gomez Isa, *Extraterritorial Duties in International Law*, in Global Justice, State Duties: The Extraterritorial Scope of Economic, Social, and Cultural Rights in International Law 51, 73 (Malcolm Langford et al. eds., Cambridge University Press 2013); Conall Mallory, Human Rights Imperialists: The Extraterritorial Application of the European Convention on Human Rights 207 (Hart Publishing 2020).

16 According to this provision, the objective of the UN is solving international problems of different nature, promoting and enhancing the respect of human rights and fundamental freedoms without discrimination. United Nations Charter, Chapter I: Purposes and Principles, Article 1(3), available at https://www.un.org/en/about-us/un-charter/chapter-1 (last accessed 3 August 2022).

nations must take actions for their protection.[17] The importance of cooperation was also mentioned, for instance in the UDHR in Articles 22 and 28.[18]

The extraterritorial application of human rights treaties has been widely discussed in the literature[19] where scholars have argued for and against it.[20] This debate has not been resolved,[21] and has gained new importance in the wake of Covid-19, where it was argued that states have an extraterritorial duty to tackle the pandemic,[22] and ensure the realization of the right to health.[23] Still, the interpretation of various provisions within human rights treaties such as the ICESCR and ICCPR with regards to this concept remains subject to

17 Chavarro, *supra* note 1058, at 92. These rights include, for instance "higher standards of living, full employment, and conditions of economic and social progress and development" in accordance with Article 55. Meanwhile, nations, based on provision 56, are expected to take joint or unilateral actions to realize them. *Id.* at Articles 55 & 56, available at https://www.un.org/en/about-us/un-charter/chapter-9 (last accessed 3 August 2022).

18 *Id.* at 91. Article 22 calls for international cooperation for the realization of the right to social security considering the resources of the UN and the state, as well as all the rights related to ensuring the dignity and well-development of a citizen's personality. Article 28 discusses the social and international order needed to protect the rights and freedoms established in the Declaration. UDHR, *supra* note 984, at Articles 22 & 28.

19 See, for instance, MARCO MILANOVIC, EXTRATERRITORIAL APPLICATION OF HUMAN RIGHTS TREATIES: LAW, PRINCIPLES, AND POLICY (Oxford University Press, 2011); Ralph Wilde, *Human Rights Beyond Borders at the World Court: The Significance of the International Court of Justice's Jurisprudence on the Extraterritorial Application of International Human Rights Law Treaties*, 12(4) CHINESE JOURNAL OF INTERNATIONAL LAW. 639–677 (2013); Sinchak, *supra* note 39, at 416–445; Hugh King, *The Extraterritorial Human Rights Obligations of States*, 9(4) HUMAN RIGHTS LAW REVIEW. 521, 521–556 (2009).

20 Todd Howland, *The Multi-State Responsibility for Extraterritorial Violations of Economic, Social, And Cultural Rights*, 35(3/4) DENVER JOURNAL OF INTERNATIONAL LAW & POLICY. 389, 402–403 (2007). See, for instance, MALLORY, *supra* note 1211.

21 Daniel Augenstein D & David Kinley, *When Human Rights 'Responsibilities' Become 'Duties': The Extraterritorial Obligations of States that Bind Corporations*, in HUMAN RIGHTS OBLIGATIONS OF BUSINESS – BEYOND THE CORPORATE RESPONSIBILITY TO RESPECT? 271, 271–294 (Surya Deva & David Bilchitz eds., Cambridge University Press 2013); Chiara Macchi, *The Transnational Dimension of International Organizations' Duty of Care Towards Their Civilian Personnel: Lessons from the Case Law on States' Extraterritorial Human Rights Obligations*, in THE DUTY OF CARE OF INTERNATIONAL ORGANIZATIONS TOWARDS THEIR CIVILIAN PERSONNEL 433, 433–456 (Andrea de Guttry, Micaela Frulli, Edoardo Greppi & Chiara Macchi eds., Springer, 2018).

22 Fons Coomans, *Responding to COVID-19: The Extraterritorial Human Rights Obligations* (Global Campus of Human Rights; 17/08/2020), available at https://gchumanrights.org/preparedness/article-on/responding-to-covid-19-the-extraterritorial-human-rights-obligations-perspective.html (last accessed 3 August 2022).

23 Benjamin Mason Meier, Judith Bueno de Mesquita & Caitlin R. Williams, *Global Obligations to Ensure the Right to Health: Strengthening Global Health Governance to Realize Human Rights in Global Health*, YEARBOOK OF INTERNATIONAL DISASTER LAW ONLINE, 3, 3-10 (2020).

controversy,[24] as the implementation of this notion remains unclear.[25] The dilemma revolves around how to create a balance between the meaningful use of extraterritoriality without creating further burdens.[26] The discussion occurred with the objective of preventing violations of human rights by individuals and corporations located in a nation's territory and impacting the rights of individuals elsewhere. Some authors claim that such an argument does not mean an endorsement of the concept of extraterritorial obligations of states.[27] Others have voiced their concerns. Gibney, for example believes that the term will be divided into extra and territorial. He argues that this will limit the interpretation of states' human rights obligations.[28]

The ICCPR, the ICESCR, and many other human rights treaties are comprised of extraterritorial obligations.[29] As water is covered within the covenant on ESC rights, the latter is examined in the following paragraphs. The ICESCR has provisions where international cooperation is required for the realization of these rights. The objective is to ensure that states with insufficient resources can seek help from other nations.[30] International human rights obligations are based on Article 2(1) of this covenant, declaring that nations must act either individually or jointly within the general framework of cooperation and assistance according to their own ability and resources. The objective is to realize the rights within the covenant using adequate means, especially legislations.[31] Accordingly, states have a duty to take all steps to ensure that citizens within their territory enjoy these rights, even if that means seeking assistance from

24 Simon Mateus, *Investigating the Extraterritorial Application of the International Covenant on Civil and Political Rights as well as the International Covenant on Economic, Social, and Cultural Rights*, 54(1) De Jure Law Journal, 70, 70–82 (2021).

25 Patricia Rinwigati Waagstein, *Justifying Extraterritorial Regulations of Home Country on Business And Human Rights*, 16 (3) Indonesian Journal of International Law. 361, 361–362 (2019).

26 Lea Raible, *Between Facts and Principles: Jurisdiction in International Human Rights Law*, 13(1) Jurisprudence. 52, 59 (2021).

27 Augenstein & Kinley, *supra* note 1217, at 271, 273–291; Khulekani Moyo, *Forced Evictions in Zimbabwe (African Commission on Human and People's Rights)*, in Litigating Transnational Human Rights Obligations: Alternative Judgments 261, 263 (Mark Gibney & Wouter Vandenhole eds., Routledge 2013).

28 Mark Gibney, *On Terminology: Extraterritorial Obligations*, in Global Justice, State Duties: The Extraterritorial Scope of Economic, Social, and Cultural Rights in International Law 32, 41 (Malcolm Langford, Wouter Vandenhole, Martin Scheinin, Willem van Genugten eds., Cambridge University Press 2013).

29 In this case, the ICJ decided that Israel violated international obligations. Therefore, it must stop building the wall, destroy the parts built in the Palestinian territory, and eliminate all the rules adopted and associated with these operations. International Court of Justice, Legal Consequences of the Construction of a Wall in the Occupied Palestinian Territory, available at https://www.icj-cij.org/en/case/131 (last accessed 3 August 2022); Leb, *supra* note 1070, at 644.

30 Chavarro, *supra* note 1058, at 93.

31 ICESCR, *supra* note 218, at Article 2(1).

other nations. There are also claims that a nation's agreement to the receipt of support means committing to help when it is needed elsewhere. This is classified as an implicit obligation.[32] States also must support the realization of human rights outside their territories. They accomplish this by providing international assistance and cooperating with nations that lack the ability to fulfill the ESC rights of their citizens.[33] The wording of this provision is vague and does not clarify the nature of the duties. However, there is a consensus that states must not commit any harm.[34]

The CESCR has indicated the potential impact of the covenant beyond the borders of a particular state. Over time, different instruments have cautiously been developed to cover this concept.[35] Based on Article 2(1) ICESCR, one can notice that there is no territorial limitation for the application of the treaty. This is why it has been stated that its drafters intended for it to have an extra-territorial effect. The idea is supported by the wording of other provisions such as Articles 11(2) and 23. Their focus emphasizes the importance of international cooperation for the realization of ESC rights.[36] The extraterritorial reach of the covenant was first introduced in GA 3, where the nature of State Parties' obligations based on Article 2(1) was examined. This resulted in the identification of positive and negative extraterritorial duties. It clearly stated that resources provided by the international community through cooperation and assistance are within the scope of Article 2(1) ICESCR.[37] According to the committee, global collaboration is a duty upon all governments, especially for the achievement of the different ESC rights.[38] It recognized the existence of extraterritorial obligations and confirmed the importance of acknowledging them by different nations.[39] Recognition was necessary since underdeveloped countries cannot ensure the domestic realization of human rights without international assistance.[40] In fact, the committee expressly mentioned the existence of an extraterritorial obligation to respect, protect, and fulfill. States are expected to not take actions affecting the enjoyment of covenant rights of

32 Leb, *supra* note 1070, at 644–645.
33 Brown & Heller, *supra* note 48, at 2249.
34 Saul, Kinley & Mowbray, *supra* note 31, at 993.
35 Coomans, *supra* note 1209, at 4.
36 *Id.* at 7–8. Article 11(2) mentions the right of all people to be free from hunger, where states have an obligation to take individual and joint measures via international cooperation comprising specific programs to achieve this objective. Article 23 states the international actions to be taken to implement the provisions of the covenant, including recommendations, technical assistance, and regional meetings. ICESCR, *supra* note 218, at Articles 11(2) & 23.
37 Office of the High Commissioner for Human Rights, CESCR General Comment No. 3: The Nature of States Parties' Obligations (Art. 2, Para. 1, of the Covenant). Adopted at the Fifth Session of the Committee on Economic, Social, and Cultural Rights, on 14 December 1990 (Contained in Document E/1991/23), General comment 3, p. 4; *Id.* at 33–34.
38 Greco, *supra* note 47, at 31. These are articles 11, 15, 22, and 23.
39 Chavarro, *supra* note 1058, at 95.
40 Gondek, *supra* note 39, at 301.

citizens outside their territories. They must also take measures to prevent and tackle violations beyond their jurisdiction, in particular by business entities. Finally, they should take collective actions to fulfill the ESC rights of individuals outside the territory.[41]

The existence of these duties has been confirmed by the ICJ. The court in 2004 issued an advisory opinion on the *Legal Consequences of the Construction of a Wall in the Occupied Palestinian Territory*, stating that both covenants apply to a state's acts beyond its territory. The court decided that Israel violated international obligations. Therefore, it must stop building the wall, destroy the parts built in the Palestinian territory, and eliminate all the rules adopted and associated with these operations.[42] Examples of rights that Israel violated include restricting access of Palestinian citizens to educational facilities and agricultural lands.[43] The court reached a similar conclusion with regards to the violation of human rights outside a state's territory in the case *Democratic Republic of Congo v Uganda*. The ICJ decided that Uganda, due to the presence of its troops in a foreign country, had a responsibility to preserve public order and safety in the occupied territory, which was not realized.[44]

The vague nature of ICESCR and the lack of clear definitions regarding its scope and aspects led to the adoption[45] of the Maastricht Principles on Extraterritorial Obligations of States in the Area of Economic, Social, and Cultural Rights in 2011.[46] These were the result of massive efforts put forth by numerous legal scholars and NGOs.[47] Initially, this resulted in the adoption of the 1986 Limburg Principles on the Implementation of the International Covenant on Economic, Social, and Cultural Rights,[48] and the 1997 Maastricht

41 United Nations Economic and Social Council, Committee on Economic, Social, and Cultural Rights, General Comment No. 24 (2017) on State obligations under the International Covenant on Economic, Social, and Cultural Rights in the context of Business Activities, 10 August 2017.

42 International Court of Justice, *supra* note 1225; Leb, *supra* note 1070, at 644.

43 Sarah Joseph, Blame it on the WTO? A Human Rights Critique 249–250 (Oxford University Press 2011).

44 International Court of Justice, Armed Activities on the Territory of the Congo (Democratic Republic of the Congo v. Uganda), available at https://www.icj-cij.org/en/case/116 (last accessed 3 August 2022).

45 Radhika Balakrishnan & James Heintz, *Extraterritorial Obligations, Financial Globalization and Macroeconomic Governance*, in Economic and Social Rights after the Global Financial Crisis 146, 150 (Aoife Nolan ed., Cambridge University Press 2014).

46 Maastricht Principles on Extraterritorial Obligations of States in the Area of Economic, Social, and Cultural Rights. Adopted on 28 September 2011.

47 Margot E. Salomon & Ian Seiderman, *Human Rights Norms for a Globalized World: The Maastricht Principles on Extraterritorial Obligations of States in the Area of Economic, Social, and Cultural Rights*, 3(4) Global Policy. 458, 458 (2012).

48 Limburg Principles on the Implementation of the International Covenant on Economic, Social, and Cultural Rights, adopted in 1986.

Guidelines on Violations of Economic, Social, and Cultural Rights.[49] These principles recognized the effects of government policies beyond states jurisdictions.[50] Therefore, they require nations to respect and safeguard human rights when acting outside their territories. They call for international cooperation and assistance based on international law applicable to ESC rights.[51] This instrument addresses various topics related to the scope of extraterritorial obligations of states; to respect, protect, and the one to fulfill. It also discusses accountability and remedies.[52]

The ICESCR is considered very important because of the efforts put into adopting it. It is expected to have a normative force[53] with regard to the establishment of economic strategies, the creation of legislation, the role of international organizations, and the activities of MNCs.[54] Further research is needed and indeed is already being conducted on the concept of extraterritorial application of human rights in the broader sense.[55] This is due to the many challenges facing its implementation mainly having the capacity to influence territories and citizens beyond a state's jurisdiction,[56] and the potential inability to affect those violating human rights.[57]

49 University of Minnesota, Human Rights Library, *Maastricht Guidelines on Violations of Economic, Social, and Cultural Rights*, Maastricht, January 22–26, 1997, available at http://hrlibrary.umn.edu/instree/Maastrichtguidelines_.html (last accessed 3 August 2022).

50 Balakrishnan & Heintz, *supra* note 1238, at 150.

51 Salomon & Seiderman, *supra* note 1243, at 458–459.

52 Maastricht Principles, *supra* note 1242, at 36.

53 Salomon & Seiderman, *supra* note 1243, at 459.

54 Balakrishnan & Heintz, *supra* note 1238, at 150.

55 See Mark Gibney et al. eds., The Routledge Handbook on Extraterritorial Human Rights Obligations (Routledge 2022); Arne Vandenbogaerde, *Extraterritorial Human Rights Obligations*, in Encyclopedia of Law and Development 84, 84–86 (Koen De Feyter, Gamze E. Türkelli, and Stéphanie de Moerloose eds., Edward Elgar Publishing 2021); Gamze Erdem Türkelli, *Extraterritorial Human Rights Obligations and Responsibility under International Law, in* The Routledge Handbook on Extraterritorial Human Rights Obligations (Mark Gibney et al., Routledge 2021); Maarten den Heijer & Rick Lawson, *Extraterritorial Human Rights and the Concept of 'Jurisdiction'*, in Global Justice, State Duties: The Extraterritorial Scope of Economic, Social, and Cultural Rights in International Law 153, 153–170 (Malcolm Langford et al. eds., Cambridge University Press 2013).

56 Sun Meng & Feng Tingting, *Extraterritorial Application of International Human Rights Conventions* (China Human Rights.CN, Mar. 6, 2022), available at http://www.chinahumanrights.org/html/2022/MAGAZINES_0306/17754.html (last accessed 3 August 2022).

57 Lea Raible, *Expanding Human Rights Obligations to Facilitate Climate Justice? A Note on Shortcomings and Risks* (EJIL: Talk!, Nov. 15, 2021), available at https://www.ejiltalk.org/expanding-human-rights-obligations-to-facilitate-climate-justice-a-note-on-shortcomings-and-risks/ (last accessed 3 August 2022).

Extra-Territorial Obligations Emerging Because of the HRWS

Transboundary water resources are unevenly distributed, and their over-utilization or pollution affects the ability of countries to realize the HRWS.[58] Extraterritorial obligations emerged since a state's actions could cause damage to other nations, impacting their access to water.[59] They impose a duty to avoid direct or indirect harm to the citizens of different countries.[60] Examples relating to this right include the inability to restrict a river flow to a point affecting the provision of basic water supply, polluting freshwater in a manner influencing the presence of fish[61] or allowing foreign stakeholders such as corporations to impact this resource, thus limiting the role of nations domestically.[62] This situation has prompted scholars to call for the establishment of a legal framework that forces states to exploit shared freshwaters equitably. Such a regime promotes the use of a basin through the extraterritorial application of the HRWS.[63] The rationale is that issues related to the inability of a state to fulfill this right, despite having all the resources and capacities, are different from those that occur if it fails to fulfill this obligation. In the latter case, individuals and groups can seek reparations. In the former case, such an option is ineffective. In this situation, new instruments must be established to hold the nations accountable. This is important because said countries may use the principle of sovereignty and other legal means to justify actions and evade responsibility.[64] One may wonder here whether such tools may result in the protection of this right.[65]

The legal basis for the latter to implement the extraterritorial obligations are the specific provisions within global instruments calling for cooperation and protection of human rights, which were mentioned earlier. These are Articles 1(3), 55(c), and 56 of the UN Charter;[66] and are human rights trea-

58 Bulto, *supra* note 46, at 496.

59 Greco, *supra* note 47, at 23–37.

60 Pedi Chiemena Obani, Strengthening the Human Right to Sanitation as an Instrument for Inclusive Development (CRC Press 2018); Lorand Bartels, *The EU's Human Rights Obligations in Relation to Policies with Extraterritorial Effects*, 25(4) European Journal of International Law. 1071, 1087 (2014).

61 Leb, *supra* note 52, at 217.

62 Bulto, *supra* note 46, at 497.

63 *Id.* at 499. The issue of seeking remedies for addressing the violation or the incapacity of a given state to realize the human right to water for its citizens has been addressed in the previous chapter.

64 *Id.* at 501–502. This is not to say that getting the reparation for victims is easy, as there is constant resistance from those that must be held accountable and even from authorities who often do not perform their duties in this regard. See, Imad Antoine Ibrahim, *Water as a Human Right, Water as a Commodity: Can SDG6 be a Compromise?*, 26(3) The International Journal of Human Rights, 469, 478–485 (2022).

65 Chavarro, *supra* note 1058, at 94.

66 UN Charter, *supra* note 1209, at Articles 1(3), 55(c) and 56; Sigrun I. Skogly, *Extraterritoriality – Universal Human Rights without Universal Obligations?*, 5, available at https://eprints

ties that highlight these duties explicitly, while others opt to include implicit language.[67] Several conventions are extremely important in this case, including the ICESCR.[68] GC 15 on the HRW recognized that nations have obligations that go beyond their jurisdictions or territories[69] by not affecting another state's capacity to provide this resource to its citizens, through, for instance, water diversion at the border.[70] In fact, it even emphasized the need to ease the implementation of this right in other countries through various types of assistance, such as financial and technical ones.[71] It stated that any agreement on trade liberalization must not prevent a country from realizing this right for its citizens.[72]All these ideas are further confirmed in paragraph 31 of the GC in the general framework of international cooperation.[73] The Comment has further developed the kind of transnational obligations that a state must realize. For instance, as said previously according to Paragraph 33, nations must take measures to restrict the ability of their citizens and corporations from breaching the HRW for the population elsewhere, as well as third parties. These include the use of political or legal means.[74]

These detailed stipulations in GC 15 highlight the nature of the extraterritorial obligations that states have. According to the CESCR, these duties are a condition for the realization of each human right mentioned in the ICESCR, including the HRW.[75] The Committee in this comment demands states to give attention to these concerns where needed, and that they must act collaboratively and avoid self-interest in considering agreements.[76] Hence, one can notice the relevance that CESCR has seen, resulting in the inclusion of such duties,[77] for the protection of the ICESCR rights in other nations, including

.lancs.ac.uk/id/eprint/26177/1/Microsoft_Word_-_Monash_-_Extraterritoriality_-_Final_draft.pdf (last accessed 3 August 2022).

67 *Id.* at 8.

68 ICESCR, *supra* note, at 218; *Id.* at 8–9.

69 General Comment 15, *supra* note 472; Paragraphs 30–36. Catarina De Albuquerque, Realising the Human Rights to Water and Sanitation: A Handbook by the UN Special Rapporteur Catarina De Albuquerque 27 (UN Special Rapporteur on the human right to safe drinking water and sanitation 2014)

70 *Id.* Coomans, *supra* note 1209, at 22.

71 Leb, *supra* note 58, at 644–645; General Comment 15, *supra* note 472, at paragraph 34.

72 Coomans, *supra* note 1209, at 22.

73 Amy Hardberger, *Whose Job Is It Anyway?: Governmental Obligations Created by the Human Right to Water*, 41 Texas International Law Journal. 533, 533–568 (2006); General Comment 15, *supra* note 472, at Paragraph 31.

74 General Comment 15, *supra* note 472, at Paragraph 31. See also Paragraphs 32, 34, 35, & 36.

75 Chavarro, *supra* note 1058, at 94.

76 Kirchner, *supra* note 986, at 485.

77 Jorge E. Vinuales, *A Human Rights Approach to Extraterritorial Environmental Protection? An Assessment*, in The Frontiers of Human Rights: Extraterritoriality and Its Challenges 177, 206 (Nehal Bhuta ed., Oxford University Press 2016).

the HRW.[78] This has been an ongoing trend in every GC adopted since 1999, such as those related to rights to food and health.[79] GC 15 covers the principal obligations of a given state within the framework of the HRW. These are related to the duties to protect, respect, and fulfill,[80] that are mentioned in detail in previous paragraphs in the comment. Adding such obligations in the transboundary context was considered controversial, as some nations were concerned that this might create legal rights in the form of assistance,[81] that are complementary to domestic states' obligations.[82] Still, a consensus has emerged with regard to ESC rights, unlike political and civil rights that apply territorially,[83] despite some nations claiming otherwise.[84]

The extraterritorial application of the HRW is based on Article 2(1) ICESCR previously discussed as well as Articles 11 and 12 of the same covenant referring implicitly to this right.[85] The general wording and application of the former provision to all human rights creates international obligations upon states to realize them.[86] This provision does not restrict the realization of these rights to a territory or jurisdiction. This means that there is nothing preventing a state from realizing them in other countries. A nation's action, in this case, can be taken individually or through international assistance and cooperation based on Article 23 ICESCR. Accordingly, states are provided specific outlets to participate in a cooperative manner with those sharing resources. It seems from the wording of the article that the list of actions that can be taken is not limited to the ones mentioned above.[87] In fact, the CESCR recognized the existence of certain obligations in the context of HRW that have extraterritorial effects on the basis of Articles 2(1), 11, and 23 ICESCR. These include respecting this right in other nations and protecting it from its own citizens

78 Sarah Joseph & Adam Fletcher, *Scope of Application*, in International Human Rights Law 119, 135 (Daniel Moeckli et al eds., Oxford University Press 2014).

79 John H. Knox, *The Ruggie Rules: Applying Human Rights Law to Corporations*, in The UN Guiding Principles on Business and Human Rights: Foundations and Implementation 51, 80 (Radu Mares ed., Martinus Nijhoff Publishers 2012).

80 General Comment 15, *supra* note 472, at Paragraph 30–36; Ripley, *supra* note 50, at 213–214.

81 Anna F.S. Russell & Stephen McCaffrey, *Tapping Transboundary Waters: Implications of the Right to Water for States Sharing International Watercourses*, in The Human Right to Water: Theory, Practice and Prospects 144, 160 (Malcolm Langford & Anna F. S. Russell eds., Cambridge University Press 2017).

82 Lisa E. Sachs & Jeffrey D. Sachs, *Health Priorities for Sustainable Development*, in Critical Issues in Human Rights and Development 186, 204 (Stephen P. Marks & Balakrishnan Rajagopal eds., Edward Elgar Publishing 2021).

83 Sumudu Atapattu, Human Rights Approaches to Climate Change: Challenges and Opportunities 89 (Routledge 2016).

84 Henry F. Carey, *The Special Rapporteur on the Human Rights to Safe Drinking Water and Sanitation: An Assessment of Its First Dozen Years*, 16(2) Utrecht Law Review. 33, 43 (2020).

85 ICESCR, *supra* note 218, at Article 2(1); 11 & 12; Cahill, *supra* note 50, at 196.

86 Bulto, *supra* note 46, at 512.

87 *Id.* at 511–512; ICESCR, *supra* note 218, at Article 23.

and companies; easing water access, the provision of aid when needed; and emphasizing its importance in global treaties focusing on aid.[88]

The 2010 Resolution on HRWS embraced the existence of the extraterritorial obligation by considering water and sanitation crucial to life and other human rights, as well as calling for the provision of financial resources, technology transfer, and capacity building.[89] This call was particularly directed to richer states.[90] These actions must take place through international assistance and cooperation with a special focus on developing countries. They must contain a final objective of providing safe, clean, accessible, and affordable drinking water.[91] One may even state that the HRC Resolution of the same year implicitly pushes towards extraterritorial obligations by calling for the creation of tools and mechanisms to promote the progressive realization of this right in served and unserved areas among many other things.[92] In a transboundary water basin, a state having such ability must help another seeking assistance by providing water to realize the obligations listed under the ICESCR. This, in turn, ensures the existence of adequate water supplies. These duties are limited, however, and have yet to be used by governments for the time being.[93] Currently, there are calls to use the extraterritorial approach for protecting the HRWS in shaping the business and human rights treaty that is being proposed.[94] Holding a state accountable on the basis of extraterritorial obligations stemming from the HRW is not an easy task. This matter will be analyzed in the following section.

88 ICESCR, *supra* note 218, at Articles 2(1), 11, and 23; Mac Darrow, *Climate Change and the Right to Water*, in The Human Right to Water: Theory, Practice and Prospects 174, 193–194 (Malcolm Langford & Anna F.S. Russell eds, Cambridge University Press 2017); Siobhan McInerney-Lankford, Mac Darrow & Lavanya Rajamani, Human Rights and Climate Change: A Review of the International Legal Dimensions 15 (World Bank Publications 2011).

89 Resolution 64/292, *supra* note 1019, at 1–3; Leb, *supra* note 1070, at 644–645.

90 Pedi Obani & Joyeeta Gupta, *Human Right to Sanitation in the Legal and Non-Legal Literature: The Need for Greater Synergy*, 3(5) WIREs Water. 678, 680–681 (2016).

91 Resolution 64/292, *supra* note 1019.

92 Resolution 15/9, *supra* note 1067.

93 Leb, *supra* note 1070, at 644–645.

94 Chiara Macchi, *Right to Water and the Threat of Business: Corporate Accountability and the State's Duty to Protect*, 35(3) Nordic Journal of Human Rights. 186, 186–190 (2017). On the proposed treaty, see Business and Human Rights Resource Center, *Summary: Third Revised Draft of the Binding Treaty on Business and Human Rights* (August 2021), https://www.business-humanrights.org/en/big-issues/binding-treaty/summary-third-revised-draft-of-the-binding-treaty-on-business-and-human-rights/ (last accessed 3 August 2022).

Challenges to the Realization of Extraterritorial Obligations of the HRWS

Despite the fact that states are responsible for the fulfillment of international obligations,[95] there are many challenges facing their implementation. The latter largely result from their inability or unwillingness to achieve their duties.[96] This applies to the realization of the HRWS. The human rights system focuses on having positive/negative responsibilities imposed upon nations. According to this, countries must either refrain from actions that impact certain rights or ensure their realization. It is very difficult to determine whether a state breached its global duties in this context.[97] They have a wide margin through which they can decide the action taken to achieve rights within international law.[98] The same questions relate to the practical implementation of the HRWS and have emerged only in the context of its extraterritorial application. In that sense, what if one state accepts the existence of such responsibilities in contrast to others? There is no way to push them to comply.[99] Traditionally, human rights obligations applied within a territory. Thus, nations held the duty of realizing ESC rights.[100]

The application of human rights treaties and instruments has been debated to a great extent in the literature. Here, numerous challenges have been established. These, however, depend on the mechanism or convention that provides the basis for the extraterritorial obligation.[101] Many have questioned the reach of human rights beyond borders and their legal basis,[102] especially as their application domestically is not taking place in many places worldwide.[103] Some argue that the drafters of covenants like the ICCPR did not intend to

95 International Commission on Intervention and State Sovereignty, *The Responsibility to Protect: Research, Bibliography, Background* 7 (International Development Research Center, Dec. 2001).

96 International Council on Human Rights, *supra* note 266, at 55.

97 Cinelli, *supra* note 63, at 181.

98 *Id.* at 183.

99 Radhika Balakrishnan, James Heintz & Diane Elson, Rethinking Economic Policy for Social Justice: The Radical Potential of Human Rights (Routledge 2016).

100 Olivier De Schutter, *Economic, Social, and Cultural Rights as Human Rights: An Introduction*, 31 (CRIDHO Working Paper 2013/2); Ute Hausmann & Rolf Künnemann, *Germany's Extraterritorial Human Rights Obligations: Introduction and Six Case Studies*, 7 (Oct. 2006).

101 See, for instance, Fons Coomans & Menno T. Kamminga eds, Extraterritorial Application of Human Rights Treaties (Intersentia Publishers 2004); Sigrun I. Skogly, Beyond National Borders: States' Human Rights Obligations in International Cooperation (Intersentia 2006); Karen da Costa, The Extraterritorial Application of Selected Human Rights Treaties (Martinus Nijhoff 2012).

102 Matthew Craven, *Human Rights in the Realm of Order: Sanctions and Extraterritoriality*, in Extraterritorial Application of Human Rights Treaties 233, 241 (Fons Coomans & Menno T. Kamminga eds., Intersentia 2004).

103 Heller, *supra* note 1141, at 276–290.

create such duties.[104] Gibney for instance, recognized that the world will ultimately be divided into *extra* and *territorial*.[105] The emergence of this concept has created great confusion concerning a state's responsibility outside its territory. The role of national and international jurisdictions and the clash between concepts of territoriality and extraterritoriality are yet to be resolved.[106] Even with a complete understanding of the nature of these obligations, their implementation in practice is very difficult.[107] Moreover, ICJ cases regarding the legal responsibility of a state in events occurring outside its jurisdiction cannot be established unless that country holds de facto control.[108] Nations also consider that human rights should only be enforced or protected within their territories.[109] There are political obstacles because countries perceive human rights agreements differently and in many situations as limiting a state's freedom to act. This reality has been highlighted in many situations where human rights breaches occurred and the international community was not able to take action.[110] This inaction was bred by the procedures within existing bodies that have the responsibility of ensuring compliance and which are considered weak and ineffective.[111]

The concept of extraterritoriality is seen by developing countries as a new way to challenge their independence and sovereignty. This is especially true in the post-colonial era, as the idea originated from laws developed in the North. This is why the notion is viewed with great suspicion,[112] in particular, in regions where cross-border investment projects are being conducted.[113] This is why there are questions concerning whether the Maastricht Principles will actually

104 Noam Lubell, Extraterritorial Use of Force Against Non-State Actors 199 (Oxford University Press 2010).

105 Gibney, *supra* note 1224, at 41.

106 Vassilis P. Tzevelekos, *Reconstructing the Effective Control Criterion in Extraterritorial Human Rights Breaches: Direct Attribution of Wrongfulness, Due Diligence, and Concurrent Responsibility*, 36(1) Michigan Journal of International Law. 129, 130 (2014).

107 Go 4 Health, *Realizing the Right to Health for Everyone: The Health Goal for Humanity*, 28 (Interim Report, Sep. 2013).

108 Sigrun I Skogly, *Extraterritoriality: Universal Human Rights without Universal Obligation*, in Research Handbook On International Human Rights Law 71, 86–90 (Sarah Joseph & Adam McBeth eds., Edward Elgar Publishing 2010).

109 *Id.* at 90–93.

110 *Id.* at 93–94.

111 Sally-Anne Way, *The Role of the UN Human Rights Bodies in Promoting and Protecting the Right to Food*, in Food and Human Rights in Development 205, 217–218 (V. 1, Wenche Barth Eide & Uwe Kracht eds., Intersentia 2005).

112 David Kinley, Civilizing Globalisation: Human Rights and the Global Economy 191 (Cambridge University Press 2009).

113 Carl Middleton, *National Human Rights Institutions, Extraterritorial Obligations, and Hydropower in Southeast Asia: Implications of the Region's Authoritarian Turn*, 11(1) Austrian Journal of South-East Asian Studies. 81, 81–97 (2018).

be relevant.[114] Other issues appear when trying to apply human rights to environmental harm beyond a state's border, as many instruments recognize different environmental rights that are subject to jurisdictional approaches. While conventions such as the ICESCR acknowledge the existence of extraterritorial obligations, others do not. There is a shortage in jurisprudence on the issue, as tribunals have not yet had the chance to address this matter within the context of human rights treaties.[115] This is not to say that there are no cases related to that, but rather a slow movement is slowly being shaped to that end.[116] Nonetheless, this reality complicates the possibility of identifying actors that are responsible for the realization of these duties. This is particularly true where environmental damage is caused through a combination of public and private errors that affect other territories.[117] In this case, this concept is crucial as a legal basis for the protection of rights outside the borders.[118]

The discussion over the implementation of the extraterritorial obligations to protect the HRWS is very relevant. It affects other potential duties. The latter includes the application of this concept to other agreements and in the context of global organizations to which the state is party or is seeking to become a party. Nevertheless, multilateralism is being attacked from many sides due to constant and growing economic and environmental crises, increasing inequalities, and competition for resources, among many other things.[119] Generally speaking, compliance with this right is more challenging than with other social and economic ones, as it has only been recently established through

114 Michael Krennerich, *The Human Right to Health: Fundamentals of a Complex Right*, in Healthcare as a Human Rights Issue: Normative Profile, Conflicts, and Implementation 23, 46 (Andreas Frewer, Heiner Bielefeldt, Martina Schmidhuer & Sabine Klotz eds., Transcript-Verlag 2018).

115 John H. Knox, *Diagonal Environmental Rights*, in Universal Human Rights and Extraterritorial Obligations 82, 86 (Mark Gibney & Sigrun Skogly eds., University of Pennsylvania Press 2010).

116 Riccardo Pavoni, *Environmental Jurisprudence of the European and Inter-American Courts of Human Rights: Comparative Insights*, in Environmental Law Dimensions of Human Rights 69, 69–106 (Ben Boer ed., Oxford University Press 2015); Zhu Mingzhe, *Environmental Rights are Now Human Rights. What Does this Mean for Climate Litigation?* (China Dialogue, September 26, 2022), available at https://chinadialogue.net/en/climate/environmental-rights-human-rights-climate-litigation/ (last accessed 3 August 2022).

117 James R. May, Global Environmental Constitutionalism 276 (Cambridge University Press 2016).

118 Jenny Gronwall, *Human Rights, Water Resources, and Governance for a Healthy and Sustainable Environment* (SIWI, Dec. 1, 2021), available at https://siwi.org/latest/human-rights-water-resources-and-governance-for-a-healthy-and-sustainable-environment/ (last accessed 3 August 2022).

119 *Id.* at 221. May, *supra* note 1310; Olivier De Schutter, International Human Rights Law 232 (Third ed. Cambridge University Press 2019).

UN resolutions.[120] The CESCR recognized this reality.[121] There are concerns regarding the manner in which a state may interpret its extraterritorial obligations and the attitude of the government towards the existence of such a duty. This is why it is important to conduct further research on the HRWS in order to clarify all potential controversies to ensure its implementation,[122] as rightfully noted by Cahill.[123] This must be conducted in the general context of IHRL, which is constantly evolving,[124] considering the growing recognition of the existence of extraterritorial obligations.[125]

Along this discussion, scholars are starting to address the interplay between the HRWS and IWL as recent efforts on the human rights front have pushed towards this debate[126] and the occurrence of several developments in this regard.

HRWS in IWL

The first IWL instruments, like the Helsinki Rules of 1966, focused on the notion of reasonable and equitable sharing. The latter considers matters like economic and social needs without providing preference to one water use over another. These mechanisms took into account the population relying on the freshwater and the availability of other resources as factors.[127] Several transboundary water treaties implicitly promote the HRWS through their provisions by giving priority to these aspects.[128] One may mention the 1909

120 Cahill, *supra* note 50, at 214.

121 General Comment 15, *supra* note 472, at paragraph 34. This paragraph states the following: "Depending on the availability of resources, States should facilitate the realization of the right to water in other countries, for example through the provision of water resources, financial and technical assistance, and provide the necessary aid when required. In disaster relief and emergency assistance, including assistance to refugees and displaced persons, priority should be given to Covenant rights, including the provision of adequate water. International assistance should be provided in a manner that is consistent with the Covenant and other human rights standards, and sustainable and culturally appropriate. The economically developed States parties have a special responsibility and interest to assist the poorer developing States in this regard".

122 Cahill, *supra* note 50, at 214.

123 *Id.* at 214.

124 Luke D. Graham, International Human Rights Law and Destitution: An Economic, Social, and Cultural Rights Perspective (Routledge 2023); Walter Kälin & Jörg Künzli, The Law of International Human Rights Protection (Oxford University Press 2019).

125 Olivier De Schutter, *Foreword: The Advance of ETOs in International Law – A Silent Revolution or a Return to the Original Promise?, in* Global Economy, Global Rights: A Practitioners Guide for Interpreting Human Rights Obligations in the Global Economy 4, 4-5 (International Network for Economic, Social, and Cultural Rights, August 2014).

126 Ahmad Nehaluddin & Gary Lilienthal, *Right to Water as a Human Right: A Critical Overview of International Instruments,* 50(4/5) Environmental Law & Policy. 299, 299 (2020).

127 This can be seen, for instance in Article V (II) 5, 6, 7, & 8 of the Helsinki Rules. See Helsinki Rules, *supra* note 353. Gupta, Ahlers, Ahmed, *supra* note 870, at 295.

128 Leb, *supra* note 1070, at 649.

Boundary Water Treaty between the US and Canada, which considered the rights, obligations, and interests of inhabitants in both countries.[129] Other examples include the Joint Declaration of Principles for Utilization of the Waters of the Lower Mekong Basin – adopted in 1975 by Cambodia, Laos, and Vietnam – which emphasized the concept of *Equality of Rights* where each nation must use the river considering its economic and social needs.[130] The WFD, in its Paragraph 24, highlights the importance of good water quality in ensuring drinking water supply for citizens.[131] The 2000 South African Development Community (SADC) Revised Protocol on Shared Watercourses mentions the population relying on the watercourse as a factor when utilizing the latter in an equitable and reasonable manner.[132] Meanwhile, the 2003 Protocol for Sustainable Development of Lake Victoria Basin reiterated the same idea and considered that serious damage or a threat may be caused to the peoples in the exercise of rights and obligations.[133] In several new treaties, an explicit reference to the HRWS is made. Among these are the Charters of Waters of the Senegal River and Niger Basin.[134] In these, the HRWS was accorded a great importance in the context of IWL.[135] In fact, the charter of the Niger Basin defined the term and included it in several of its provisions when addressing equitable and reasonable utilization.[136]

The slow development of this concept within water agreements and instruments is understandable, given that the discussion concerning this right intensified only in the last couple of decades.[137] This in addition to the fact that

129 The Boundary Water Treaty of 1909, Article IX & X, available at https://www.ijc.org/sites/default/files/2018-07/Boundary%20Water-ENGFR.pdf (last accessed 3 August 2022).

130 Joint Declaration Of Principles for Utilization of the Waters of the Lower Mekong Basin, Signed by the Representatives of the Governments of Cambodia, Laos and Vietnam to the Committee for Coordination of Investigations of the Lower Mekong Basin, Signed At Vientiane On 31 January 1975, Articles X & XI.

131 Leb, *supra* note 1070, at 649. Directive 2000/60/EC of the European Parliament and of the Council of 23 October 2000 establishing a framework for Community action in the field of water policy.

132 Revised Protocol on Shared Watercourses in the Southern African Development Community (SADC) signed in 2000, Article 3(8) a(iii).

133 Protocol for Sustainable Development of Lake Victoria Basin signed on 29th November 2003. Article 48(2) & 5(3) c.

134 Kirchner, *supra* note 986, at 484.

135 Leb, *supra* note 1070, at 648–650. The right to water was mentioned in several provisions of the Niger Basin Water Charter and the Charter of Waters of the Senegal River.

136 International Environmental Agreements (IEA) Database Project, Charter of Waters of the Senegal River, 2002, available at https://iea.uoregon.edu/treaty-text/4462 (last accessed 3 August 2022); Niger Basin Authority, Executive Secretariat, The Niger Basin Water Charter, 2011, available at http://www.abn.ne/images/documents/Charte_Eau/niger_basin_water_charter_certified_copy.pdf, Articles 1(11); 4 & 9 (last accessed 3 August 2022).

137 Inga T. Winkler, *The Human Right to Water*, in Research Handbook on International Water Law 242, 242 (Stephen C. McCaffrey, Christina Leb & Riley T. Denoon eds., Edward Elgar Publishing 2019).

water resources in the transboundary context are not equally distributed and impacts the implementation of water rights.[138] This reality resulted in calls for the adoption of a specific treaty tackling the HRWS,[139] while others see legal pluralism as the way forward to balance the various binding and non-binding instruments.[140] The importance of freshwaters from an environmental perspective and for the continuity of human life constitutes an evolution in the perception of this resource. Thus, it can no longer be viewed solely through an economic lens. Hence, new non-economic criteria have been adopted and included within IWL. In particular, a focus on the ecosystem has been added. Meanwhile, social factors are beginning to be taken into consideration.[141] The result has been the adoption of many soft and hard environmental instruments tackling water resources, such as Agenda 21. The latter, in its Chapter 18, has pushed towards the inclusion of social and environmental issues within IWL.[142] Even GC15 stressed the importance of social and human needs in the transboundary context as they must be considered when tackling the equitable utilization of watercourses.[143] The concept of sustainable development applicable to shared waters was the primary element that led to the inclusion of environmental and social concerns within this field. This notion led to the emergence of a compromise solving the long-standing conflict between the principle of equitable and reasonable utilization and the obligation to not cause significant harm. Hence, the UNWC and the UNECE Water Convention included it within their provisions.[144]

Both conventions included the concept of vital human needs, which was given priority over any other uses.[145] According to the ILC, these are satisfied when enough water is supplied to sustain adequate consumption and aid in the growth of food.[146] These can be further expanded for vulnerable populations within countries where the food supply is connected to the existence of

138 Zheng & Spijkers, *supra* note 668, at 12.

139 Ndjodi Ndeunyema, *Unmuddying the Waters: Evaluating the Legal Basis of the Human Right to Water under Treaty Law, Customary International Law, and the General Principles of Law*, 41(3) MICHIGAN JOURNAL OF INTERNATIONAL LAW. 455, 457 (2020).

140 Joseph W. Dellapenna, *International Water Law in 2070*, 46 (7/8) WATER INTERNATIONAL. 1116, 1127 (2021).

141 Tanzi, *supra* note 61, at 268. On the ecosystem approach, see, for instance, McIntyre, *supra* note 898, at 1-14; McIntyre, *supra* note 156, at 88–95.

142 *Id.* at 268–269. Chapter 18 of Agenda 21: Protection of the Quality and Supply of Freshwater Resources: Application of Integrated Approaches to the Development, Management and Use of Water Resources, Objective 18.8, United Nations Conference on Environment & Development, *supra* note 114.

143 General Comment 15, *supra* note 472, at 11.

144 UNWC, *supra* note 184, at Article 24 (2) a; UNECE Water Convention, *supra* note 431, at Preamble & Article 3 (1) i; LEB, *supra* note 52, at 202.

145 *Id.* at 270. The concept of sustainable development was included within Article 24(2)(a) of the UNWC while it was implicitly mentioned in the UNECE water convention.

146 LEB, *supra* note 52, at 202.

fisheries in the freshwater source.[147] Even though the provisions within IWL agreements and their instruments apply only to states, these rules include the objective of the HRW when allocating transboundary waters. Thus, these nations must give special attention to these requirements.[148] Their scope is limited in comparison to the scope of the HRW. The latter encompasses, in addition to human survival and cultural perspectives, the progressive enhancement of living situations comprising access to available freshwaters.[149] The scope of vital human needs determined by the ILC was implemented in the UNWC. Here, the interpretation of the texts of the Draft Convention shows that the satisfaction of this necessity requires paying particular attention to the provision of this resource for protecting human life, which includes inter alia water for drinking and agriculture to avoid hunger.[150] Despite its limitation, these necessities were given primacy over any other use of an international watercourse,[151] although the protection offered was seen as inadequate, especially as the convention applies only to states.[152] The restraint does not mean that the provision addressing this issue is inconsistent with the HRWS.[153] On the contrary, it is considered to support this right,[154] in the transboundary context creating a legal obligation upon each state to implement it.[155] Its importance can be seen in other water instruments. This is because nations can no longer ignore these necessities and prioritize other interests.[156] This notion is supported through environmental instruments and the treaty practice conducted at the river-basin level.[157]

In contrast, there are water conventions and instruments that have made reference to or supported the HRW. In fact, the 1992 UNECE Water Convention and the 1999 London Protocol on Water and Health implicitly promoted it. For instance, the water convention recognizes the need to consider future generations in the management and use of current water

147 Paul Stanton Kibel, Riverflow: The Right to Keep Water Instream 202 (Cambridge University Press 2021).
148 Kirchner, *supra* note 986, at 484.
149 Leb, *supra* note 52, at 202.
150 Ziganshina, *supra* note 1012, at 117.
151 Article 10(2) states that "In the event of a conflict between uses of an international watercourse, it shall be resolved with reference to Articles 5 to 7, with special regard being given to the requirements of vital human needs." UNWC, *supra* note 184, Article 10(2).
152 Antoinette Hildering, *The Impact of a Human Right to Water on the Sustainable Balance of Water Uses under the UN Watercourses Convention*, 16(2) Utrecht Law Review. 7, 10–13 (2020).
153 Robert C. Palmer, Damien Short & Walter E. Ted Auch, *The Human Right to Water and Unconventional Energy,* 15(9) International Journal of Environmental Research and Public Health. 1, 11 (2018).
154 *Id.*
155 Hildering, *supra* note 1348, at 10–13.
156 International Law Association, *supra* note 479; Bourquain, *supra* note 479, at 48-49.
157 Owen McIntyre provides many examples of such treaty practice. McIntyre, *supra* note 722, at 109.

supplies.[158] The protocol has no explicit reference to the HRW but mentions access to drinking water for everyone as one of the targets, without providing guidance as to how such a target can be achieved.[159] Despite that, it seems that it is relevant to the HRWS given its provisions related to access to water. Tanzi has analyzed its importance, concluding that it satisfies all the main duties of GC 15 at a minimum level.[160] There are instruments that refer to both concepts. The Berlin Rules have made a reference to vital human needs in Article 14 and HRW in Article 17.[161] Accordingly, states must support their citizens in the realization of this right. They are obligated, in particular, when the individuals do not have the capacity to satisfy their own demands.[162] McIntyre, along with others, noted the relevance of mentioning both concepts.[163]

The general principles of IWL are important for the protection of individual needs in terms of water. In accordance with the obligation to not cause significant harm, polluting this shared resource in a manner that renders it inadequate for human consumption in another state leads to a breach of this concept.[164] Water necessities, according to the notion of equitable and reasonable utilization, must be protected. Furthermore, they must take factors such as economic and social requirements of the different basins and hydrologic situations into consideration. Several viewpoints and opinions exist here. Scholars such as Bourquain argue that the application of this principle means that a sufficient quantity of water must exist to satisfy basic human needs. McCaffrey goes further in his interpretation, claiming that the existence of this obligation contradicts hydrological realities as in the case of shared water basins where there are scarce water resources. A state must use the existing water to guarantee the human needs of its own population. As such, nations must cooperate in the latter case to satisfy the wants of their citizens, such as providing water from alternative sources. The debate over the interpretation of these principles

158 UNECE Water Convention, *supra* note 431, at Article 2(5)C.

159 Protocol on Water and Health to the 1992 Convention on the Protection and Use of Transboundary Watercourses and International Lakes, done in London, on 17 June 1999, Articles 4 (2) a; c; (3); Article 5 (e); Article 6 (1) a; 2 (a) (c) (f) (j) (n); Gavouneli, *supra* note 17, at 315–316.

160 Tanzi, *supra* note 61, at 272–275.

161 Gavouneli, *supra* note 17, at 315. Article 14(1) of the Berlin Rules states that, "In determining an equitable and reasonable use, States shall first allocate waters to satisfy vital human needs". Article 17 discusses, in detail, several points supporting the right of access to water and the ways that states must implement such right. For instance, in 17(1), the instrument recognizes that, "Every individual has a right of access to sufficient, safe, acceptable, physically accessible, and affordable water to meet that individual's vital human needs." International Law Association, *supra* note 479.

162 Gupta, Ahlers, Ahmed, *supra* note 870, at 296.

163 McIntyre, *supra* note 539, at 323. See also, for instance, Owen McIntyre, *The Human Right to Water and Global Administrative Law: Mutually Supporting Concepts?*, in Globalization and Ecological Integrity in Science and International Law 208, 219 (Laura Westra, Klaus Bosselman, Colin Soskolne eds. Cambridge Scholars Publishing 2011).

164 Leb, *supra* note 1070, at 646–647.

does not, however, negate their importance. Rather, it can provide protection to vital human needs where international water mechanisms state that they must be granted attention.[165] This is particularly the case as more scholars see this concept as an equitable mechanism to tackle the conflicts of uses between nations sharing a water resource.[166] The following section will examine the application of the HRWS to transboundary groundwaters.

HRWS in the Context of TBAs

The literature on the relationship between the HRWS and IWL is only emerging. Meanwhile, there remain relatively few studies discussing the issue of TBAs in the context of this right.[167] The fact that it was only adopted recently may have led to this situation. The lack of treaties regulating shared groundwaters is another reason. This is especially true since IWL developed instruments and conventions that primarily dealt with surface waters. Hence, there are very few mechanisms by which one can examine the HRWS as it pertains to TBAs.[168] The main instrument that can be examined is the Draft Articles on the Law of Transboundary Aquifers. The explicit focus on TBAs compared to the UNWC or the UNECE Water Convention makes this analysis useful.[169] The Draft Articles do not include a provision that focuses on the HRWS. Its purpose is the regulation of water use among nations sharing TBAs,[170] despite the reliance on groundwater for various needs, including domestic ones.[171]

In accordance with Article 4 of this instrument related to the principle of equitable and reasonable utilization, when using the TBA, states must focus on benefiting long term from the water. They are expected to create holistic, comprehensive utilization plans independently or jointly, considering current and future generations and potential new sources for the nations sharing the aquifer. Finally, countries must ensure the constant efficient functioning of the aquifer or aquifer system when using it.[172] Article 5 states the factors that must

165 *Id.* at 647.

166 Clive Vinti, *The Treaty on the Lesotho Highlands Water Project and the Principle of "Equitable and Reasonable Utilization"*, De Jure Law Journal. 328, 345 (2021).

167 Some of these studies have been extensively analyzed by the author, given their relevance to the topic of this chapter.

168 María Milanés-Murcia, *The Application of the General Principles and Key Obligations to Internationally Shared Groundwater, In* Research Handbook on International Water Law 147, 151 (Stephen C. McCaffrey, Christina Leb & Riley T. Denoon et al ed., Edward Elgar Publishing 2019).

169 For instance, the UNWC mentions that vital human needs must be given priority in conflicts between different uses of an international watercourse.

170 Draft Articles, *supra* note 515, at Article 1.

171 McCaffrey, *supra* note 463, at 5.

172 Draft Articles, *supra* note 515, at Article 4; Gavouneli, *supra* note 17, at 305–309.

be considered including paying special regard to vital human needs.[173] This suggests the existence of a HRWS. The concept is used in Article 17 concerning emergency situations. In these cases, aquifer states must take the necessary actions to meet these needs.[174] No explicit mention of the HRWS can be found in the framework conventions such as the Draft Articles, UNWC, or the UNECE Water Convention. This is understandable since they were adopted before the formal recognition of this right in 2010.[175] It is in this context that proposals were made for the adoption of a draft convention on the HRWS,[176] which has been incorporated into other international water agreements, as mentioned earlier.[177]

The models mentioned here explicitly include the HRW. The focus of some of these conventions is on surface water. Treaties like the Niger Basin Water Charter cover groundwater resources within their scope. These references were in accordance with Article 11 of the Charter.[178] Another example is the Water Charter of the Lake Chad Basin. This covers surface water and groundwater where the HRWS are expressly mentioned in many articles. For example, provision 4 serves this purpose.[179] Meanwhile, the HRW is considered one of the factors when applying the equitable and sustainable utilization obligation.[180] Conventions such as the Niger Basin Water Charter and the Water Charter of the Lake Chad Basin did not make any reference to vital human needs, despite their explicit inclusion within other framework conventions and instruments.[181] There are examples of water agreements where neither the HRWS nor vital human needs were mentioned. For instance, the Revised Protocol on Shared Watercourses in the SADC, signed in 2000, did not use these terms.[182] An explanation for not including the HRWS is that it was formally recognized afterward. Still, its drafters could have mentioned the

173 *Id.* at Article 5(2).

174 *Id.* at Article 17 (3).

175 Both the UNWC and the UNECE Water Convention became enforceable after the formal recognition of the right to water and sanitation through UN resolutions.

176 Clark, *supra* note 1111, at 239.

177 Russell & McCaffrey, supra note 1277, at 170.

178 Article 11 states explicitly the adoption of policies for tackling groundwater and surface water. The terms groundwater and transboundary groundwaters are also mentioned in Article 1 related to definitions. See, Niger Basin Water Charter, *supra* note 1332, at Article 11; *Id.* at 170.

179 For instance, Article 4 states that, "Water Charter aims to fulfilll the following specific goals: … c) Groundwater management along with the establishment of principles and rules on transboundary groundwater management." See also, Article 11 & 17. Water Charter of the Lake Chad Basin – English version, Version of the 8 April 2011, available at https://www.africanwaterfacility.org/fileadmin/uploads/awf/Projects/MULTIN-LAKECHAD-Water-Charter.pdf (last accessed 3 August 2022).

180 *Id.* at Article 13.

181 See, Niger Basin Water Charter and Water Charter of the Lake Chad Basin.

182 SADC Revised Protocol, *supra* note 1328.

concept of vital human needs, especially since it was signed only two years after the adoption of the UNWC.[183]

Several challenges and opportunities emerged when attempting to apply the HRWS to TBAs. The impact of this right is that the state is bound to its obligation to provide freshwater to its citizens, regardless of market rules.[184] In that sense, shared aquifers are primarily used for satisfying the survival needs of the population, as humans cannot live without water.[185] Groundwater would not be seen as a profit-oriented resource because states have the obligation to provide it without considering whether citizens have the capacity to afford it.[186] This is not to say that people have no responsibility to bear, but rather that in the case of an inability to meet basic water needs, it must be provided by the government from any reservoir.[187] The HRWS applicable to TBAs would mean that the priority of aquifer use is to satisfy basic needs.[188] This remains the case despite other uses that are important.[189] The right imposes another obligation on states, as nations have to improve water management practices to reach the stated objective.[190] Many suggestions have been made, such as enhancing the water governance system by involving all stakeholders, the public, and the private sector.[191] Any improvement is very welcome given the importance of groundwater in the overall supply, the protection of ecosystems, and the well-being of humans.[192] Studies have been conducted

183 *Id.*

184 Eckstein & Eckstein, *supra* note 1, at 687.

185 Manohar Pawar, Water and Social Policy 44 (Palgrave Macmillan 2014).

186 Eckstein & Eckstein, *supra* note 5, at 255.

187 Bourquain, *supra* note 1197, at 151.

188 Villar, *supra* note 6, at 96.

189 National Academies of Sciences, Engineering, and Medicine, *Future Water Priorities for the Nation: Directions for the U.S. Geological Survey Water Mission Area*, 9 (Washington D.C., The National Academies Press, 2018).

190 Villar, *supra* note 6, at 96.

191 José Galizia Tundisi, *Water Resources in the Future: Problems and Solutions*, 22(63) Estudos Avançados. 7, 16 (2008). Improving water management practices has proved to be quite effective in reaching better water governance, see for instance, Akhter Ali; Dil Bahadur Rahut; Khondoker Abdul Mottaleb, *Improved Water-Management Practices and their Impact on Food Security and Poverty: Empirical Evidence from Rural Pakistan*, 20(4) Water Policy. 692, 692–711 (2018).

192 The United Nations World Water Development Report 2015: *Water for a Sustainable World* 13 (2015); *Id.* at 13. Scholars are already examining the so-called groundwater footprint as a measurement to highlight that many great aquifers are being overexploited. This applies, in particular, to Asia and North America. Tom Gleeson et al., *Water Balance of Global Aquifers Revealed by Groundwater Footprint*, 488(7410) Nature. 197, 197–200 (2012).

to provide recommendations[193] and ensuring an adequate decision-making process.[194]

Prioritizing groundwater for survival purposes instead of being subject to market rules is very relevant if one takes into consideration the impact of commercial companies on this resource. For instance, in India, groundwater withdrawal for commercial reasons has negatively affected aquifers.[195] The latter, for example, is being used by corporations such as Coca-Cola for selling soft drinks.[196] This is because it is considered a better source for drinking water.[197] This impact of a human rights approach to water, in accordance with the UN Resolutions of 2010, is expected to affect legislation and policies of states in a similar manner to other legislation, such as the right to food.[198] The existence of numerous questions and uncertainties concerning the meaning and implementation of the HRWS complicates its application.[199] The latter must be realized in the context of shared aquifers where there is an urgent need to ensure consensus among the nations through legal and institutional arrangements,[200]

193 See, ANTHONY J. JAKEMAN ET AL., *Integrated Groundwater Management: An Overview of Concepts and Challenges*, in INTEGRATED GROUNDWATER MANAGEMENT 3, 3–20 (Anthony J. Jakeman et al. eds., Springer 2016); Marios Sophocleous, *Review: Groundwater Management Practices, Challenges, and Innovations in the High Plains Aquifer, USA – Lessons and Recommended Actions*, 18(3) HYDROGEOLOGY JOURNAL. 559, 559–575 (2009).

194 Anna Schlattmann, Na'ama Teschner & Christina von Haaren, *"Who May Use Scarce Water? An Expedition into the Normative Basis of Sustainable Decision-Making Norms for Sustainable Water Use*, 23(3) WATER POLICY. 556, 556–560 (2021).

195 David Hall & Emanuele Lobina, *Conflicts, Companies, Human Rights and Water – A Critical Review of Local Corporate Practices and Global Corporate Initiatives*, 1–26 (A report for Public Services International (PSI) for the 6th World Water Forum in Marseille, March 2012).

196 *Id.* Coca-Cola and PepsiCo plants in Kerala were held accountable by the Indian government in 2004. The government found that the companies caused water pollution, depleted groundwater, and affected crop yields. This reality impacted the right of citizens living close to the plants to have access to water that is safe to consume. KAITLIN Y. CORDES, *The Impact of Agribusiness Transnational Corporations on the Right to Food, in* ACCOUNTING FOR HUNGER: THE RIGHT TO FOOD IN THE ERA OF GLOBALIZATION (Olivier De Schutter & Kaitlin Y Cordes eds., Hart Publishing Ltd 2011).

197 Maya Velis, Kirstin Conti & Frank Biermann, *Groundwater and Human Development: Synergies and Trade-Offs within the Context of the Sustainable Development Goals*, 12(6) SUSTAINABILITY SCIENCE. 1007, 1009 (2017).

198 Varady et al., *supra* note 16, at 37. There was previous legislation providing protection for water. See, Tomasz Nalecz, *Sustainable Use and Protection of Groundwater Resources – Transboundary Water Management – Belarus, Poland, Ukraine Project as a Step for Establishing Integrated Transboundary Groundwater Management East of EU*, in TRANSBOUNDARY AQUIFERS IN THE EASTERN BORDERS OF THE EUROPEAN UNION: REGIONAL COOPERATION FOR EFFECTIVE MANAGEMENT OF WATER RESOURCES 1, 1 (Tomasz Nalecz ed., Springer 2010).

199 NELSON & QUEVAUVILLER, *supra* note 302, at 184.

200 GREG HOBBS, ALISON FLINT, AND CHRISTIE HENKE, *Sharing Water – A Necessity for Peace in a Changing World*, in THE RIGHT TO WATER AND WATER RIGHTS IN A CHANGING WORLD 55, 55 (Michael R. van der Valk & Penelope Keenan eds., Papers presented at a colloquium held on 22 September 2010 in Delft, the Netherlands 2011).

as TBAs are being relied on by at least 2 billion peoples globally.[201] This must occur in a manner that does not directly hinder the rights and interests of other states, nor indirectly impact those of the population.[202] This idea is still contested because of the concept of vital human needs being applied in IWL.

Transboundary Groundwater as a Vital Human Need

IWL has been developed to address states' obligations and duties, not the rights of individuals and groups.[203] New issues like climate change have pushed scholars to call for more flexibility in water agreements.[204] In this context, the concept of vital human needs covered within the framework means guaranteeing water to sustain life in any capacity related to survival and well-being. This is less comprehensive than the HRW, which also includes enhancing progressively existing conditions, cultural values, and acceptability.[205] Vital human needs signify that minimum supply must be provided to individuals, where such amount must be calculated on a per capita basis for citizens relying on it for direct consumption[206], and where such a calculation would allow minimum use of water for the functioning of society and the prevention of health issues.[207] A recent interpretation of the term by the ILA includes sanitary needs and the water required for sustaining a household.[208] This concept was used by some to create a compromise among nations sharing freshwater, particularly in regions suffering from conflicts. Here, this notion would be used to satisfy the needs of states, ignoring geographic considerations and historic claims.[209] The argument is that water allocation, in this case, must take into consideration the real necessities of each party and whether certain nations have the capacity to provide assistance.[210]

201 Kerry Schneider, *Water Cooperation: Cooperation over Shared Waters is a Critical Aspect of Water Governance (SIWI)*, available at https://siwi.org/undp-siwi-water-governance-facility/work-areas/water-cooperation?iproject=undp-siwi-water-governance-facility (last accessed 3 August 2022).

202 He, *supra* note 1075, at 490.

203 Bulto, *supra* note 1116, at 312.

204 Magsig, *supra* note 537.

205 Leb, *supra* note 1070, at 648.

206 Bulto, *supra* note 1116, at 313.

207 Beaumont, *supra* note 861, at 483.

208 International Law Association, *Water Resources Law: Fourth Report* (Paper presented at the Berlin Conference, Berlin, Germany, 2004).

209 Hillel Shuval, *Meeting Vital Human Needs: Equitable Resolution of Conflicts over Shared Water Resources of Israelis and Palestinians*, in Water Resources in the Middle East: Israel-Palestinian Water Issues – From Conflict to Cooperation, 1, 3 (Hillel Shuval & Hassan Dweik eds., Springer 2007).

210 *Id.* at 15.

The UNWC and the Draft Articles adopted different approaches to reaching this objective.[211] According to Article 10 of the UNWC, in case no treaty or custom exist, all uses of a shared watercourse are equal.[212] In accordance with the vital human needs mentioned in Article 10(2), the UNWC prohibits states from conducting any action that will explicitly or implicitly affect another nation's ability to provide basic water needs to its population.[213] Any conflict between the factors must be resolved considering the principle of equitable and reasonable utilization and the obligation to not cause significant harm.[214] Based on this, many scholars have claimed that the Watercourses Convention, despite its stated intentions, is not dedicated to ensuring access to clean and safe water for current citizens and groups as well as future generations.[215] The Draft Articles provide special weight to vital human needs when an assessment of the different uses is taking place in accordance with Article 5(2).[216] It has been said that this provision grants stronger protection than the UNWC, as the special weight is accorded beforehand and can prevent a conflict.[217] One explanation of this approach concerns the role of groundwater in satisfying the drinking needs of over half the world's population. It serves the development and evolution of the concept of HRW globally.[218] In both mechanisms, there is no obligation to provide, nor do they impose a duty to satisfy these needs before others. Rather, it includes a responsibility to pay special attention to them.[219] The recognition of the existence of vital human needs through the UNWC in 1997 was crucial to the further development of the concept of the HRW. This notion is the closest to the acknowledgment of this right within water conventions and the Draft Articles.[220] According to McCaffrey, focusing explicitly on this idea is understandable given human reliance on water for survival in contrast to other uses where its reduction would not cause serious threats to life.[221] Unlike these instruments, the UNECE Water Convention did not tackle this concept directly but focused on meeting the needs of the present generation without affecting those of future ones.[222] Still, the substantive

211 Leb, *supra* note 1070, at 640–653. There is a consensus on the definition of vital human needs, see Bulto, *supra* note 1116, at 312–313.
212 UNWC, *supra* note 184, at Article 10.
213 *Id*; Cinelli, *supra* note 63, at 181.
214 *Id*. Leb, *supra* note 1070, at 640–653.
215 Ellen Hey, *The Watercourses Convention: To What Extent Does It Provide a Basis for Regulating Uses of International Watercourses?*, 7(3) REVIEW OF EUROPEAN, COMPARATIVE & INTERNATIONAL ENVIRONMENTAL LAW. 291, 291 (1998).
216 Draft Articles, *supra* note 515, at 5(2).
217 Leb, *supra* note 1070, at 640–653.
218 Sindico & Pateiro, *supra* note 859, at 398.
219 Leb, *supra* note 1070, at 648.
220 McCaffrey, *supra* note 463, at 276.
221 MCCAFFREY, *supra* note 722.
222 UNECE Water Convention, *supra* note 431, at Article 2 (5) C.

provisions of the treaty are being interpreted in a way that highlights the protection of these needs.[223]

There are many different types of utilization of groundwater in places where aquifers are the only source. These include drinking, agriculture, industry, human domestic needs, and support for terrestrial and aquatic ecosystems. Giving priority to vital human needs in this context means providing the necessary and sufficient amount for human survival, such as for drinking and agricultural purposes.[224] Classifying groundwater as such has great implications. Since it is vital to human survival, civil society organizations argue that governments should provide this resource for free or at an extremely reduced price.[225] Despite the implicit recognition of the importance of groundwater as a vital human need within the UNWC Convention and the Draft Articles, there are no other provisions that grant strong protection to the HRW.[226]

The importance of the concept of vital human needs to access groundwater lies in the fact that in many regions, it is considered the only drinking water supply. Hence, Article 10 of the UNWC does not help as it does not provide a priority of use to groundwater.[227] In the Draft Articles, this concept has been integrated within the principle of equitable and reasonable utilization.[228] Article 17 confirms the priority given to vital human needs in cases of emergency situations.[229] The Draft Articles' special regard to this notion was added after amendments made by the ILC. These changes altered the previous version.[230] The approach outlined in this instrument emphasizes the basic needs of the population before evaluating other uses.[231] The Draft Articles provide a special status to vital human needs implicitly in Article 16, related to technical cooperation with developing states.[232] This concept, applicable

223 David J. Devlaeminck, Reciprocity and China's Transboundary Waters: The Law of International Watercourses 81 (Routledge 2021).

224 Report of the International Law Commission, available at https://books.google.it/books?id=KD_t-V9PxYEC&pg=PA209&dq=Groundwater+as+a+vital+human+need+in+international+water+law&hl=en&sa=X&ved=0ahUKEwiUtqPxm9zjAhVGy6QKHbLfB-gQ6AEISzAG#v=onepage&q=Groundwater%20as%20a%20vital%20human%20need%20in%20international%20water%20law&f=false 209 (last accessed 3 August 2022).

225 Jayyousi, *supra* note 32, at 329.

226 Bourquain, *supra* note 1197, at 51.

227 UNWC, *supra* note 184, at Article 10; Marcella Nanni, *Legal Aspects of Groundwater Management: An Overview* 9–10 (2015), https://hydrologie.org/BIB/Publ_UNESCO/SOG_Transboundary_aquifers_and_International_Law/Documents/Regional%20meeting%20Americas/Papers/Legal%20Aspects%20of%20Groundwater%20Management%20An%20Overview.pdf (last accessed 3 August 2022).

228 Draft Articles, *supra* note 515, at Article 4 & 5; Christina Leb, *Dig Deep: Conflict Prevention through Protection of Basic Water Rights*, 4 (International Conference "Transboundary Aquifers: Challenges and New Directions" (ISARM 2010).

229 Draft Articles, *supra* note 515, at Article 17; *id.* at 4.

230 Stephan, *supra* note 851, at 40.

231 Leb, *supra* note 1424, at 5.

232 Draft Articles, *supra* note 515, at Article 16; McIntyre, *supra* note 411, at 245.

in the context of TBAs, gains further importance if one follows the interpretation of McCaffrey that hydrologically disadvantaged states should be the main ones benefiting from a global instrument supplying water to ensure these necessities,[233] and as aquifers are considered a vital natural resource[234] that is highly vulnerable.[235] This becomes further complicated when one considers the implementation of this notion, taking into account the energy and food sectors under the water-energy-food nexus umbrella.[236] Given this ongoing debate, the following section shall address the interplay between the HRWS and this concept.

Between Human Rights Agreements and IWL

Historically, it has been noted that IWL was not able to cope with the challenges associated with the satisfaction of the basic human need for water. This opinion existed despite developments in the last few decades. The principal factor of limitation is the fact that this regulatory framework applies to shared freshwaters. Meanwhile, the problems associated with the fulfillment of existing necessities are national and international.[237] The resolutions and declarations adopted since the Stockholm Conference of 1972 have not made a distinction between the concept of water as a human right or as a vital human need. The use of these terms may lead one to believe that they are the same. This is not accurate and shows a lack of understanding of both notions and the potential implications of their usage.[238] In reality, it is very easy to confuse both, as considering water a vital human need is the basis upon which human rights frameworks have been built.[239]

An interaction between two different international legal regimes - IHRL and IWL - is taking place under the umbrella of PIL.[240] This is as these fields, among

233 Stephens, *supra* note 192, at 28.

234 Christina Fraser, *Transboundary Aquifers, A Global Outline 2021* (International Groundwater Resources Assessment Center, 2021), available at https://www.un-igrac.org/stories/transboundary-aquifers-global-outline-2021 (last accessed 3 August 2022).

235 Yoshihide Wada & Lena Heinrich, *Assessment of Transboundary Aquifers of the World – Vulnerability Arising from Human Water Use,* 8 Environmental Research Letters. 1, 1–13 (2013).

236 Waseem Ahmad Qureshi, *The Role of International Law in the Food-Energy-Water Nexus,* 28(1) Buffalo Environmental Law Journal. 1, 8–9 (2021).

237 Bourquain, *supra* note 1197, at 50.

238 Biswas, *supra* note 1128, at 209–225. Article 2 of the Stockholm Declaration dealt briefly and vaguely with water as a natural resource that must be protected for current and future generations.

239 Claudious Chikozho & Everisto Mapedza, *Free-Market Economics and Developmental Statism as Political Paradigms: Implications for Water Governance Theory and Practice in Developing Countries*, in Freshwater Governance for the 21st Century 51, 70 (Eiman Kara red., Springer, Cham 2017).

240 Palak Katta, *International Water Law: An Overview*, 4(3) International Journal of Law Management & Humanities. 3691, 3694 (2021).

others mainly IEL, have evolved creating synergies between each regime.[241] Examining the interplay aims to understand the situations in which nations operate together. As such, global frameworks act as outlets for communication that allow water issues to be addressed.[242] The difference between both legal systems is that IWL is applicable in the case of shared water resources, while IHRL applies to all states that are members of the ICESCR. Here, factors such as geographical or hydrological connections are irrelevant. Nations have an obligation under IWL to apply procedural rules like the exchange of information to fulfill their duties. Under human rights agreements, the obligation of cooperation is satisfied via means of technical and economic assistance.[243] Bulto, in this context, argues that IWL provides the basis for the application of extraterritorial human rights obligations to water, including the positive and negative duties.[244] Through the analysis of paragraphs (31-35) in GC 15, it was noted that the CESCR was seeking to make reference to inter-state norms and duties that are applicable to shared watercourses. These measures include those mentioned in the UNWC and relate to the extraterritorial application of the HRW.[245] It is in this context that Hildering, for instance, discussed the *human right to water for vital human needs.*[246] It is worth mentioning that this is not the only notion that has been analyzed in the understanding of the interconnection between the principles of IWL and other fields. Scholars, for instance, have analyzed the potential impact of the SDGs on the development of this framework.[247]

The principal question that must be posed here is whether classifying water as a human right or a basic need will change anything in practice. Would using one concept facilitate an increase in water access?[248] There is a lack of research on how IHRL can impact the rights and duties of states in the transboundary water context and how these two areas can coexist.[249] Human rights rely on agreements between nations sharing freshwaters because their fulfillment may produce some expenses. These incurred costs are associated with the realization of the same rights in other nations that share a water supply.[250] Water conventions like the UNWC do not directly recognize a HRWS, but support

241 Ellen Hey & Alberto Quintavalla, *How International Water Law Connects to Environmental Law and Human Rights*, in Elgar Encyclopedia of Environmental Law 190, 190 (Michael Faure ed., Edward Elgar Publishing, 2021).
242 Cinelli, *supra* note 63, at 185.
243 Chavarro, *supra* note 1058, at 1110–1111.
244 Takele Soboka Bulto, The Extraterritorial Application of the Human Right to Water in Africa 179 (Cambridge University Press 2014).
245 Vinuales, *supra* note 1273, at 206–207.
246 Hildering, *supra* note 1348.
247 Spijkers, *supra* note 752, at 39.
248 Biswas, *supra* note 1128, at 209–225.
249 Shirani, *supra* note 772, at 50.
250 *Id.* at 74

its implementation.[251] Article 6 of it is related to the factors of equitable and reasonable utilization. It includes the social and economic needs of the watercourse states and the population dependent on it. Read in conjunction with Article 10(2), in case of conflict between different uses, special regard shall be given to vital human needs.[252] According to Bulto, vital human needs and the HRW are ideas that are concurrent with one another. The former represents the minimum required for the implementation of the latter.[253] The application of IWL principles does not always lead to the realization of the HRWS and may result in human rights violations. For instance, the construction of dams on a particular river permitted on the basis of this framework may affect the lives of the people living downstream. In that sense, the application of IWL means that states must realize vital human needs, but not the HRW,[254] The main objective remains ensuring access to water for poor and marginalized communities.[255] This argument is supported by McCaffrey who claims that nations do not have a responsibility to guarantee sufficient water in the shared context so that other states can satisfy the basic needs of their citizens as each country has its population as a priority regardless of the amount of existing water. In such situations, governments must compromise to find a reasonable solution.[256]

In contrast, there is a claim that IWL and the HRWS are mutually interconnected and that international law is pushing towards the consolidation of the latter via the former. Despite separate legal systems, these regimes seem complementary.[257] Implementing the equitable and reasonable utilization principle requires that special attention is provided to vital human needs. Satisfying this requirement means realizing the HRWS. It also implies that protection will be provided in cases where this right is not supported by nations who are members of water agreements. This principle has been connected to the obligation to fulfill, wherein states must help in the realization of the HRWS in other nations. Accordingly, governments sharing a water resource must distribute it in an equitable manner, prioritizing vital human needs and treating all citizens of countries sharing the resource equally.[258] Non-compliance with the no-harm rule also affects the HRW, particularly the population living near the shared freshwater, and impacts other human rights like the right to health and food.[259] This is because it is considered as supplementing the

251 Cinelli, *supra* note 63, at 185.
252 *Id.* at 186–187.
253 Bulto, *supra* note 1440, at 53.
254 Shirani, *supra* note 772, at 76–78.
255 Jayyousi, *supra* note 32, at 329–339.
256 Shirani, *supra* note at 772.
257 Tanzi, *supra* note 61, at 284–285.
258 Chavarro, *supra* note 1058, at 106.
259 Shirani, *supra* note 772, at 79–80.

HRWS.[260] Accordingly, states must refrain from causing harm to the water resource, which corresponds to the responsibility to respect. It also requires nations to prevent third parties from causing harm, which is comparable to the duty to protect.[261] The responsibility to not cause significant harm is a substantive principle that upholds that damage caused by a state can affect the HRW of a population elsewhere. In this regard, this principle can only be invoked by states, not individuals. In the Pulp Mills case, the ICJ stated that the environment encompasses many elements, including the quality of life and human health.[262] This statement highlights the connection between IWL and human rights.[263] Because of the importance of this connection, some claim that the weakness of water agreements is due to ignoring human rights treaties related to water.[264] Therefore, IWL must be transformed using the principles of human rights as guidance. The objective is to improve the resiliency of the legal system and achieve the SDGs associated with this resource and the ecosystem. The traditional structure of IWL is being challenged by the HRWS, which requires a change in this structure by adopting human rights principles.[265]

Conclusion

The human rights system focuses on imposing positive/negative obligations upon states. Nations must refrain from interfering in the realization of certain rights while carrying a duty to ensure the fulfillment of others. The first is primarily concerned with civil and political rights. The latter is mainly related to ESC rights.[266] According to Article 12 of the ILC's Draft Articles on Responsibility of States for Internationally Wrongful Acts, an obligation is

260 Naho Miramuchi & Margot Hurlbert, *Reflecting on Twenty Years of International Agreements Concerning Water governance: Insights and Key Learning*, 22 International Environmental Agreements: Politics, Law and Economics. 317, 321 (2022).

261 Chavarro, *supra* note 1058, at 106–107.

262 Steven Freeland, *Human Rights, the Environment, and Conflict: Addressing Crimes against the Environment*, 2(2) International Journal on Human Rights. 113, 113 (2005); World Court Digest, Gabcíkovo-Nagymaros Project (Hungary/Slovakia) Judgment of 25 September 1997 I.C.J. Reports 1997, p. 7, available at https://www.mpil.de/de/pub/publikationen/archiv/world-court digest.cfm?fuseaction_wcd=aktdat&aktdat=214000000301.cfm (last accessed 3 August 2022).

263 The Pulp Mills Case is a dispute between Argentina and Uruguay related to the construction and operation of pulp mills in Uruguay. These are near an international river called the Uruguay River. This waterway is shared between Argentina and Uruguay. See McIntyre, *supra* note 675, at 124–144.

264 Shirani, *supra* note 772, at 83.

265 Julie Gjørtz Howden & Claudia Ituarte-Lima, *Realizing the Human Right to Clean Water: Time to Rethink the Legal Architecture?* (20 November 2017), available at http://www.unrisd.org/resilience-howden-ituarte (last accessed 3 August 2022).

266 Cinelli, *supra* note 63, at 181.

violated when state acts do not comply with it.[267] It is very difficult to determine whether a government breached its responsibilities by failing to act or prohibiting the enjoyment of certain rights.[268] IHRL offers a limited response to the management and use of TBAs. IWL is viewed as a solution where nations that share water resources fulfill the needs of individuals. Its principles that prioritize domestic uses and vital human needs protect the core content of human rights obligations.[269] In a transboundary context, water issues cannot be solved by relying on a right that was agreed upon globally. Instead, cooperation among nations holds better chances.[270] IWL can lead to the realization of human rights duties by applying its main principles.[271] Both regulatory frameworks can be harmonized when they overlap.[272]

The extraterritorial obligation deduced from the call for providing international assistance and cooperation has raised concerns. These duties were directed towards developing countries. It has been argued here that wealth transfer can be one of its main motives. This doubt is further strengthened since providing assistance does not necessarily correlate to ensuring access to water.[273] Even in cases where governments have an obligation to do so under IHRL, IWL seems to balance all interests. In the opposite case, water can become inexpensive or even free. This is not sustainable since low prices lead to higher consumption and less incentive to conserve.[274] Free water means that the costs of providing it must be paid through other means like taxes.[275] To offer this resource, it is more important to focus on the causes that actually prevent its access.[276] IWL does not tackle all the issues and does not deal with matters such as corruption. These are reserved for states and must be dealt with internally.[277] Nonetheless, protecting freshwaters like TBAs requires good governance where the HRWS does not fulfill this objective.[278]

267 Draft articles on Responsibility of States for Internationally Wrongful Acts, with commentaries. Text adopted by the International Law Commission at its 53rd session in 2001 and submitted to the General Assembly as part of the Commission's report covering the work of that session (A/56/10).

268 Cinelli, *supra* note 63, at 181.

269 Leb, supra note 1070, at 650.

270 Ved P. *Nanda, Emerging Trends in the Use of International Law and Institutions for the Management of International Water Resources*, 6(3) Denver Journal of International Law & Policy. 239, 242 (1976).

271 Chavarro, *supra* note 1058, at 108.

272 Greco, *supra* note, 47, at 23–37.

273 Pardy, *supra* note 941, at 910–911.

274 *Id.* at 912.

275 *Id.* at 914.

276 *Id.* at 917.

277 See the provisions of the UNWC and the UNECE Water Conventions.

278 Pardy, *supra* note 941, at 920.

It is in this context that scholars are calling for the harmonization of IWL and IHRL.[279] In that sense, this resource, including TBAs, must be primarily used for providing drinking water and for the production of food.[280] This suggestion means that current groundwater uses for industrial purposes[281] must be stopped. It is only to be consumed in the situation mentioned above considering vital human needs.[282] In contrast, there are calls for the adoption of an alternative approach. For instance, Carlson suggests the use of the HRWS to develop obligations or prohibitions on government activities affecting TBAs.[283] He stated that the incorporation of this right within the Draft Articles increases the chance of its adoption as a convention. He cites examples of conventions that gained acceptance because they were based on human rights. For instance, the Convention on the Rights of the Child.[284]

Thus, the Draft Articles must be revised to provide further flexibility and clarity so that this instrument might have a chance of ratification. This proposal is very logical since IWL and basin-specific agreements require a lengthy amount of time before adoption. This ensures that the recognition of the HRWS for populations sharing a freshwater resource occurs at the drafting stage.[285] It follows the trend that agreements established at the regional and basin levels combine human rights and international cooperation obligations.[286] It is not clear, though, whether the incorporation of such a provision within IWL instruments is desirable. It may contradict some concepts. This is especially true in cases where the realization of this right may not lead to an equitable and reasonable utilization of the shared water.[287]

279 Greco, *supra* note 47, at 26.

280 Gavouneli, *supra* note 17, at 316–317.

281 See, for instance, E. Custodio & M.R. Llamas, *Intensive Use of Groundwater: Introductory Considerations*, in Intensive Use of Groundwater: Challenges and Opportunities 3, 3–10 (M. Ramon Llamas & E. Custodio eds., A.A. Balkema Publishers 2002).

282 Adele J. Kirschner & Katrin Tiroch, *The Waters of Euphrates and Tigris: An International Law Perspective*, 16(1) Max Planck Yearbook of United Nations Law Online. 329, 365 (2012).

283 Carlson, *supra* note 14, at 1411–1412.

284 *Id.* at 1433.

285 Karina Vink, *Transboundary Water Law and Vulnerable People: Legal Interpretation of the 'Equitable Use' Principle*, 39(5) Water International. 743, 749 (2014).

286 Leb, *supra* note 1070, at 650.

287 J. M. Verschuuren, *The Right to Water as a Human Right or a Bird's Right: Does Cooperative Governance Offer a Way Out of a Conflict of Interests and Legal Complexity?*, in Water governance in motion: Towards Socially and Environmentally Sustainable Water Laws 359, 359–387 (P. Cullet, A. Gowlland-Gualtieri, R. Madhav, & U. Ramanathan Eds., Cambridge University Press 2010).

6 Harmonizing International Water Law while Considering the Human Right to Water and Sanitation

Building on the previous analysis, this part will provide arguments as to why the HRWS should be included in water instruments. This chapter will simultaneously seek to answer the question of how to best harmonize IWL. The rationale adopted is based on a practical and pragmatic approach to international law, despite the added value of idealistic solutions. In the author's opinion, the survival of the global legal order is based on its ability to solve common challenges.[1] This should be the main objective of any regulatory framework to avoid inadequacy. Unfortunately, the recent history of treaties shows that numerous ones were unable to reach their stated goal. Though many reasons are cited, utopian language and text has played a role.[2] This, in addition to the pick-and-choose strategy used by the states that sign and ratify agreements considering their interests, makes a realistic approach to this issue the most appropriate.[3]

Arguments for the Inclusion of a HRWS Provision within IGL

The HRWS Has a Broader Scope Than the Concept of "Vital Human Needs"

The confusion between the concept of vital human needs and the HRWS stems from the fact that these two notions are interconnected. One provides the basis for the other. States, through the former, recognized the existence of

1 See, Anu Bradford & Omri Ben-Shahar, *Efficient Enforcement in International Law*, 12(2) Chicago Journal of International Law. 375, 375–431 (2012); Joshua Kleinfeld, *Skeptical Internationalism: A Study of Whether International Law Is Law*, 78(5) Fordham Law Review. 2451, 2451–2530 (2010); Mortimer N. S. Sellers, Republican Principles in International Law: The Fundamental Requirements of a Just World Order 52–57 (Palgrave Macmillan 2006).

2 Kenneth Anderson, *Remarks by an Idealist on the Realism of the Limits of International Law*, 34(2) Georgia Journal of International and Comparative Law. 253, 253–284 (2006); Sam Muller & Marcel Brus, *The Decade of International Law: Idealist Dream or Realist Perspective?*, 3(3) Leiden Journal of International Law. 1, 1–14 (1990).

3 Oona A. Hathaway, *International Delegation and State Sovereignty*, 71 Law and Contemporary Problems. 115, 115–149 (2008).

DOI: 10.4324/9781003537724-7

the latter before its adoption. That same right provides the necessary support for vital human need through its scope.[4] Despite the impression that IWL and IHRL are two separate fields, they are intertwined since human rights treaties also apply to transboundary water issues.[5] This has already been acknowledged by different organizations and scholars. These have identified the intersectoral relationship between the HRWS and good governance of resources. For instance, in its 2019 World Water Development Report, the United Nations Educational, Scientific and Cultural Organization recognized the interplay between the realization of this right and environmental management as a whole.[6] The UNWC and the Draft Articles both contain provisions related to vital human needs, as was mentioned earlier. TBAs are subject to this notion within the watercourse convention. In the 2008 instrument, this tem is mentioned twice. In Article 5, it is directly related to factors relevant to equitable and reasonable utilization. In Article 17, it is associated with emergency situations. Article 5 imposes an obligation upon states to provide special regard to vital human needs in determining precedence for the use of TBAs. Article 17 provides aquifer states with legal support to take measures to meet these necessities in emergency situations.[7] The UNECE Water Convention does not contain a similar provision, although the 1999 Protocol on Water and Health does incorporates the HRWS.[8]

The definition of the concept incorporated in IWL instruments, as mentioned earlier, states that careful consideration is necessary to the maintenance of water resources.[9] Ensuring that basic water needs of individuals are met is an idea supported by scholars within the legal and human rights fields. It is upheld by experts from bodies like the WHO. Many conferences and customary international law support and stress the existence of a right for individuals to satisfy their water necessities.[10] This term, along with others, has been criticized as to what exactly constitutes a vital human need.[11] The notion was conceived as being misplaced and overemphasized. Instead, it should have been included within the factors related to equitable and reasonable utilization.

4 Bulto, *supra* note 1113, at 313–314.

5 BOURQUAIN, *supra* note 1197, at 206.

6 The United Nations World Water Development Report 2019: *Leaving No One Behind* 36 (United Nations Educational, Scientific and Cultural Organization, 2019).

7 UNWC, *supra* note 184; Draft Article, *supra* note 451, at Article 5(2) and 17(3).

8 Protocol on Water and Health, *supra* note 1355, Article 9(b); ATTILA TANZI, *The Global Water Treaties and Their Relationship, in* RESEARCH HANDBOOK ON INTERNATIONAL WATER LAW 44, 53 (Stephen C. McCaffrey, Christina Leb and Riley T. Denoon eds., Edward Elgar Publishing 2019).

9 EYAL BENVENISTI, *The Role of Third Parties in Promoting Collective Action Among Riparians, in* RESOLUTION OF INTERNATIONAL WATER DISPUTES: PAPERS EMANATING FROM THE SIXTH PCA INTERNATIONAL LAW SEMINAR 201, 216 (Permanent Court of Arbitration. International Bureau, Permanent Court of Arbitration ed., Kluwer Law International 2002).

10 McGraw, *supra* note 993, at 158.

11 Talozi et al., *supra* note 690, at 912–913.

Also in the UNWC, there was a failure in the definition of the meaning of *special regard*, which should be given to these needs. This led to an inability to stress the importance of human rights. Similar problems can be noted in the Draft Articles. This is why, some suggested adding clear human rights considerations within the factors related to equitable and reasonable utilization.[12] Already, there are calls for expanding the definition of vital human needs to include any capacity necessary for a having a decent life.[13] Scholars highlighting the use of IHRL and the HRWS in the transboundary context supported this idea.[14]

It is now known in the legal community that vital human needs refers to the basic minimum elements of the HRWS.[15] The provisions related to this notion are binding within the UNWC. This is in contrast to the above mentioned right.[16] This reality begs the question of its relevance when the HRWS is already adopted, has broader scope, and offers better guarantees to citizens in the domestic and transboundary situation.[17] This follows the general nature of human rights in form and content.[18] The focus is on TBAs since the Draft Articles are not currently binding and require updating and amendment. The HRWS can be included within the instrument replacing vital human needs. This would provide more guarantees to citizens while also binding force to this right since it would constitute a provision within a treaty. Having such an article related to water needs of the population taking precedence over other elements is crucial. This makes sense because of the life-threatening situations that result from the lack of this resource.[19] Hence, why not increase the scope of this right by including the HRWS in lieu of vital human needs? Paragraph 31 of GC 15 provides a basis for such inclusion by stating that nations must respect other countries capacity to provide water based on international cooperation. The latter prohibits governments from impacting this right implicitly or explicitly in other places.[20]

If the obligation to respect the HRWS is based on IWL and not IHRL, it does not matter if the state that breached it has signed human rights conventions.[21] Another paragraph that provides such basis is 34, which asserts

12 Traversi, *supra* note 55, at 479–480.

13 Vink, *supra* note 1481, at 68.

14 Russell, *supra* note 1198, at 269; Russell & McCaffrey, *supra* note 1277, at 169. On this see, McCaffrey, *supra* note 944, at 371; Patricia Birnie, Alan Boyle & Catherine Redgwell, International Law and the Environment 565 (Oxford University Press 2019).

15 Bulto, *supra* note 1437, at 53.

16 *Id.* at 54.

17 McCaffrey, *supra* note 947, at 221–232; Tignino, *supra* note 169, at 78.

18 Ko Hasegawa, *The Possibility of the Human Right to Environment – From a Viewpoint of Legal Philosophy*,in The Global Community Yearbook of International Law and Jurisprudence 2021 63, 76 (Giuliana Ziccardi Capaldo ed., Oxford University Press 2022).

19 McCaffrey, *supra* note 947, at 221–232.

20 General Comment 15, *supra* note 472, at Paragraph 31.

21 McIntyre, *supra* note 539, at 323.

that countries should work across geographical boundaries to ensure access to water for all humans.[22] This should be read as though nations are required to ensure the existence of sufficient water for the realization of this right.[23] Paragraph 35 provides an explicit basis for the respect of the HRW pertaining to transboundary use by ensuring its incorporation within current and future treaties and the implementation of existing ones with this in mind.[24] All of these obligations fall in the framework of the extraterritorial application of the HRWS. Their implementation provides a solid basis, not only for supporting vital human needs, but also the inclusion of the HRWS within agreements.

The definition of vital human needs provided by the ILC is limited in comparison to the HRW defined within GC 15 and HRC Resolution which emphasizes the importance of water for sustenance, the realization of mental and emotional health, and as an aspect related to human dignity.[25] Both the UNWC and the Draft Articles, recognize a special regard to them.[26] In the author's opinion, this is no longer enough. This is why, the inclusion of a provision related to HRWS within IWL is beneficial for human rights regimes as the existing compliance as well as reporting mechanisms and procedures have failed to protect individuals located in a state whose rights have been violated by another. This loophole persists because it lies beyond territorial jurisdiction. Here, affected individuals lack legal means to address human rights violations.[27] Including a HRWS within water agreements would provide the necessary binding force for it. Furthermore, governments would be obliged to comply with all the provisions of the agreement.[28] This suits perfectly its relevance as the one with the most consequences in international law given its vitality to humans as well as living beings within ecosystems.[29] In fact, this right is being considered in the context of 2030 Agenda beyond global regulations.[30]

It Is Becoming a State Practice

IWL has an important role to play in the realization of the HRWS. It has been developing to address the lack or absence of such right, where the status and

22 General Comment 15, *supra* note 472.
23 MCINTYRE, supra note 539, at 323.
24 General Comment 15, *supra* note 472, at Paragraph 35.
25 Leb, *supra* note 52, at 202; HRC Resolution, *supra* note 1020; General Comment 15, *supra* note 472.
26 Leb, *supra* note 52, at 206.
27 *Id.* at 213.
28 UNWC, *supra* note 184.
29 Trigueros, *supra* note 370, at 600.
30 Rio Hada et al., *The Human Rights to Water and Sanitation and the 2030 Agenda for Sustainable Development* (Office of the United Nations High Commissioner for Human Rights & UNESCO World Water Assessment Programme, 2019).

wording of instruments affects it.[31] The provisions of water agreements may not violate the HRWS but could do so when different states are competing over the same water.[32] Despite the relevance of social aspects related to this resource and their inclusion in water laws at the domestic and international levels, this remains the case.[33] Yet, the HRWS is now being incorporated as a part of customary IWL considering its broad scope. It is viewed as such despite the absence of priority of use within existing treaties and instruments.[34] This shift has occurred because the human rights lens has focused on water issues since the adoption of this right.[35] It has already been argued, that water laws and policies are necessary to protect humans and water systems.[36] Globally, the HRWS is not the solution for the water crisis. However, it is relevant where problems go beyond the scope of human rights. In fact, the latter are limited to the safeguard of human dignity and survival and must be supplemented with environmental law and IWL to realize sustainability.[37]

Human rights represent just one dimension of global water governance that includes inter alia law, policy and economic considerations.[38] Water management requires that synergies between IWL and the HRWS are adequately addressed.[39] If this is accomplished, it will ensure that both fields benefit. A human rights approach to water strengthens laws concerning this resource and vice versa.[40] The HRWS is already included within certain water agreements. Primary examples are the Senegal Water Charter where numerous principles have been laid out.[41] For instance, Article 4 emphasizes the need to distribute water for the benefit of the population.[42] Another example is the 2008 Water Charter of the Niger Basin,[43] including considerations of the HRWS and IWL in the preamble and defining the former. It incorporated factors associated

31 Obani & Gupta, *supra* note 1004, at 33.
32 Bourquain, *supra* note 1197, at 207.
33 Brunner et al., *supra* note 1126, at 425.
34 Gupta, *supra* note 62, at 126.
35 Grazia Scocca, *Strengthening International Water Security: The European Union's Proposal*, 5(2) World Water Policy. 192, 197 (2019).
36 Craig Anthony (Tony) Arnold, *Water Privatization Trends in the United States: Human Rights, National Security, and Public Stewardship*, 33(3) William & Mary Environmental Law and Policy Review. 785, 790 (2009).
37 Cavallo, *supra* note 1022, at 199.
38 Joyeeta Gupta et al., *Policymakers Reflections on Water Governance Issues*, 18(1) Ecology and Society. 35, 35 (2013).
39 Asanga Gunawansa, Lovleen Bhullar & Sonia Ferdous Hoque, ***Introduction***, in Water Governance: An Evaluation of Alternative Architectures 1, 1–43 (Asanga Gunawansa & Lovleen Bhullar eds., Edward Elgar Publishing 2013).
40 David Boyd, *The Right to Water: A Briefing Note* 2 (High-Level Expert Group Meeting, The Global Water Crisis: Addressing an Urgent Security Issue, March 21-23, 2011, Canada, Toronto).
41 Russell & McCaffrey, *supra* note 1277, at 170–171.
42 Charter of Waters of the Senegal River, *supra* note 1332, at Article 4.
43 Russell & McCaffrey, *supra* note 1277, at 170–171.

with equitable and reasonable utilization of the HRWS of the basin population within Article 4. The charter covered the payment of fees emerging from water uses in provision 9. The payment applies where explicit mention was included stating that this right must be guaranteed.[44] A final example is the Water Charter of the Lake Chad Basin where the right is seen as necessary, especially for human dignity. Therefore, measures of various types are to be taken to reach it.[45] The Charter included Provision 77 on the right of civil society and grassroots community organizations to bring actions before courts for environmental protection purposes including water protection.[46]

The protocol on Water and Health to the UNECE Water Convention indirectly includes the HRWS. It aims to improve management by protecting human health and well-being. It was adopted to maintain access to water and proper sanitation.[47] The importance of water for drinking purposes was stressed through many of its provisions. Articles 4, 5, and 6 are the best examples of this. For instance, Article 4 emphasized in Part 2 the need to provide healthy water free from diseases and its protection from pollution.[48] Meanwhile, provision 6 confirms the necessity of ensuring access to drinking water and sanitation to realize the goals of the protocol.[49]

The inclusion of a HRWS in this context makes sense. Demands on this limited resource are growing constantly because of population increase and better living standards.[50] Such incorporation is important because numerous conventions do not cover the rights of individuals in terms of water and sanitation[51] For instance, the agreement between the US and Mexico of 1944 on the Utilization of Waters of the Colorado and Tijuana Rivers and of the Rio Grande, does not include any provision on the HRWS or vital human needs.[52] The Mekong Agreement, adopted in 1995 between Cambodia, Laos, Thailand, and Vietnam has the same issue.[53] Given the recent inclusion of HRWS provision within certain transboundary agreements, it would seem more logical to have a similar ones within IWL. This includes the Draft Articles given its current non-binding nature and as numerous TBAs are still in need of a treaty.

44 Water Charter of the Niger Basin, supra note 1329, Articles 4 & 9.
45 Water Charter of the Lake Chad Basin, *supra* note 1375, at Article 72.
46 *Id.* at article 77.
47 Russell & McCaffrey, *supra* note 1277, at 171,
48 Protocol on Water and Health, *supra* note 1355, Article 4.
49 *Id.*, at Article 6.
50 Luis Santos Pereira, Ian Cordery & Lacovos Lacovides, Coping with Water Scarcity: Addressing the Challenges (Springer 2009).
51 Ripley, *supra* note 29, at 9.
52 Utilization of Waters of the Colorado and Tijuana Rivers and of the Rio Grande, Treaty Between the United States of America and Mexico Signed at Washington 3 February 1944. And Protocol Signed at Washington 14 November 1944.
53 Agreement on the Cooperation for the Sustainable Development of the Mekong River Basin, adopted 5 April 1995.

The incorporation of such rights within water agreements helps with tackling the growing challenges and pressures on shared freshwaters coupled with an inadequate and inconsistent response.[54] It would also contribute to reducing tensions between human rights and environmental protection. Each field is seeking to take priority over the other. Concerning transboundary water management, the two could somehow be balanced through IWL's focus on both concerns.[55] The latter can be viewed as the appropriate outlet.[56] This is not to say, that including such rights is not challenging. Its definition, scope, and implementation at the national level alone is facing huge problems.[57] Still, covering it within specific legal frameworks for water cooperation is a must.[58]

It Provides a Binding Force to the HRWS Given Its Non-Binding Nature Globally

The adoption of the HRWS holds great importance to the international community, states, civil society organizations, etc. Even when nations deny its existence, clear obligations have emerged and are undeniable in this regard. These include expectations to protect, respect, and fulfill. Compliance mechanisms and procedures have been put in place to monitor implementation. Numerous challenges mentioned in previous chapters are noted in practice and are still complicating its achievement.[59] The legal foundation for this right is based on the 2010 Resolutions and many other ones and documents,[60] while its legal evolvement is constantly debated in the literature.[61] In customary international law, the HRWS has not yet become binding. This is despite

54 Anders Jägerskog, Mark Zeitoun, and Anders Berntell, *Addressing Transboundary Water Management Challenges: Getting it Right* 5 (Report 25; Stockholm International Water Institute, SIWI 2009).

55 Trigueros, *supra* note 370, at 599.

56 Pardy, *supra* note 941, at 910–911.

57 Amber Wutich et al., *Fairness and the Human Right to Water: A Preliminary Cross-Cultural Theory*,in The Social Life of Water 220, 220–221 (John R. Wagner ed., Berghahn Books 2013).

58 Danijel Javorić Barić, *Water Agreements in Central Asia and their Impact on Human Rights*, 50(1) Pravnik. 123, 123–130 (2016).

59 Maude Barlow, *Forward*, at xv–xvii and Farhana Sultana & Alex Loftus, *The Right to Water: Prospects and Possibilities, in* The Right to Water: Politics, Governance and Social Struggles 1, 1–10 (Farhana Sultana & Alex Loftus eds., Earthscan 2012). Other actors include, for instance, foreign investors and MNCs. These also have an obligation to comply with this right. Farouk El-Hosseny, Civil Society in Investment Treaty Arbitration: Status and Prospects 153 (Brill/Nijhoff 2018).

60 Winkler, *supra* note 1029; Also see on this Bronwen Morgan, *The Regulatory Face of the Human Right to Water*, 15 Journal of Water Law. 179, 179–187 (2004).

61 Amparo Sereno, *Human Right to Water and Sanitation: Water for All vs. Full Cost Recovery*, 4 Frontiers in Water. 1, 1–5 (2022).

the numerous documents adopted,[62] as well as the different global legal instruments.[63] The right emerged from non-binding mechanims. Its achievement is progressive in nature. Other factors may play a bigger role in solving the freshwater crisis than its simple recognition. These include, for instance, proper water governance.[64]

Discussion over the interplay between water laws and the HRWS has been ongoing for few decades. Scholars have examined this debate in national and international contexts.[65] Consideration of this relationship requires taking into account various factors such as governance regimes, politics, and history. This entails careful consideration of each shared freshwater,[66] and including the HRWS as a provision within water agreements. This carries importance given that water management has always been associated with the law in the past.[67]As there is no way to enforce a HRWS outside a binding treaty, a citizen cannot directly demand the state to provide such right.[68] It has also been argued that this is not enforceable by courts since its content is not specific.[69] Compliance is hard to assess as there is a lack of precise guidelines and conditions.[70] This led, in certain circumstances, to ambiguous outcomes in practice.[71] Many nations echo this view, recognize the existence of human rights,

62 Winkler, *supra* note 1029, at 95–100; also see on this Morgan, *supra* note 1543, at 179–187.

63 Giupponi & Paz, *supra* note 1130, at 323–330.

64 Thielbörger, *supra* note 1117, at135.

65 Peter Howsam, *Water Law and the Right to a Basic Water Supply*, 16(3) Waterlines. 4, 4–7 (1998); Travis J. Hyer, *Considering Ecuador's New Water Law through the Lens of Indigenous Rights Under International Law*, 3 Willamette Environmental Law Journal. 63, 63–96 (2015); Bettina Lange & Mark Shepheard, *Changing Conceptions of Rights to Water? – An Eco-Socio-Legal Perspective*, 26(2) Journal of Environmental Law. 215, 215–242 (2014); Joshua Getzler, A History of Water Rights at Common Law (Oxford University Press 2004).

66 Anne Hellum, Patricia Kameri-Mbote & Barbara van Koppen, *The Human Right to Water and Sanitation in a Legal Pluralist Landscape: Perspectives of Southern and Eastern African Women*, in Water is Life: Women's Human Rights in National and Local Water Governance in Southern and Eastern Africa 1, 9 (Anne Hellum, Patricia Kameri-Mbote & Barbara van Koppen eds., Weaver Press 2015).

67 Erkki J. Hollo, *Introduction; The Concept and Traditions of Water Management Law*, in Water Resource Management and the Law 1, 1 (Erkki J, Hollo eds., Edward Elgar Publishing 2017). On the future see, Andrea Ballestero, A Future History of Water (Duke University Press 2019).

68 Hilal Elver, *The Emerging Global Freshwater Crisis and the Privatization of Global Leadership*, in Global Crises and the Crisis of Global Leadership 107, 121 (Stephen Gill ed., Cambridge University Press 2011).

69 Thielbörger, supra note 1117, at102.

70 Jennifer Schiff, *Measuring the Human Right to Water: An Assessment of Compliance Indicators*, 6(1) WIREs Water. 1, 1 (2019).

71 Jennifer Schiff, *Masquerading as Compliance: Tracing Canada's Policy Implementation of the Human Right to Water*, 8(2) Journal of Human Rights Practice. 264, 264 (2016).

but acknowledge that they are not legally enforceable.[72] This does not mean that there are no successful cases where a HRWS was enforced in the domestic context.[73] Nonetheless, this is domestically and not internationally.[74]

No sanctions can be imposed on states that do not fulfill this right. This is the case despite the argument that they can reduce violations and be used as a tool for the enforcement of international law.[75] It has been noted that they can have negative effects on the fulfillment of human rights. Some accept these effects as inevitable.[76] If compliance cannot be guaranteed and sanctions cannot be imposed, there must be another way in which the HRWS can be enforced in the transboundary context. Otherwise, it would be left to the states. Meanwhile, stakeholders who are influenced by their particular interests tend to define and apply this concept in a way that suits their agenda.[77] In disputes between states and investors over the HRWS and large investment projects, this is clear.[78] IWL can solve this issue, as it requires that different interests are taken into account in its applicability.

The many challenges facing IWL do not mean that this field cannot tackle the question of the HRWS as it pertains to transboundary water. On the contrary, water lawyers are seeking to solve existing issues through it.[79] In this, the shortcomings of this field are being addressed to tackle water security and global environmental changes.[80] Such efforts are being made despite the general focus in MEAs on ensuring states rights to reasonably exploit natural resources.[81] A nation may support the HRWS by providing assistance to other

72 Michael Rebell, *The Right to Education in the American State Courts, in* The Future of Economic and Social Rights 137, 139 (Katharine G. Young ed., Cambridge University Press 2019).

73 Maria Onestini, *Human Right to Water: Argentine Cases, Human Rights – Are They Enforceable?* in Water Resource Management and the Law 118, 124 (Erkki J. Hollo ed., Edward Elgar Publishing 2017).

74 Winkler, *supra* note 1029.

75 Baek, Buhm Suk, *Economic Sanctions Against Human Rights Violations* 1 (Cornell Law School Inter-University Graduate Student Conference Papers. Paper 11, 2008).

76 Coomans, *supra* note 1206, at 10; Jonathan Trebble-Greening, *Raising the Stakes: Creating an International Sanction to Generate Corporate Compliance with Data Privacy Laws,* 2019(2) Columbia Business Law Review. 763, 779 (2019).

77 Priscila, Neves-Silva & Heller, *supra* note 32, at 664.

78 Tamar Meshel, *Human Rights in Investor-State Arbitration: The Human Right to Water and Beyond,* 6(2) Journal of International Dispute Settlement. 277, 277–307 (2015).

79 Tarlock, *supra* note 734 & 740; A. Dan Tarlock, *Water Security, Fear Mitigation and International Water Law (Symposium),* 31(3) Hamline Law Review. 703, 703–728 (2008); Muhammad Mizanur Rahaman, *Principles of International Water Law: Creating Effective Transboundary Water Resources Management,* 1(3) International Journal of Sustainable Society. 207, 207-233 (2009); Patricia Wouters, *Water Security: What Role for International Water Law?,* inHuman and Environmental Security: An Agenda for Change 166, 166–181 (Felix Dodde ed., Earthscan Publications 2005).

80 Wouters & Moynihan, *supra* note 182, at 350.

81 Ryan Stoa, *International Water Law Principles and Frameworks: Perspectives from the Nile River Basin,* in Nile River Basin: Ecohydrological Challenges, Climate Change and Hyd-

ones to ensure access for its citizens in exchange for securing other interests. This can include having the right to build dams on rivers, which would provide electricity and allow selling it.[82]

It is in this context that IWL must be viewed as the appropriate legal field. The HRWS can be included as a provision within the water agreements, instead of having the concept of vital human needs. Developments made in IHRL should serve as guidelines for the implementation of the broad and vague HRWS provisions that would be incorporated. It is worth noting that already supranational courts such as the European Court of Human Rights, the Inter-American Human Rights Court as well as investment tribunals have promoted this right through their cases.[83]

The HRWS in the Context of Different Suggestions for the Harmonization of IGL

Transboundary groundwater governance has led actors like the UNECE to create an Inventory of this resource in Europe.[84] Despite such attempts, only a global comprehensive instrument may provide the guidelines necessary for the management of TBAs. Under these, the HRWS can be included. The Draft Articles represented the first ever mechanism to provide recommendations and ways for the management of shared aquifers.[85] The expectations are that this instrument would bridge the gaps when it comes to this resource.[86] It has the potential of making great contributions to the progressive development and codification of IWL. This possibility exists given the sophisticated

ROPOLITICS 581, 586 (Assefa M. Melesse, Wossenu Abtew & Shimelis G. Setegn eds., Springer 2014).

82 For instance, on this point see, Imad Antoine Ibrahim, *Water Governance in the Mekong After the Watercourses Convention 35th Ratification: Multilateral or Bilateral Approach?* 36(1) INTERNATIONAL JOURNAL OF WATER RESOURCES DEVELOPMENT. 200–220 (2020); Aibek Zhupankhan, Kamshat Tussupova & Ronny Berndtsson, *Could Changing Power Relationships Lead to Better Water Sharing in Central Asia?* 9 WATER. 1–17 (2017); MWANGI S. KIMENYI & JOHN MUKUM MBAKU, GOVERNING THE NILE RIVER BASIN: THE SEARCH FOR A NEW LEGAL REGIME (Brookings Institution Press 2015).

83 The Rt Hon Lady Justice Arden, *Water for All? Developing a Human Right to Water in National and International Law*, 65(4) INTERNATIONAL & COMPARATIVE LAW QUARTERLY. 771, 777–779 (2016); Ursula Kriebaum, *The Right to Water Before Investment Tribunals*, 1 BRILL OPEN LAW. 16, 16 (2018).

84 G.E. Arnold & Zs. Buza´s, *Economic Commission for Europe Inventory of Transboundary Ground Water in Europe*, 43(5) GROUNDWATER. 669–678 (2005). 1–10

85 GANOULIS & FRIED, *supra* note 861, at 148.

86 KIRSTIN I. CONTI, NENO KUKURIC & JOYEETA GUPTA, *Groundwater and Security, in* HANDBOOK ON WATER SECURITY 161, 173 (Claudia Pahl-Wostl, Anik Bhaduri, Joyeeta Gupta eds., Edward Elgar Publishing 2016).

understanding offered through it to aquifers.[87] Its importance lies in its added value considering the governance of TBAs which was absent before.[88]

The future of TBAs governance relies on determining the final form of the Draft Articles and the efficiency of whatever shape this instrument may take.[89] It is worth mentioning that globally, the UNWC, the UNECE Water Convention, and the Draft Articles apply to shared aquifers. Differences and similarities, however, were noticed in the scope and the principles adopted.[90] Given the current status of the latter instrument, the following sections will tackle suggestions made by different scholars while also pointing out what would best fit the attempt to harmonize IGL and IHRL. Before doing so, the next section will discuss the need to amend this mechanism.

Amending the Draft Articles

This instrument has received significant criticism by scholars and states. The same actors have considered it an achievement in itself, despite drawbacks. The focus should be on improving and strengthening it due to its importance to the international community and nations. In case the Draft Articles should be adopted as a binding treaty, there remains a need to amend it to harmonize IWL. This is especially true, given the changes and updates that have occurred in recent years with the enforceability of the UNWC and the alteration in the status of the UNECE Water Convention. Amendments are needed to solve controversies, contradictions, and overlaps between the Draft Articles and the UNWC. It is also necessary to consider the provisions of UNECE Water Convention that received less focus because its status changed only recently. Hence, the modifications required should not have the explicit purpose of harmonizing IWL by solving problems and issues related to the UNWC and Draft Articles only excluding the UNECE Water Convention. Here, several changes were suggested. Among them, adding a provision related to the HRWS is a must and should replace the concept of vital human needs in IWL. This is because it contains broader scope and is more accepted by the international community, states, civil society organizations, and populations. The existence of a body of detailed documents, resolutions, and instruments that provide much-needed details on the ways this right can be implemented in practice is an added value. This does not mean that this notion will completely disappear sine the UNWC and other non-binding instruments directly cover it.[91]

Along this amendment, the list of potential changes has been discussed in a previous chapter. These examined issues and problems are debated in

87 McCaffrey, *supra* note 463, at 292.

88 Tanzi, *supra* note 341, at 206–207.

89 Puri & Villholth, *supra* note 560, at 367.

90 Stephan, *supra* note 28, at 48.

91 See for instance Article 19 of the Watercourses Convention.

the literature. These include, for instance, the need to consider the relationship between the Draft Articles and the existing water conventions.[92] This will strike a balance between having broad and general provisions to provide flexibility to the states also giving sufficient details to guarantee the protection of TBAs.[93] Other suggestions comprise amending this instrument to reflect the language within the UNWC concerning permanent sovereignty over natural resources[94] and ensuring compliance of the definitions of the terms used with the scientific and hydrological realities focusing on groundwater rather than the geological formation.[95] Scholars called to consider the interconnection between surface water and groundwater;[96] adding a requirement for states to conduct EIAs;[97] incorporating provisions reflecting the current practices for oil and gas exploration and exploitation, highlighting how states can be given flexibility in the management of shared aquifers;[98] and so on.

Once the amendment of the Draft Articles occurs, the question that remains is what type of instrument should be established? The response will depend on many factors. These include the potential success of each form, the most appropriate way for the harmonization of IWL, states positions, and many other issues that may create obstacles before its efficient use in practice.

Potential Ways for the Harmonization of IWL

There are several suggestions made to that end mainly keeping the Draft Articles as a non-binding instrument and adopting it as either an independent convention or a protocol to the UNWC.

Maintaining the Draft Articles as a Non-Binding Instrument

Numerous states have expressed their views of having the Draft Articles as a non-binding instrument,[99] given the need for more scientific research on the topic before adopting a treaty.[100] This is crucial since further understanding of TBAs and their connection to surface water is required.The rationale is that

92 Pronto & Wood, *supra* note 496, at 570.
93 Carlson, *supra* note 14, at 1434–1434; Allan, Tignino & Loures, supra note 12, at 251.
94 Stoa, *supra* note 866, at 545.
95 Traversi, *supra* note 55, at 472–473.
96 Dellapenna & Loures, *supra* note 586, at 274.
97 Traversi, *supra* note 55, at 472–473 and 486–487.
98 Carlson, *supra* note 14, at 1433.
99 United Nations International Law Commission, *Yearbook of the International Law Commission 2008*, Vol. II, Part 1; 78 (Documents of the Sixtieth Session, United Nations, New York and Geneva, 2014).
100 Laurence R. Helfer & Timothy Meyer, *The Evolution of Codification: A Principal-Agent Theory of the International Law Commission's Influence, in* Custom's Future: International Law in a Changing World 305, 305–331 (Curtis A. Bradley ed., Cambridge University Press 2016).

this instrument represents the most significant attempt for the codification of this resource.[101] It will still hold high authoritative value in this case.[102] This is true, especially as it lacks the support of states in its current form,[103] and as many problems must be solved.[104] Governments shifted toward having the Draft Articles as a non-binding document. The suggestion is to adopt it as a declaration of principles reflecting its current content. This ensures that the provisions of any instrument are not diminished beyond the scope of enforceability as nations would no longer object. Many see such a declaration as an essential step in the process of adopting a future convention.[105] Keeping this instrument as non-binding demands consideration of the risks in negotiations over its status when they are re-opened. Renegotiation may not necessarily lead to the improvement of the text. Even if solutions are reached, there is a high probability that this mechanism may not be adopted as a convention undermining its authority.[106] The importance of a non-binding tool in this context is that it reduces the potential for conflict by mitigating legally complex issues that may be contested.[107]

Another proposal is treating the Draft Articles as guidelines. This would facilitate their replication at the local and regional level by states sharing TBAs mitigating the emergence of legal conflicts between this instrument and the UNWC.[108] Others suggested maintaining the status quo since the language has changed in the Resolutions following its adoption. Here, states are recommended to use the Draft Articles when negotiating. This language seems to be approved in situations where numerous nations typically oppose a non-binding document like a UN declaration. Countries have argued that the current instrument lacks maturity and that they need time to understand and examine it to determine whether it should hold relevance in the future. It seems that many governments still lack proper awareness when it comes to the issue of TBAs. States have argued for maintaining the status quo since the Draft Articles have been annexed to a UN Resolution providing them flexibility in considering local needs and the specificities of each TBA.[109] The rationale justifying this concerns the difficult process that the UNWC underwent before being adopted and ratified. Another reason is the need for urgent action for

101 Sands et al., *supra* note 432, at 344.

102 Kerstin Mechlem, *International Groundwater Law in the Euphrates and Tigris Region, in* Water Law and Cooperation in the Euphrates-Tigris Region: A Comparative and Interdisciplinary Approach 21, 35 (Aysegul Kibaroglu et al eds., Brill /Nijhoff 2013).

103 Stoa, *supra* note 866, at 543; Conti, Kukuric, & Gupta, *supra* note 1566, at 173.

104 Russell & McCaffrey, *supra* note 1277, at 170.

105 Eckstein & Sindico, *supra* note 56, at 37–38.

106 Tanzi, *supra* note 341, at 207.

107 Mark E. Villiger, Customary International Law and Treaties: A Manual on the Theory and Practice of the Interrelation of Sources 120 (2d ed., Brill/Nijhoff 1997).

108 Stoa, *supra* note 866, at 547.

109 Eckstein & Sindico, *supra* note 56, at 38.

the management of shared aquifers. There are already examples of how the Draft Articles, in their current status, have positively affected the management of TBAs. For instance, the Guarani aquifer agreement benefited from it. In this, it provided a framework and guidelines for nations drafting the treaty. In this instance, the status quo is viewed favorably.[110]

A non-binding instrument is preferable given the lengthy negotiations that would be required to reach a solution. An early codification may interrupt the current evolution of norms and principles related to this field, especially given the hidden nature of groundwater.[111] It allows the progressive development of rules applicable to TBAs. In many instances, nations comply with a non-binding instrument in a similar manner to where there is a binding one. The rules could be developed faster to remedy this gap since they won't be subject to a similar negotiation process. Under ordinary negotiating procedures, political interests would constitute an obstacle.[112] International law, applicable to TBAs, is still nascent. A non-binding instrument would allow the development of a concrete regulatory framework. It would also address the problem of overlaps between it, the UNWC, and the UNECE Water Convention.[113]

There are many advantages for having a non-binding instrument. Established literature includes articles and studies comparing the impact of hard or binding mechanisms. Comparison has led scholars to either support having binding or soft ones. They have provided arguments backing their claims. With the emergence of new types of tools that may be soft in nature but have a binding force, this debate is far from over.[114] When it comes to the Draft Articles, the rationale and the arguments behind having it as a non-binding instrument are solid. Given the sensitivity of the topic and the difficulty of reaching consensus among the different nations, the context of this argument comes into clearer

110 Stoa, *supra* note 866, at 547.
111 Mechlem, *supra* note, 394 at 77–78.
112 *Id.* at 78.
113 Traversi, *supra* note 55, at 473.
114 On this point see for instance, Alan Boyle, *The Choice of a Treaty: Hard Law versus Soft Law*, in The Oxford Handbook of United Nations Treaties 101, 101–118 (Simon Chesterman, David M. Malone, Santiago Villalpando eds., Cambridge University Press 2019); Laurence R. Helfer & Ingrid B. Wuerth, *Customary International Law: An Instrument Choice Perspective*, 37(4) Michigan Journal of International Law. 563, 563–609 (2016); Arnold N. Pronto, *Understanding the Hard/Soft Distinction in International Law*,48 Vanderbilt Journal of Transnational Law. 941, 941–956 (2015); Sumudu Atapattu, *International Environmental Law and Soft Law: A New Direction or a Contradiction?*, in Non-State Actors, Soft Law and Protective Regimes: From the Margins 200, 200–226 (Cecilia M. Bailliet ed., Cambridge University Press 2012); Gregory C. Shaffer & Mark A. Pollack, *Hard vs. Soft Law: Alternatives, Complements, and Antagonists in International Governance*, 94 Minnesota Law Review. 706, 706–799 (2010); Arnold N. Pronto, *Some Thoughts on the Making of International Law*, 19(3) European Journal of International Law. 601, 601–616 (2008); Pierre-Marie Dupuy, *Soft Law and the International Law of the Environment*,12(2) Michigan Journal of International Law. 420, 420–435 (1991).

focus. As such, if the purpose is to have general rules that states can use for drafting water agreements, then having a soft mechanism makes sense.

However, if the purpose is the harmonization of IWL with IHRL, then a non-binding instrument is not the best approach. There is a need to amend the Draft Articles to solve contradictions and overlaps between it, the UNECE Water Convention, and the UNWC. Additionally, including a provision related to the HRWS within this instrument instead of using the concept of vital human needs is a must. Once amended, the Draft Articles should be adopted as a binding mechanism in the form of either a protocol or an independent treaty. This would fulfill the objectives of harmonization of IWL and tackles the HRWS.

Adopting the Draft Articles as a Protocol to the UNWC

Having the Draft Articles as a protocol to the UNWC is one of the suggestions raised.[115] For the time being, no such mechanism exists.[116] Protocols have been established in international law to tackle specific challenges. One can mention the 2010 Nagoya Protocol on Access and Benefit-Sharing,[117] the Cartagena Protocol on Biosafety of 2000,[118] the Madrid Protocol on Environmental Protection of 1991,[119] and the Montreal Protocol on Substances that Deplete the Ozone Layer of 1987.[120] Protocols addressing shared freshwaters have been adopted in many regions. For examples, the SADC Water Protocol was created to address the water challenges in the Southern African region.[121] One

115 Kirstin I. Conti, *Factors Enabling Transboundary Aquifer Cooperation: A Global Analysis* 9 (IGRAC Publication, 2014).

116 Sahana Rao, *Governance of Water Resources Shared by India and Pakistan under the Indus Waters Treaty: Successful Elements and Room for Improvement*, 25 New York Environmental Law Journal. 108, 114 (2017).

117 Secretariat of the Convention on Biological Diversity, Montreal, Nagoya Protocol on Access to Genetic Resources and the Fair and Equitable Sharing of Benefits Arising from their Utilization to the Convention on Biological Diversity (United Nations, 2011).

118 United Nations, Cartagena Protocol on Biosafety to the Convention on Biological Diversity (Montreal, 2000).

119 Protocol on Environmental Protection to the Antarctic Treaty (the Madrid Protocol), adopted in 1991.

120 Montreal Protocol on Substances that Deplete the Ozone Layer (with annex). Concluded at Montreal on 16 September 1987. See in general, Elisa Morgera, Matthias Buck & Elsa Tsioumani (eds), The 2010 Nagoya Protocol on Access and Benefit-sharing in Perspective: Implications for International Law and Implementation Challenges (Martinus Nijhoff Publishers 2013); Marie-Claire Cordonier Segger, Frederic Perron-Welch, Christine Frison, Legal Aspects of Implementing the Cartagena Protocol on Biosafety (Cambridge University Press 2013); Francesca Trombetta-Panigadi, *The Exploitation of Antarctic Icebergs in International Law*, *in* International Law for Antarctica 225, 236 (Francesco Francioni & Tullio Scovazzi eds., Kluwer Law International 1996).

121 Revised Protocol on Shared Watercourses, *supra* note 1328.

can mention the Protocol on Water and Health of 1999,[122] and the one on Civil Liability and Compensation for Damage, caused by the Transboundary Effects of Industrial Accidents on Transboundary Waters to the 1992 UNECE Water Convention and to the 1992 Convention on the Transboundary Effects of Industrial Accidents.[123]

Some organizations advocated for the adoption of the Draft Articles as a protocol to the UNWC. This suggestion did not receive support at the UN level. The rationale is that there is a need to ensure the harmonization of IWL through a holistic approach. This would guarantee that the field is well-developed and codified. Another reason is the need for good governance of surface and groundwater. This is justified by the fact that, in many cases, they are interconnected.[124] Such recognition would provide the basis for a cohesive legal structure.[125]

Since the UNWC has served as a basis for the preparation of the Draft Articles and the development of international law pertaining to TBAs, adopting this instrument as a protocol to it seems like a logical choice.[126] Those opposing argue that it would not ensure that groundwater and surface water are given equal treatment. This is because a protocol supplements a treaty and holds a lower value. This is especially true given that the UNWC is a framework convention. Groundwater regulation is not simply tackling some details related to it, but rather, establishing the main principles and rules that apply.[127] Those arguing for a protocol see it as the basis for later creating a stable framework for water management integrating surface and groundwater.

The protocol will include new provisions related to sustainability, prevention, and precaution. Its scope will be expanded. Many scholars are calling for amending the Draft Articles to include all types of aquifers, especially those connected to transboundary freshwaters and have recharge zones in multiple states.[128] A protocol would consider the interconnectivity between surface water and groundwater and account for the specific characteristics of each aquifer. The Draft Articles would be adopted as a protocol after having been

122 Protocol on Water and Health, *supra* note 1355.

123 Protocol on Civil Liability and Compensation for Damage Caused by the Transboundary Effects of Industrial Accidents on Transboundary Waters to the 1992 Convention on the Protection and Use of Transboundary Watercourses and International Lakes and to the 1992 Convention on the Transboundary Effects of Industrial Accidents; Sabine Brels, David Coates, and Flavia Loures, *Transboundary Water Resources Management: The Role of International Watercourse Agreements in Implementation of the CBD* 32–33 (Secretariat of the Convention on Biological Diversity, CBD Technical Series No. 40, 2008).

124 Eckstein & Sindico, *supra* note 56, at 38–39.

125 Christian Behrmann & Raya Marina Stephan, *The UN Watercourse Convention and the Draft Articles on Transboundary Aquifers: The Way Ahead* 5 (UNESCO-IAH-UNEP Conference, Paris, 6–8 December 2010).

126 *Id.* at 5.

127 Mechlem, *supra* note 468, at 820.

128 Dellapenna & Loures, *supra* note 584, at 218.

amended to include much-needed updates and changes. The UNWC and the Draft Articles deal with the same natural resource, at a different hydrological cycle phase. Any action affecting surface water will have an impact on groundwater and vice versa. Hence, creating two separate conventions is not a logical solution.[129] Dellapenna and Loures argue further that, through a protocol to the UNWC, it would be possible to have groundwater as the object of regulation in place of aquifers.[130]

The difference between surface water and groundwater does not require the adoption of a new convention since the increased scientific understanding of TBAs allows for having a unified regime. The focus should remain on the interconnectivity between these two resources and reducing fragmentation of IWL. This, however, can only occur if the varying legal instruments are harmonized.[131] Many of the provisions of the Draft Articles are similar to the ones of the UNWC. This is why a protocol makes more sense than an independent convention.[132] Similarities can be found between the Draft Articles and the UNECE Model Provisions on Transboundary Groundwaters.[133] The idea of having the Draft Articles as a protocol of the UNWC was backed by countries like Italy at the beginning of the drafting process.[134] Among the many arguments made was that the protocol would consider TBAs' vulnerabilities to pollution and potential overexploitation and using existing UNWC provisions to that end. Additionally, a protocol would prevent confusion as to which treaty would apply in the case that more than one exists and holds binding status. The UNWC also covers TBAs, which increases the potential for conflicts when nations base their claims on two different conventions that address similar matters.[135]

The above-mentioned arguments represent valid reasons for the adoption of the Draft Articles as a protocol to the UNWC, and are feasible from a legal perspective. The UNWC lacks the presence of institutional bodies that can connect the treaty with the latest scientific developments or monitor its implementation. This reality affects its ability to adapt to changes like the adoption

129 *Id.* at 221–222.
130 *Id.* at 277.
131 Vick, *supra* note 563, at 205.
132 Nilüfer Oral, *The International Law Commission and the Progressive Development and Codification of Principles of International Environmental Law*, 13(6) FIU Law Review. 1075, 1086–1087 (2019). On this point see also, Waseem Ahmad Qureshi, *The IWT and the UNWC: Commonalities and Differences*, 23(1) Ocean and Coastal Law Journal. 87, 87–145 (2018).
133 Renee Martin-Nagle & Stephanie Hawkins, *Transboundary Aquifers*, in Research Handbook on Freshwater Law and International Relations 305, 322 (Mara Tignino & Christian Bréthaut eds., Edward Elgar Publishing 2018).
134 WWF, *Position Paper: The ILC Draft Articles on the Law of Transboundary Aquifers* 3 (66th Session of the UN General Assembly, 6th Committee Meeting – 18 October 2011, Agenda Item "The Law of Transboundary Aquifers").
135 *Id.* at 4–5.

of new instruments and treaties such as the UNECE Water Convention. Several developments that have occurred in the last decades make this suggestion less appropriate. These will be examined in the following section. The author will focus on one particular suggestion that, according to him, constitutes the most adequate way for the harmonization of IWL and IHRL. The latter is having the Draft Articles as a separate and independent convention.

Adopting a New Convention

The adoption of a treaty represents the most appropriate way for the harmonization of IWL as well with IHRL. The Draft Articles could be used as a basis for the negotiation among the different nations. This would occur through an intergovernmental process. A new convention would be signed by different nations and ratified over time. Numerous states backed this option initially, but such support began to fade. There are many reasons to object to this suggestion, mainly several disagreements concerning whether the draft articles clash with other existing instruments and differences regarding particular provisions.[136]

Politically, challenges have been noted. The first is that a new convention may not have the necessary support needed to ratify it. That is, unless countries believe in its importance.[137] The second is a disagreement over the scale in the sense that some nations believe that global rules are a necessity. Others point out that specific aquifer agreements would be more effective. Supporters of the first view argue that global regimes can integrate local issues and provide solutions to them.[138] Other challenges pointed out are socio-economic, and affect the local management of TBAs. These include disruption due to economic, political and other types of interests. Supporters of a universal treaty claim that having it does render local solutions obsolete.[139]

The idea of adopting the Draft Articles as a convention would be an upgrade to the status of the instrument.[140] It was intentionally created to address TBAs and is more appropriate to provide the necessary framework for states sharing groundwater.[141] The potential overlap with the UNWC can be accepted where contradictions between them can be excluded. Instead, stressing on their complementary aspects would allow interpretation of the Draft Articles in a manner that conforms with the provisions of the watercourse convention.[142] Specific rules and principles can emerge in the framework of this mechanism. There is

136 Eckstein & Sindico, *supra* note 56, at 35–36.
137 *Id.* at 36.
138 *Id.* at 37.
139 *Id.* at 37.
140 Tanzi, *supra* note 341, at 207.
141 Traversi, *supra* note 55, at 473–474.
142 Behrmann & Stephan, *supra* note 1608, at 6.

a high likelihood that such a treaty would become enforceable because of the existence of few ones related to TBAs.[143]

The Draft Articles and the UNWC represent two separate instruments within the same regime. Having the former as a convention is perfectly in line with fragmentation of international law. This is based on many factors including the increasing technicalities of issues being tackled. The Draft Articles are more technical, given the specific knowledge and expertise needed to govern shared aquifers.[144] Despite the complicated process of adopting and ratifying it as a treaty, it is still worthwhile.[145] Moreover, several differences can be noticed when it comes to its provisions, in comparison to the UNWC. This is why, an independent convention may be more appropriate.[146] It also falls within the ILC two-steps approach. The second one focuses on seeing the potential of having a convention at a later stage while also recognizing that this may take some time to be achieved.[147] For the time being, the Draft Articles did not reach sufficient approval rates to be adopted as a convention. This process is expected to take time and effort.

Given all of the above, the author supports the adoption of the Draft Articles as a separate convention. Firstly, groundwater holds much more importance than surface water. It represents two thirds of the existing freshwater available. It is invisible and can be easily polluted. The current and reckless means of extracting it may lead to its depletion.[148] There is a need to make sure that it is given its much-needed value through a treaty that expressly covers all types of TBAs.[149] Another reason for this is for the harmonization of IWL. The provisions of the Draft Articles can be amended to take into account the provisions of the Watercourse Convention, solving the overlaps and contradictions between the different provisions.[150] Additionally, the UNECE Water Convention has officially been ratified as a global convention in 2014 and its provisions tackle surface water and groundwater. The treaty has already established a UNECE

143 *Id.* at 820.

144 Vick, *supra* note 563, at 202.

145 Quadri, *supra* note 515, at 6.

146 Zeitoun, *supra* note 200, at 949–968.

147 Mikhail Kalinin, *Are There Any Transboundary Aquifers in Belarus?*, inTransboundary Aquifers in the Eastern Borders of The European Union: Regional Cooperation for Effective Management of Water Resources 87, 88 (Tomasz Nałęcz ed., Springer 2010).

148 See in general, Feng Huang et al., *Environmental Groundwater Depth for Groundwater-Dependent Terrestrial Ecosystems in Arid/Semiarid Regions: A Review*, 16(5) International Journal of Environmental Research and Public Health. 73, 763 (2019); UN Water, *Groundwater Overview: Making the Invisible Visible* (Produced by IGRAC (International Groundwater Resources Assessment Centre, in cooperation with UNESCO-IHP, IAH, IWMI and with contributions of many UN Water Members and Partners, 2018)); Wolfgang Kinzelbach et al., *Sustainable Groundwater Management – Problems and Scientific Tools*, 26(4) Episodes. 279–284 (2003).

149 Behrmann & Stephan, *supra* note 1608, at 5–7.

150 See for instance, Dellapenna & Loures, *supra* note 586 & 607.

Secretariat assisting countries looking to join the Convention and has adopted *Model Provisions on Transboundary Groundwaters* that were highly influenced by the Draft Articles.[151] Addressing the question of harmonization through the lens of UNWC/Draft Articles is no longer valid. This needs to consider the UNECE Water Convention that has similar importance.

The adoption of the Draft Articles as an agreement results in the harmonization of IWL and IHRL. Having a protocol to the UNWC means that the provisions of the watercourse convention have higher value than the ones of the 2008 instrument. Among those, Article 10(2) related to vital human needs compared to the new ones to be included within the Draft Articles and related to the HRWS.[152] Nations that are parties to the UNWC may attempt to use Article 10(2), instead of the HRWS one, to satisfy basic obligations. They could justify it as the provisions of the UNWC are more important than the Draft Articles because of its status as a treaty. Hence, having the Draft Articles as a convention would better suit the purpose of harmonizing IWL and IHRL, considering the urgent need for legal action for the protection of TBAs.

Conclusion

This chapter focused on providing a nuanced approach on how the harmonization of IWL can occur. It studied how synergies between IWL and the HRWS can be considered. This could still be the case despite the fragmentation of international law. The author first provided arguments as to why the HRWS should be included as a provision within the Draft Articles. It proceeded to discuss how to fit this suggestion into the harmonization of IWL. Several ideas were presented in this regard. After examining them, the author is of the opinion that the Draft Articles should be adopted as a convention. This should occur after efforts are made toward proper amendments based on which provisions can be added. Whatever suggestion followed will have advantages and disadvantages. This is especially true as external factors will affect the efficiency of any form the Draft Articles shall take – mainly states

151 See, Attila Tanzi, *The Economic Commission for Europe Water Convention and the United Nations Watercourses Convention: An Analysis of Their Harmonized Contribution to International Water Law* (United Nations Economic Commission for Europe, Water Series № 6, 2015); United Nations Economic Commission for Europe, Convention on the Protection and Use of Transboundary Watercourses and International Lakes, *The Water Convention: Responding to Global Water Challenges* (United Nations, New York and Geneva, 2018).

152 UNWC, *supra* note 184, at Article 10(2).

interests, lack of ability to ensure states compliance, or simply lack of capacity by developing nations to implement the provisions.[153] Holding a convention, despite the above mentioned challenges, and uncertainties,[154] represents the most pragmatic approach toward the harmonization of IWL. This promotes the creation of synergies between IWL and the HRWS.

153 On these external factors see for instance, Carmela Lutmar, Cristiane L. Carneiro & Sara McLaughlin Mitchell, *Formal Commitments and States Interests: Compliance in International Relations,* 42(4) International Interactions. 559, 559–564 (2016); Mark A. Pollack, *Who Supports International Law, and Why?: The United States, the European Union, and the International Legal Order,*13(4) International Journal of Constitutional Law. 873, 873–900 (2015); Jack L. Goldsmith & Eric Posner, The Limits of International Law (Oxford University Press 2006); A. A. Fatouros, *International Law and the Third World,* 50(5) Virginia Law Review. 783–823 (1964).

154 See for instance, Samantha Besson, *State Consent and Disagreement in International Law-Making. Dissolving the Paradox,* 29(2) Leiden Journal of International Law. 289–316 (2016); Emily O'Brien & Richard Gowan, *What Makes International Agreements Work: Defining Factors for Success* 1–28 (New York University, Center on International Cooperation, September 2012); Andrew T. Guzman, *Against Consent,* 52(4) Virginia Journal of International Law. 747, 747–790 (2012); Andrew T. Guzman, *The Design of International Agreements,* 16(4) European Journal of International Law. 579, 579–612 (2005).

Conclusion

Water as a resource is vital for society, economic development, and political stability. Its availability, accessibility, and protection from degradation represent a huge challenge to all nations.[1] The 21st century is witnessing an increase in attention to it,[2] where international law, global organizations, and various stakeholders are vital to its governance.[3] Its importance has led to several debates concerning its classification, and its management is very complicated. Politicians, scientists, lawyers, and other actors have been attempting to address this topic, wherein different political and administrative systems need to find a compromise. The latter is necessary, especially since two-thirds of existing freshwater available to humans is groundwater.[4] Thus, it deserves special attention, and strict rules must be established.[5]

The increasing focus on TBAs begs the question of what kind of regulations should be adopted to tackle it.[6] The specifics surrounding groundwater resources make their management extremely different from surface water. Rules that address their particular characteristics need to be formed.[7] Their governance is complicated due to the involvement of various stakeholders and the use of tools and mechanisms at different levels.[8] The situation further worsens when one considers that these factors increase the probability of

1 Itzchak E. Kornfeld, Sprawl, *Sustainable Development and the Preservation of Groundwater Resources*, 23 Temple Environmental Law & Technology Journal. 41, 48 (2004).
2 Francesco Sindico, *Water Governance in the Aftermath of RiO+20*, 16(2) International Community Law Review. 236, 236–237 (2014).
3 *Id.* at 239. See on this, Claudia Pahl-Wostl, Joyeeta Gupta & Daniel Petry, *Governance and the Global Water System: A Theoretical Exploration*, 14(4) Global Governance. 419, 419–435 (2008).
4 Nalecz & Puri, *supra* note 561, at 2–3.
5 Traversi, *supra* note 55, at 488; see on this, Emily Brophy, *The Importance of Regulating Transboundary Groundwater Aquifers*, 10(1) Sustainable Development Law & Policy. 19, 19–81 (2009).
6 Tanzi, *supra* note 341, at 193.
7 Mechlem, *supra* note 394, at 79.
8 Neal (Patrick) et al., *supra* note 1071, at 268.

DOI: 10.4324/9781003537724-8

conflicts over it.[9] Climate change adds another layer of complexity,[10] as well as globalization. Due to all of this, cooperation between nations is a must.[11]

From a legal point of view, collaboration is the cornerstone of international law where states' consent is the only means of implementing global frameworks.[12] There are already examples of countries cooperating in their management of TBAs.[13] This is a necessity from a legal and political perspective.[14] The international community has the task of promoting collaboration between nations sharing freshwaters, eliminating reasons for conflict, and fostering sustainable water management and environmental protection. In this case, IWL offers the basis for the realization of these objectives.[15] In fact, TBAs are no longer ignored. One can now notice a change as the pressure on water resources has been growing. This led to increasing awareness about TBAs and the importance of cooperation through adequate rules.[16] This is why there has been an evolution within the laws applicable to it due to the development of scientific knowledge in addition to the environmental trends and degradation occurring worldwide.[17]

Before the occurrence of these changes, numerous attempts were made to understand the role that international law can play in the governance of shared freshwaters.[18] This has been taking place since the 60s and 70s to establish regulatory frameworks applicable to it.[19] Further progress and evolution of IWL have been ongoing in the last decades.[20] International law applicable to TBAs is still in its initial stages. Early advancements that occurred led to the emergence of non-binding rules. The combination of soft law and sporadic rules related to groundwater meant that a body of IGL was developing before the Draft Articles. The challenges facing the instrument need to be addressed before its adoption as a treaty or any other form.[21] Its effectiveness is based on its interplay with the rest of the water conventions and instruments.[22] The

9 Jarvis, *supra* note 1082, at 393–410; see on the developments taking place in this field, Varady, Scott & Megdal, *supra* note 568, at 1–6.
10 Joseph W. Dellapenna, *International Water Law in a Climate of Disruption*, 17(1) Michigan State University College of Law Journal of International Law. 43, 59 (2008).
11 McCaffrey, *supra* note 463, at 14.
12 Wouters, *supra* note 637, at 88.
13 Aureli & Eckstein, *supra* note 1084, at 550.
14 Armin Rosencranz, *Transboundary Waters on the Subcontinent*, 40 Environmental Policy & Law. 331, 336 (2010).
15 Dellapenna, *supra* note 1647, at 60.
16 Stephan, *supra* note 342, at 162.
17 *Id.* at 163.
18 Benvenisti, *supra* note 410, at 384–415.
19 Nanda, *supra* note 1466, at 258.
20 Wouters, *supra* note 637, at 97.
21 Mechlem, *supra* note 362, at 222.
22 Rieu-Clarke & Kinna, *supra* note 547, at 30–31.

ILC, in drafting it, has adopted a pragmatic approach.[23] Its formation and current discussion over its final status highlight how international law is constantly evolving.[24] The Draft Articles are the closest instrument that takes into account the particularities of groundwater resources and hold future prospects of becoming binding.[25] The legal protection of TBAs is necessary to protect this resource.[26] The amendments to the provisions of the Draft Articles mentioned in previous chapters are needed.[27] Regardless of its future status, what matters is whether states embrace its principles and provisions and implement them in practice. This is how the effectiveness of this instrument will be measured in the long term.[28]

Nations need to use the Draft Articles in their negotiation process for the adoption of regional, basin level, and bilateral water agreements addressing TBAs.[29] These treaties are vital since IWL cannot address every specific issue.[30] State practices in the field of TBAs are slowly emerging.[31] This is vital given the current state of international law that is highly fragmented.[32] Another important element is that decision makers and lawyers, when adopting rules, need to be fully aware of the hydrological realities to ensure their full understanding of water resources and the water cycle. The decision-making process needs to include a scientific basis to reach decisions and legal provisions that are sound. Only the combination of a science-based approach with legal and policy mechanisms offers the best protection for shared freshwaters.[33]

Even if the management of TBAs is basin-specific, numerous countries still lack the necessary mechanisms despite the efforts made to that end.[34] Moreover, groundwater governance is usually fragmented across different

23 Matz-Lück, *supra* note 525, at 134–150.
24 Wouters, *supra* note 637, at 143.
25 Mechlem, *supra* note 466, at 162.
26 Frink, *supra* note 599, at 530.
27 McIntyre, *supra* note 411, at 254.
28 Eckstein & Sindico, *supra* note 56, at 42.
29 *Id.*
30 Stephens, *supra* note 191, at 34.
31 Stephan, *supra* note 456, at 44.
32 On these points see, Tomer Broude, *Keep Calm and Carry On: Martti Koskenniemi and the Fragmentation of International Law*, 27(2) Temple International & Comparative Law Journal. 279, 279–292 (2013); Tullio Treves, *Fragmentation of International Law*, XVI(27) Agenda Internacional. 213, 213–253 (2009); Andrzej Jakubowski & Karolina Wierczyńska, Fragmentation vs. the Constitutionalisation of International Law: A Practical Inquiry (Routledge 2016); Matthew Lister, *The Legitimating Role of Consent in International Law*, 11(2) Chicago Journal of International Law. 663, 663–691 (2011); Eva Kassoti, *Beyond State Consent? International Legal Scholarship and the Challenge of Informal International Law-Making*, 63 Netherlands International Law Review. 99, 99–131 (2016).
33 Eckstein & Eckstein, *supra* note 5, at 258.
34 Nanni, *supra* note 1423, at 1.

agencies affecting its protection.[35] Global instruments like the Draft Articles are very important. In its work, the ILC has been trying to harmonize the universal rules applicable to freshwater resources, and those at the regional and basin levels. In reality, both levels of regulatory frameworks are extremely important where international rules constitute the basis for the adoption of regional and basin-level agreements.[36] Without IWL, states would find it very hard to develop basin-specific water agreements in the absence of guidelines and technical expertise.[37] There are reasons to be optimistic. Positive developments have occurred in the last decade with the enforceability of the UNWC and the UNECE Water Convention becoming global. The fact that discussions are taking place concerning the future fate of the Draft Articles is just another cause to be optimistic.[38] Such optimism must be carefully weighted as the success of any water treaty also depends on linking it to other issues such as trade and human rights.[39]

35 *Id.* at 5.

36 Laurence Boisson de Chazournes, *Comment: Trends in the Law Applicable to Freshwaters*, in Peace through International Law 157, 171 (Georg Nolte ed., Springer 2009).

37 Eckstein, *supra* note 53, at 581.

38 Stoa, *supra* note 855, at 544–548.

39 Dellapenna & Gupta, supra note 531, at 449–450. Such links are also acknowledged at the national level. See, for instance, Jonathan R. Eaton, *The Sieve of Groundwater Pollution Protection: A Public Health Law Analysis*, VI Journal of Health & Biomedical Law. 109, 109–146 (2010).

Index

FSC
www.fsc.org
MIX
Papier | Fördert gute Waldnutzung
FSC® C083411

Kolibri 360 GmbH
Ferdinand-Jühlke-Straße 7
99095 Erfurt, Deutschland
produktsicherheit@kolibri360.de